Patterson for Alabama

To Jim & Pat Martin

da appreciation four your dedication
and service to Alabama Republicans

Gene L. Howard
'12

Frontispiece: A satisfied John Patterson on the night of his victory over George Wallace.
(Photo courtesy Jim Cannon.)

Patterson for Alabama

The Life and Career
of John Patterson

Gene Howard

THE UNIVERSITY OF ALABAMA PRESS
Tuscaloosa

Copyright © 2008
The University of Alabama Press
Tuscaloosa, Alabama 35487-0380
All rights reserved
Manufactured in the United States of America

Typeface: Goudy

∞

The paper on which this book is printed meets the minimum requirements of American National Standard for Information Sciences-Permanence of Paper for Printed Library Materials, ANSI Z39.48-1984.

Library of Congress Cataloging-in-Publication Data

Howard, Gene L., 1940–
    Patterson for Alabama : the life and career of John Patterson / Gene Howard.
        p.   cm.
    Includes bibliographical references and index.
    ISBN 978-0-8173-1605-1 (cloth : alk. paper) — ISBN 978-0-8173-8056-4 (electronic : alk. paper) 1. Governors—Alabama—Biography. 2. Lawyers—Alabama—Biography. 3. Judges—Alabama—Biography. 4. Alabama—Politics and government—1951- 5. Alabama—Social conditions—20th century. 6. Phenix City (Ala.)—History—20th century. 7. Alabama—Biography. I. Patterson, John, 1921 Sept. 21- II. Title.
    F330.3.P27H68 2008
    976.1′063092—dc22
    [B]

2007042108

Contents

Preface and Acknowledgments

This is a story about a remarkable period in Alabama history and some of the people who made it remarkable. From the 1950s through the 1970s, southern history provides many stories of the good and the bad as the Old South made the awkward, sometimes painful, transition to a more modern era. This is the setting for the people and events the reader will encounter in this book.

This is not, strictly speaking, an academic book. It is, however, a documented account. Although it is primarily about Albert and John Patterson, it also looks at how Alabama struggled to enjoy the benefits of efficient state government during a time when the South went through the terror and turmoil of the civil rights movement.

The most important resources in compiling this story were the cooperation of John Patterson and Patterson family members and the contributions from those who had significant roles in the Patterson administration. Official documents and personal information were made available without restriction or control, and at no time did John Patterson attempt to influence my treatment of the material. He was candid in his disclosures and encouraged those close to him to be the same.

A note about the documentation. As my intention was to tell a story, rather than to produce an analytical study of the man and the times, I have not interrupted the narrative flow with copious note numbers. An endnote number appears at the end of a passage on a particular topic, which may extend over several paragraphs; citations for the passage are grouped together in the endnote.

Acknowledgments are always necessary with a work of this nature. I am indebted, among others, to the following for their contributions in getting the manuscript ready for publication. Maxine Rose and George Whitesell were instrumental in helping me meet the standards of the University of Alabama Press. Through the years, members of the University of Alabama history department, especially William Barnard and Gary Mills, offered important counsel pertaining to the context of the period. Valuable information also came from the personal collections of Charles Meriwether, Hilda Coulter, Harry Cook, and Hugh Bentley. Jim Cannon of Phenix City permitted me to use selections from his valuable collection of photographs. Ray Jenkins provided observations about the characters and events in the last gasps of Phenix City's criminal empire, as well as John Patterson's time in public service. I'm grateful to my wife, Janice, who helped collect information and diligently proofed the draft of the manuscript. Many libraries and archives provided material, including the John F. Kennedy Library in Boston.

One final comment. The occurrences during this period continue to lie heavily on the consciousness of most Alabamians. Dark newspaper headlines and news reports about racial conflict created a negative image of the state that still persists for those watching from afar. Yet the people of Alabama, black and white, have moved on to a new and more progressive era. Not everything is perfect, nor do we expect it to be, but important changes have opened many doors that were previously closed and have improved the prospect of a better life for everyone.

I trust readers will find value in the time they invest in reading this story.

I have enjoyed working on it for the past two decades.

Patterson for Alabama

1
Looking for a Rainbow in Phenix City

It is characteristic of human nature to discount recognized risks when making critical decisions and focus instead on promising aspects of a venture. And it was this characteristic that led Albert Patterson to move his family to Phenix City, Alabama. In 1933, at the height of the Great Depression, he decided to live and work in a town remarkable for its violence and corruption. The move would create within his family a life of contrasts between good and evil and bring them to a historic confrontation with the town's century-old decadence. But those who knew Patterson well understood that he was not a reckless person. He would not expose his young family to the criminal environment that thrived on the banks of the Chattahoochee River—not without good reason.

Albert Patterson saw in Phenix City the possibility of financial success, something that otherwise seemed out of reach at that point in his life. In exchange for that opportunity he would accept whatever risks came with living there. Patterson wanted a better chance at succeeding in the legal profession. For five years he had struggled to establish a law practice in Alexander City. The Depression was not the best time for starting new careers or business ventures, and nothing indicated that the future would be any different. So on a hot summer day in 1933, after telling his wife that he was driving over to Russell County, Albert Patterson went to get a better feel for Phenix City.

He saw something he hadn't seen for a while in Alabama: a thriving economy. Streets were crowded with shoppers, and the town, as well as neighboring Columbus, Georgia, across the Chattahoochee River, was bustling with business and trade. The difference from Alexander City and the rest of Depression-era Alabama was startling. Patterson spent the morning riding around Phenix City and Columbus, and he took a walking tour through the Russell County courthouse that overlooked the river. He was impressed with the downtown and looked at some homes in the Pine Hill neighborhood. It didn't take him long to decide that his prospects would be decidedly better in Russell County—even if it was a showplace for corruption. Back home late that afternoon, he told his wife, Agnes, that they were moving to Phenix City. Without hesitation she agreed, and the family began packing their meager belongings.

The Pattersons—Albert, Agnes, and their three sons—moved within days so that Albert could restart a law career that had thus far been disappointing. Their kinfolk in Tallapoosa County didn't want them living in a place like Phenix City, and back home at the family farm in Goldville in northern Tallapoosa County, Albert's father, Delona Patterson, warned him that he didn't know what he was getting his family into. Nonetheless, the Pattersons left Alexander City reasonably aware of what they could expect in Phenix City. In any case, Albert and Agnes felt they were in no position to be overly particular, and they believed they could safely live and raise their family there.

Throughout the South dirt farmers and cotton mill workers scratched and fought for survival during the Depression while inhabitants of Phenix City prospered. The reason was geographic: The town lay just across the Chattahoochee River from the thriving metropolis of Columbus, Georgia, which owed a major share of its prosperity to Fort Benning, the nearby army infantry training base. The Phenix City–Columbus area teemed with commerce and industry, apparently unaffected by the economic disaster that had all but stalled the economy of the rest of the nation. It was this stark difference that Albert Patterson saw when he drove over from Alexander City looking for a place to relocate a law practice that was going nowhere.

Five years earlier the family had left Opelika for the same reason, after Patterson's first attempt at a law career stalled. Alexander City proved to be no different; few clients had hard cash to pay for his professional services. Albert Patterson had a row of German machine-gun bullets permanently embedded in his right leg and he managed to keep his family supplied with the bare essentials with a World War I disability check of less than one hundred dollars a month. Debts piled up because all too frequently he was paid for his occasional legal work with farm produce, homemade syrup, or chickens.

The Pattersons' life had long been a mixture of hard work, near poverty, and the sacrifices that Albert and Agnes made to acquire an education. To help the family overcome their financial straits, Agnes Patterson taught elementary school. Their eldest son, John, had a *Birmingham Post* paper route. With the money he made, he bought his own clothes, charging them to the account he maintained at Froshins, a downtown department store.

Even with family help, Albert Patterson saw little hope in continuing to wrestle with problems that were clearly beyond his control. One bright moment occurred during the Alexander City period, however. A group of townspeople elected him spokesman for a four-car caravan that traveled to nearby Warm Springs, Georgia, to encourage New York governor Franklin Roosevelt to seek the presidency on the Democratic ticket. According to Judge Jack Coley who coordinated the visit, Patterson spoke commendably. Yet not long afterward he decided it was time to move on.[1]

Albert Patterson found his rainbow in Phenix City. Within a decade, he had achieved the kind of personal success that had previously eluded him. The city of about twenty-five thousand had a reputation as the most sinister place in Alabama, perhaps even the South. Seemingly, it had always been that way. One historical narrative said the town had been named Girard at an earlier time, and described it as "a loosely organized community in the 1800s that became a refuge for gamblers, murderers, thieves and drunks trying to escape the law across the river in Columbus. It bloomed as a colony of villains who cohabited with the Indians and reveled in corrupt freedom, making regular criminal excursions into Georgia and returning to sanctuary in Girard." The surrounding population, the account went on, was highly indignant at the behavior of the depraved villagers, and referred to it as "Sodom," the city on the plains of Jordan notorious for its wickedness.[2]

The rutted dirt streets of Phenix City were crowded with young soldiers, college students from nearby Auburn University, and visitors looking for fun and excitement. Revelers had their choice of virtually every kind of vice: open debauchery, booze, gambling, prostitution, narcotics. There was even an abortion ring. The town was economically dominated by the underworld characters that masterminded the rackets. The same band of hoods held the local government in a death grip and, through judicious payoffs, kept state and federal authorities from interfering. For Albert Patterson, Phenix City's primary sources of income—crime and corruption—meant legal work and plenty of it; soon he was able to settle his Alexander City debts.

Albert Patterson had fought in a world war, returned home crippled for life, and become an educator in an effort to develop a respectable professional career. He taught school, even in one-roomers. He turned to law in his late thirties, spending summers at Cumberland Law School in Tennessee, working on his law degree in hopes of finding success in another profession.

John Patterson was twelve when the family settled in Phenix City. Small of stature like his mother's people, the Bensons from Sunny Level, he was entirely content with the rural adventures to be found in small towns and on his grandfather's Goldville farm, where he had been born on September 21, 1921. John found Phenix City seductive. He explored the forbidden streets and alleys, often playing war games with his friends on a hill south of town, referred to as either Confederate or Ku Klux Hill. At the time John was unaware that his great-grandfather John Love Patterson—a conscripted miller from Hackneyville—had helped dig the rifle pits when the Confederate Army rallied one final time to fight what some consider the last battle of the Civil War. A better-than-average athlete, Patterson developed a passion for baseball, playing all the positions. Articles in the local papers noted that his bat often provided the margin of victory for his team.

Young Patterson was predictably awed by Phenix City and neighboring Columbus, which he considered one big town. "There was always something to do. Columbus was the center of a lot of sports activity, baseball and football games," he recalled. It was a stimulating world for a teenager. Ignoring his parents' warnings and determined to satisfy his curiosity, he spent his spare time downtown hanging out at honky-tonks, flophouses, and clip joints like Heavy's Place, the Manhattan Club, the Silver Dollar Cafe, Pat Murphy's, and the most celebrated dive of all—Ma Beachie's Swing Club. He watched bartenders rebottle unconsumed beer and knew bar girls and whores on a first-name basis; he also knew that the Bridge Grocery did not have as much as a can of sardines on the premises. In a short time Patterson became friends with the colorful characters up and down the strip that ran along Fourteenth Street, the only paved street in town and the one that brought the nightly trade over from Columbus.[3]

None of this changed his work habits, however, and he soon found work at King's Grocery in the downtown business district. King's was one of several stores in a local chain that offered delivery service. John earned ten to fifteen cents a trip delivering boxes of groceries by bicycle around the two cities. A large poolroom, where gambling was the primary activity, was across the street from the grocery store; a whole battery of slot machines lined the walls and the proprietor took bets on professional baseball. It became John's favorite haunt. He spent his spare time betting on baseball, playing the "bug"—the lottery—and dropping nickels in the slots.[4]

Growing up in Phenix City was distinctly different from growing up almost anywhere else in 1930s America. A normal American childhood customarily revolved around a combination of family, school, and religion of some sort. John Patterson came of age in a place where huge sums of money were wagered; sex, whiskey, and drugs were openly for sale; and local authorities profited by looking the other way. Living with widespread corruption, Phenix City citizens had learned to accept the town's character. John Patterson went to school with the children of the gamblers, madams, and casino owners and didn't find anything unusual in his relationship with them. Respectable families attended church (surprisingly, there were more churches than honky-tonks) and warned their children about going down to the strip. Still, many of the boys took their lunch money and played slot machines conveniently installed in a grocery store across the street from the school, provided with wooden stools so the smaller children could reach the levers. In spite of the appearance of moral chaos, the environment didn't seem to affect the children, who tended to look at the town's strange character as normal adult fun and games.

John Patterson had positive elements in his life: Sundays spent with his family at Trinity Methodist Church, his father's professional standing in the community that came to include a seat on the local school and draft boards, and his mother's teaching career. Nevertheless, John seemed drawn to the dark side of town in defiance of his parents' admonitions. A favorite amusement was to go downtown with some friends and hang out at the bars on Fort Benning's payday. The youngsters watched as a steady procession of soldiers entered the bars then left with one of the working girls. John also had a more than casual relationship with one of the whorehouses in the North Highlands section of Columbus, often spending summer evenings swinging with the girls on the front porch and earning pocket money by running errands for the madam. From 1933 through 1939 John Patterson tried to balance two dissimilar worlds: the one in which his stern and demanding father tried to keep him from mischief and ruin and the one that offered easy money and excitement.

Except for a hobo adventure that he and his friend Sidney Pelham took at age sixteen—a grand southeastern tour made by thumbing and riding the rails—Phenix City was the most formative experience of his youth. This was also when his independence became more pronounced. He was a good student, excelling in English and math, but he also played cards, shot craps, and drank wildcat whiskey in a small coppice at the edge of town. In the summers, he and neighborhood boys fished in the rapids at the river's fall line. He didn't smoke and the last time his father took his razor strap to him was when someone told on him for drinking at Charlie's Frog Eye Saloon. "He beat the hell out of me," Patterson remembered. The razor strap was not Albert's only form of punishment. Whenever the Patterson boys broke a family rule, they were made to lie under their parent's bed for extended periods of time. That was particularly embarrassing when the boys were almost grown or the family had company over for a visit.[5]

John's first experience with adult frustration came in his senior year of high school, when he tried to discuss postgraduation plans with his father. Except to say that he wanted his son to go to college, Albert brushed aside further discussion of the subject. John wanted to go to the University of Alabama, but he needed his father's financial support, support that John thought Albert was avoiding. John was offered another choice when the owners of King's grocery chain asked him to manage one of their stores after graduation. John was reluctant to accept the offer because he did not want the grocery business to be his life's work. He wanted advice and a financial commitment from his father.

He waited, often talking with his mother about his discouragement, yet anticipating that his father would eventually address the matter—but nothing happened. Eventually, John realized he had to make his own career decision. The only choice besides college or the grocery business was the military, which had held a fascination for Patterson since he came to Phenix City. He had toured Fort Benning for special events and was impressed by the sheer size of the installation. The fort, named after Confederate general Henry Lewis Benning, was experiencing a massive construction boom during Patterson's initial visits. Federal work projects directed by the Roosevelt administration enabled the army to convert what had been an old plantation into a first-rate infantry training school. It would eventually encompass 187,000 acres, with about 12,000 of those acres in Alabama. John ate in mess halls that served more food than he had ever seen in his entire life, and he took particular interest in long rows of cannon in the artillery units. "This appeared to be the only real choice I had at the time," he recalled. "Even at graduation time my father never said a word about college, which was very upsetting. So I began thinking more and more about the military." Military service was not unheard of in the family. Albert had been wounded in an assault against the Germans at Saint-Etienne during World War I, and been decorated for his service, and two of John's great-grandfathers were Confederate Army veterans.[6]

John first attempted to enlist in the navy but was turned down because he was too young. Dejected, Patterson kept his job at the grocery store, resentful of his father's seeming indifference. Many evenings he entertained himself with the nightly activity along the strip, occasionally dating one of the girls from the Pine Hill neighborhood where the Pattersons lived, idly marking time as he waited for something to give his life a more meaningful turn. Finally in March 1940, dismayed that his life was going nowhere and with war under way in Europe and Asia, he walked over to the Columbus post office and enlisted in the army. Since he was still not of enlistment age, he had to have his father's signature, a requirement that seemed ironic to him: "I walked back to my father's office and waited outside like any other client until he could see me. He studied the paper for some time and looked at me only briefly. He agreed to sign the enlistment paper under one condition; that I stick it out to the bitter end, come what may. I agreed, and that night I slept at Fort Benning."[7]

John Patterson was now part of a peacetime army of fewer than a hundred thousand men—his future firmly set for the next five years.

2
From El Guettar to the University

The nation was mobilizing its military and industrial base to meet the demands of World War II when Corporal Patterson came home on leave in March 1942. For some time he and Gladys Broadwater, whom he had dated regularly before enlisting, had been corresponding frequently and seriously. Gladys was a senior at Central High School and somehow in all the talking and writing, the idea of getting married "just came up and we agreed on it," according to Patterson. They obtained a marriage license in Opelika and drove down to Seale to get married in the old courthouse. But when Patterson returned to base he was convinced they had made a foolish decision.[1]

If Patterson was dismayed by the marriage, he soon got over it. In June 1942, he received an appointment to Officer Candidates School (OCS) at Fort Sill, Oklahoma. The "ninety-day wonder" taunt didn't rankle him, and he graduated with high marks. He was especially gratified to write his father about his achievement.[2]

Patterson's high scores at OCS landed him an assignment with army administration at General Eisenhower's headquarters in London, where—with car and driver—he delivered military documents around the city, including Number Ten Downing Street and the British War Office. He became friends with Kay Summersby, Eisenhower's English driver, although he remembered nothing that hinted of her alleged affair with Ike. Drinking beer with friends at local pubs, Patterson often startled them with his knowledge of the conduct of the war and with surprisingly accurate predictions of many of the Allies' tactical moves. He did not tell them that, on the sly, he was reading the documents during the delivery runs.

Like many American soldiers Patterson wanted to get closer to the war. He got his wish when he took part in the invasion of North Africa, going ashore at Algiers to help set up Eisenhower's headquarters. Installed in an office at the palatial Saint George Hotel in Algiers, he was responsible for issuing medals, citations, and decorations to the Allied forces. It was an assignment that any infantryman would envy, nevertheless he lay awake at night watching as German planes bombed the city and harbor, wanting desperately to get into the fight. Inevitably, whenever he and Kay Summersby met during the North Africa invasion, the discussion quickly reverted to their personal complaints; he wanted to get into the war and she wanted to go home.[3]

His fortunes changed one day in the hotel dining room, when by chance he found himself seated for dinner with the inspector general and the surgeon general of the U.S. Army. The two dignitaries looked him over carefully and immediately asked: What's a young man like you doing in a place like this? Patterson couldn't have written a better script himself and quickly launched into a lengthy explanation of his London and Algiers duty, and how he wanted an assignment with an artillery unit. The officials listened without comment as they finished the meal. The next day, Patterson was assigned to the 1st Battalion of the 17th Field Artillery, in desert training at the time, and given command of a platoon with six 37-mm antitank guns. Excited about being part of the world conflict, he promptly wrote his family about his new assignment, and predicted that he was going to "kick hell out of the Huns."[4]

Patterson's first combat experience came at El Guettar, in the North Africa campaign, a pivotal World War II battle that will be analyzed and studied for generations. On March 23, 1943, his battery took part in a twenty-four-hour pitched battle supporting Patton's forces as they dueled with the Tenth Panzer Afrika Korps in the desert. Military historians portray it as a Homeric battle, with American forces entrenched in the hills and the Panzers rumbling toward them in parade ground formation across the desert floor. The Germans, in an effort to awe the green American troops, led with their infantry followed by rows of tanks in what observers said looked like a grand assault in the style of the American Civil War.

Patterson's artillery battalion was entrenched in the overlooking hills, pouring out a steady stream of fire, turning back the German advance again and again throughout a day and night of spine-tingling assaults.

The spectacular attacks by the Germans would stand as an unmatched personal experience: "I have never been involved in anything that equaled the Battle of El Guettar; it was the longest day of my life. Those of us who survived formed friendships that have lasted the rest of our lives." The next day a thoroughly drained and battle-weary Patterson received a letter from back home: the navy was ready to consider his enlistment now that he had reached the proper enlistment age.[5]

His involvement in the war was just beginning. His unit took part in seven campaigns in Italy, Sicily, Germany, and France, expending more than 150,000 rounds of ammunition according to a unit newsletter. Pleased that he was contributing to the success of the Allied campaign, John wrote to his parents describing how he ate Thanksgiving dinner "standing knee deep in water and mud with shells flying overhead." In Hopfen am See, Germany, he led a small task force that intercepted a convoy of Germans trying to escape across the Austrian border—taking 450 prisoners. During the campaign, Patterson was promoted to captain, cited for meritorious service, and awarded the Bronze Star for his performance in France and Germany.[6]

As the war success was elevating his rank and giving him a sense of great personal satisfaction, his battalion received cease-fire orders—the war was over. "We were chasing Germans through the Alps at the time of the cease-fire, and we wanted to finish the job," he recalled. While most of the world celebrated Germany's surrender, Patterson and his men sat around in bitter disappointment late on a May night in 1945, while the officers of the battalion drank beer and played poker in a German *gasthaus*. In the dead of night, Patterson said he could not resist the temptation to fire one last round. Walking out to the unit's row of silent cannon, he rattled the whole village awake with one final thunderous round.[7]

With victory, an old dilemma resurfaced for John Patterson. He had now spent more than a fifth of his life away from home and had developed broad but vaguely defined expectations for himself. At twenty-four, he still did not know what he wanted to do with his life. In fact, he wasn't even in a real hurry to return home; the military had given him a taste of the kind of success he had wished for in Phenix City.

In early September 1945, when Patterson arrived at Fort McPherson in Atlanta, a crusty sergeant major unwittingly helped him make a decision. For six months the army had made overtures to John about making military service a career. Anticipating a furlough to visit with his parents and mull the idea over, Patterson was startled when the sergeant major told him rather curtly that he had to decide immediately. The brusque handling of the matter angered him and he told the sergeant major that he was getting out of the army. Perhaps naively, he thought someone in Washington really cared about what he had done for his country and would give him time to think about the matter.[8]

Albert and Agnes Patterson brought John's young wife, Gladys, with them when they met him in Atlanta. During the homecoming, Albert said something startling, a statement John would like to have heard following his high school graduation. Albert said John had better hurry over to the university while there was still time to enroll for the fall term. John had not reenlisted in the army; he had his GI benefits plus the money he had saved, more than five thousand dollars, a significant sum; and now his father was telling him to go to college. In a matter of days, John rented an apartment for Gladys in Phenix City and left for Tuscaloosa and the University of Alabama, just as his father had entered college after fighting in World War I.

Patterson was typical of WWII veterans who became students at the university. Older, experienced men who were serious about getting an education, they knew how to work and play in ways completely foreign to younger students straight out of high school. John took a room in a boarding house and began his studies, majoring in political science and history while considering a career in public administration. He found college intellectually demanding and often taxing, but it couldn't compare to the mental and emotional rigors of his wartime experiences.

Only weeks after he entered the university John and Gladys decided to end their marriage. It was an amiable divorce with Albert Patterson serving as Gladys's lawyer. The reason given for dissolution was "voluntary abandonment from bed and board," inaccurate but sufficiently legal to end the relationship.[9]

By the time his divorce was final, John had settled into university life and was enjoying himself. Academics, social life, sports, new people: "It was all I imagined it would be," he said. "I felt good about what I was doing because I was finally getting somewhere with my life." Toward the end of his freshman year he turned his attention to the law. It seemed like an inevitable choice; his family assumed that he was getting an education so he could return to Phenix City and practice law with his father. The degree requirements in those days could be satisfied in four years; two years of prelaw with another two years of actual law study. This apprenticeship in Patterson's professional education set a permanent course for his life, satisfying a compelling need to have a life's work that he would find satisfying. And others were beginning to take note. "We thought he had a good future, if he continued to work as he did in school," recalled Harry Hayden, one of his law professors.[10]

He moved into the Alpha Tau Omega fraternity house and roomed with Joe Robertson of Birmingham. Robertson, square-jawed with a crew cut, had put in a year at West Point. Similarities in their backgrounds made them natural allies. They studied and partied together, even sharing a plaid suit and a single white shirt for dates. They were part of a larger group of older students that included Jimmy Walker of Clanton, "Red Bay" Smith of Red Bay, and Joe Kellett from Fort Payne. The group enjoyed convivial male college rituals, often piling into the two-toned green Oldsmobile that John's father had given him and driving down to Greene County where, unlike Tuscaloosa, liquor was legal. Often they headed for a big, barnlike roadhouse with sawdust on the floor, to drink beer and tell war stories.[11]

When the social side of university life became too much of a distraction, John left the fraternity house to room at Mrs. Cummings's near the campus. He avoided campus politics, which his group regarded as frivolous. Nor did he indicate any great desire to involve himself in politics of any sort, though his friends believed he displayed leadership qualities. Irby Keener of Centre said of Patterson, "He was a man's man. People seemed to gravitate to John, and they were especially impressed that during the war he had been an officer." Robertson, who spent a good deal of time with John in college, said that Patterson was somewhat of an enigma, a person not given to emotion and who would not easily reveal his innermost thoughts. However John was building a growing circle of loyal friends and acquaintances that would form a core of support later in his life.[12]

Early in John's second year at Alabama during the fall term, Jimmy Walker arranged a date for John with Mary Joe McGowin from Clanton. "Jimmy talked excitedly about John, telling me that he was something special, and that I should go out with him," Mary Joe recalled. She did. Within a week John gave her his fraternity pin and not many weeks later they were seriously discussing marriage. The courtship lasted a year. John was in law school when they married on October 19, 1947. The Reverend John Carlisle Miller officiated. With lots of Pattersons and McGowins in attendance, the Methodist Church at Clanton overflowed. Sibley McGowin, local lumber merchant, held an equally crowded reception at his home. Albert Patterson stepped in as John's best man when Joe Robertson went to the hospital for an emergency appendectomy.[13]

Certain difficulties had to be overcome before Mary Joe's family would agree to the marriage. After Mary Joe brought John home to meet her family for the first time, Sibley McGowin checked into Patterson's background. His curiosity was piqued when he learned Albert had been elected to the state senate in 1946 and practiced law in lawless Phenix City. When McGowin and his wife discovered that John had been previously married and divorced they were alarmed; Mary Joe was crushed by the revelation. John explained the brief marriage to the McGowins, why he and Gladys had eventually divorced, even his father's role in the matter. Mary Joe said John was able to answer the family's more serious concerns: "He was always able to charm his way out of anything." Wedding plans were allowed to continue, but the McGowins clearly had some concerns about their new son-in-law.[14]

John Patterson completed law school in the summer of 1949, after struggling to pay for his schooling and maintain an apartment for Mary Joe and himself without support from either family. Despite the economic strain, he was beginning to see some positive results. Like his military career, law school had been a real confidence builder. The Farrah Order of Jurisprudence, a university society reserved for top law students, recognized his scholastic work, and Patterson's classmates elected him secretary of the Law School Student Government Association. The faculty chose him for membership to the board of editors, a select group of students who managed the *Alabama Law Review*.

Patterson was eager to complete his education and return to Phenix City to practice law. Mary Joe was pregnant, and his savings were getting uncomfortably low. "I wanted to buy a house, make some money, and start building a reputation as a good lawyer," he explained. "At the same time, my father was starting a statewide campaign for lieutenant governor and he kept telling me to hurry up and finish school, there was plenty of work in Phenix City." John Patterson received his law degree in August 1949 and moved a very pregnant Mary Joe into a small basement apartment in his family's home in Pine Hill. He was admitted to the Alabama State Bar on September 15; three days later, Albert Love Patterson III was born in a Columbus hospital.[15]

John Patterson had just turned twenty-eight when he started practicing law in Phenix City. He reflected the prevailing southern temperament in his thinking and reasoning. He believed that everyone should be treated fairly, black and white, but he felt no inclination to oppose general conventions on race, especially now that he was offering his services to the public. He was also a staunch Democrat in a one-party state where fewer than ten thousand blacks voted.

The Patterson and Patterson law firm was located on the second floor of the Coulter Building in the heart of Phenix City, a short block from the Russell County courthouse. The Chattahoochee River and the sprawling metropolis of Columbus lay in a panoramic view beyond their hilltop offices. Initially, John's legal work was simple and uncomplicated: real estate transactions, property title searches, contracts, personal injury actions, and criminal cases. He said his father watched his work closely and offered advice, which "I never failed to follow."

The first years of John and Mary Joe's marriage were simple and routine. Despite Phenix City's abundance of places to drink, gamble, and party, there was little social interaction among the townspeople outside of church. And there was, as in all southern towns, a social and geographic boundary between blacks and whites.

Stretching for more than a mile south of Girard was the lower section of town; impoverished blacks lived there as best they could in neighborhoods referred to as "Sugartown," "Punkin Bottom," and "Silk Shirt Alley." Black folks had their own schools, churches, and movie theater. They also had their own juke joints, with gambling, liquor, prostitution, and lottery tickets for sale. These services, for blacks and whites, were under the control of Hoyt Shepherd and the uptown mob.

The South Girard elementary and high school provided black families the rudiments of education for their children under the South's "separate but equal" education system. Blacks acquired another educational option when the Mother Mary Catholic School was established in 1941 by the missionary Salvatorian Fathers and Vincentian Sisters to educate poor black children. Blacks customarily were employed as porters, domestics, kitchen help, and day laborers, with many black men being loosely retained by the mob for various tasks. Georgia blacks who lived in "Kinfolks Corner," the black section across the river from lower Girard, walked across the Dillingham Street Bridge to visit with their Alabama friends and listen to some of the earliest rock-and-roll music. Fats Domino often entertained at Red Cook's Original Barbecue, where the lottery paid out forty to sixty dollars each day. Many blacks were avid lottery players. All knew to avoid conflict with the Ku Klux Klan. When Klansmen and their law enforcement collaborators got dolled up in their white robes and hoods, crosses blazed on Ku Klux Hill. Blacks and poor whites took particular care not to provoke anyone connected with these perpetually mean-spirited criminals. White folks around town took comfort in knowing that blacks "knew their place."[16]

About the time John Patterson returned to Phenix City, the gangsters' influence was at its peak, attracting thousands each night to Phenix City's Mardi Gras style revelry. Since there were no stores where brand-name goods could be bought, most citizens crossed the river bridge and shopped in Columbus. There was no reason for respectable people to be seen about town after working hours. Patterson said the only exception he and Mary Joe made to this custom was the occasional dinner at the Yellow Front restaurant on Dillingham Street, owned by one of the gambling kingpins; it had a Chinese chef.

Just as John was getting comfortable with his legal career and starting to generate badly needed income, Albert Patterson launched his statewide campaign for lieutenant governor. The race, the first that John had witnessed closeup, created a rift between the two men. John was shocked and angered at how political considerations preempted the family legal business. These were not his expectations for a career in the law. There were daily demands on Albert's time that John found irritating and of little value to the business. Heated arguments erupted when John felt that his father was spending too much time away from the office or when too many visitors, who were not clients, were hanging out in their law offices. As the election neared, tension between father and son increased. John Patterson said, "I was determined to avoid any personal involvement in politics."[17]

3
Praying the Devil Out of Town

John Patterson said that his first months back in Phenix City were a revelation. "I didn't realize how aggressively my father had become involved in Russell County politics." Away for more than a decade, John, in his brief visits back home, had had only brief glimpses of what he now recognized as a dangerous political conflict. He also saw how deeply his father had come to hate the town's corrupt power structure. By the time John graduated from high school, Albert Patterson had broadened his community activities into veterans affairs and educational and fraternal activities, earning him considerable prominence throughout Russell County. However, John Patterson had been away during the formative period of a citizens' revolt against the gambling empire and he wondered about the wisdom of a confrontation with the traditional power structure. Albert Patterson was preparing to oppose people whose interests he had previously represented.[1]

Early in his law practice, Albert Patterson had had a working relationship with people associated with Phenix City's notorious gambling empire. That connection was evident in 1945, when he made a successful run for the Lee and Russell counties senate seat in the Alabama legislature. A heated three-man race saw him win without a runoff, polling almost the same percentage of votes in neighboring Lee County as in his home county of Russell. Albert could not have won without an alliance with the local gambling kingpins who controlled the election machinery in Russell County. The election clearly linked Patterson to Phenix City's power brokers. "We were realistic about practicing law in a place like Phenix City," John Patterson explained about the law firm. "We handled all kinds of legal work for the local people, which naturally included the gambling crowd."

Accommodating underworld characters as part of their clientele generated income for the Pattersons. During his first decade in Phenix City, Albert Patterson defended some of the city's leading criminal figures, the most notable being Grady and Hoyt Shepherd. The Shepherds were indicted for the murder of Fate Leeburn, a member of a rival crime organization across the river in Columbus. The brothers, who hired virtually every attorney in town, including Patterson and a young lawyer named Arch Ferrell, were acquitted without having to testify. Patterson received a handsome thousand dollar fee for his work. Later, Albert also defended "Head" Revel against extradition proceedings connected with a Florida murder charge. While he did occasional legal work for them, Patterson was never in a position of obligation to the crime organization. Family and friends recall that underworld figures attempted to fraternize with Albert, but he distanced himself from them. John remembers that their attempts to chat with him on the street were met with silence: Albert would simply ignore the conversational gambit, walk around them, cane in hand, and continue on.[2]

Nevertheless, the mob's electoral muscle sent Patterson to the senate, and there he acquired a new political ally in Jim Folsom. The 1946 Alabama gubernatorial race saw the rise of a political phenomenon in James E. "Big Jim" Folsom. Democratic Party leaders didn't take Folsom's bid for governor seriously, although he had made a respectable showing in the 1942 race. He lacked the traditional support of courthouse politicians and had no impressive financial backers. Knowing this, Folsom made his case by appealing directly to Alabama's plain folks. The customary hillbilly band entertained the crowds while Folsom, brandishing a corn-shuck mop and using laughably outrageous speeches to damn special interests and their politicians, passed a bucket for donations. Folsom enjoyed baiting big city newspapers and frequently referred to the *Montgomery Advertiser* as little more than a fish wrapper. One political observer said Folsom excited a "religious contagion" among the voters. However he did it, Folsom confounded political experts and in 1946 the lumbering six-foot-eight-inch insurance salesman was elected governor of Alabama.[3]

Albert Patterson became a Folsom ally soon after the election, although he had supported Handy Ellis for governor, as had the local political bosses. Patterson and Folsom had the same political philosophies: both men were steeped in populism and Roosevelt's New Deal policies. They saw the government's role as being responsive to the people and their economic problems—ideals that they earnestly hoped to develop in the Alabama legislature.

When the first session convened in 1947, Folsom had little influence in the House and was met with open hostility in the Senate. Albert Patterson became one of the administration's few allies when both sides turned to bitter fighting that almost grounded the governor's populist agenda. The Senate divided along conservative/liberal lines, with the opposition forming the "economy block." Composed mainly of representatives from Alabama's Black Belt counties, the cotton kingdom south of Montgomery, it was led by Walter Givhan, Bruce Henderson, and Sam Engelhardt. This group, segregationists to the man, opposed passage and funding of the administration's "People Program." Patterson was one of a small group of senators who supported legislation for improvements in the state's education and highway systems. He further supported Folsom by attempting—unsuccessfully—to obtain confirmation for the governor's nominees to state boards.[4]

Patterson became Folsom's political ally for the usual reasons: to help his constituency back home with their many needs and to strengthen his legislative influence. While the administration courted his favor in the hostile Senate chambers, they made the natural assumption that he was also closely allied with the Phenix City crowd. It was an erroneous conclusion. Folsom learned the truth after he took office. He sent for Patterson, instructing him to "tell the boys to get the black bag ready and bring it over here Monday morning." Albert, who knew that the underworld routinely paid off state officials, angrily told Folsom to get it himself and, leaning heavily on his cane, stamped out of the governor's office.

According to the historian George Sims, the incident did no real harm to the Folsom-Patterson relationship; Albert later persuaded the governor to have the gamblers' henchman Arch Ferrell appointed as district attorney in the newly created Twenty-Sixth Judicial Circuit Court for Russell County. Patterson also received the governor's appointment to a committee to investigate the conditions of Alabama's prison system, which resulted in revealing a scandal in the pardon and parole system—corruption was so pervasive that prisoners gained freedom through political favors and bribery. The relationship between Albert and Big Jim remained cordial during the first session, and when Folsom visited Phenix City he stayed overnight with the Pattersons. Mrs. Patterson solved the problem of sleeping accommodations for the governor's considerable height by moving a cedar chest to the foot of the guest bed.[5]

During his first session Albert Patterson coauthored some important bills and guided them through the legislature. True to his populist leanings, he cosponsored with Rep. George Wallace the act that created the first trade school in Alabama, and he cosponsored the Wallace-Cater Act that authorized the issue of state bonds for industrial expansion. Both these bills represented a major effort by the state to attract new industry and begin programs to train skilled workers.

Early in the second session Patterson and Folsom's relationship was shattered by the patronage appointment of a probate judge in Lee County. As the ranking legislator, Albert expected someone of his choosing to fill the post, but the governor appointed the nominee of the other members of the Lee Country delegation. Sims believes this appointment angered Patterson to the extent that he broke all political ties with the governor, throwing his support to the "economy block" faction.[6]

Albert Patterson did not put himself at risk when he broke with the governor. Folsom's popularity had been seriously damaged by a highly publicized paternity suit and a tendency to get roaring drunk in public. The rift liberated him from the Folsom stigma and accommodated Patterson's latest political venture. By the end of the session, Patterson was stumping the state as a candidate for lieutenant governor.

Albert Patterson never explained, publicly or privately, why he invested so much of his life seeking political office. What little is known comes from sifting through a few brief speeches and some campaign correspondence in his personal files. Apparently he thought politics would be the most effective method of accomplishing his goals with regard to community involvement and educational improvement. Organized crime and education were Patterson's two most frequently mentioned topics. A speech written for the lieutenant governor's race touched on the major concerns of Alabamians in 1950 and completed Patterson's platform: states' rights and local self-government, old age pensions and welfare, the corrupt state prison system, party loyalty, reapportionment, roads, veteran's services, and segregation. Other than jobs and industry, the speech was tailored for the primarily rural electorate across the state.

Friends and family believed Albert Patterson was attracted to politics because of his education, his agrarian background, and his altruistic faith, which had been instilled in him in country churches. This impression is confirmed by a comment penciled in at the bottom of one of his speeches: "My philosophy: Live & help others live."

The lieutenant governor, the second highest official in Alabama's state government, was a part-time constitutional office and involved few responsibilities other than presiding over the Senate. Customarily, the office attracted only casual interest during statewide elections, prompting many to regard it as little more than a "beauty contest." But in 1950 the race was crowded with seven candidates, including James B. Allen, a well-known state senator from Gadsden. Albert's inaugural race had occurred the year before when he ran unsuccessfully for delegate to the National Democratic Convention. John, who was finishing law school at the time, got his first political experience speaking on behalf of his father at schoolhouse rallies and box suppers around Tuscaloosa County.

Albert had no real political organization; his finances—all his own money— were limited; and his extended family did most of the campaigning. His campaign style consisted of talking with friends and neighbors and an occasional speech about issues of interest. Advertising money was scarce; friends of Patterson, including his politically astute brother Lafayette, attempted to make up the difference with a scattering of radio ads in major markets across the state. Patterson finished a weak third in the May state primary and Allen eventually won the lieutenant governor's position. County vote totals show with striking clarity Patterson's favor with the Phenix City machine. Almost 90 percent of Russell County's votes went to Patterson, a feat he was unable to match elsewhere, even in his home county of Tallapoosa.[7]

After the convincing defeat, Albert Patterson turned his attention back to Phenix City, his political fervor more subdued and with a long list of campaign debts to settle. He expressed no further interest in politics to his family and friends. The only comment he made to his supporters was that he would pay his bills and get back to his law practice, which by now included his son as his law partner.

Meanwhile, seeds for change were being sown across a city that had earned a well-merited epithet: the Wickedest City in the United States. What was to become a civil revolution began as a simple and improbable movement: citizens started meeting in their churches for around-the-clock prayer vigils, seeking divine help in ridding the town of crime and widespread evil. The gambling interests had all but neutralized the civic action of the local Christian community or at least forced it into sullen and resentful silence. Prayer meetings may have seemed like an unlikely answer to a problem that had existed for more than a century. But for the good people of Phenix City it seemed their only hope. Civil authorities did not function in matters of vice and crime; state authorities ignored the town like grandparents ignoring the bad behavior of an unruly child; and Hilda Coulter, one of the early advocates for a clean city, noted that casino owners hedged against federal intervention by buying the proper federal gaming licenses, filling out income tax returns that accurately reported their earnings, and paying off the authorities.

Out of a sense of desperation, the churches turned to the only source of help accessible to them, the supernatural. The prayer meetings began in early 1950 and continued regularly with few results other than bolstering the hopes of the congregations involved. A few ministers attempted to persuade leading crime figures to give up criminal activity, and when two of the town's mayors died from heart attacks in quick succession, some ministers wanted to take credit for their unexpected deaths. The reform group was astonished that many locals defended the city's domination by a lawless element, citing generous contributions to charities made by the gamblers, who were particularly generous with church building funds. Talk heard around town was that gambling was an innocent pastime and the people who ran the casinos and bars weren't such a bad lot.[8]

Immorality had been the hallmark of the town since territorial days, but not until 1916 did state authorities move to purge criminal activities from the town. Alabama attorney general William Logan Martin led a sizable party of state agents into the town for what has been called the largest liquor raid ever made in the South. Martin was forced to raise private money to stage the raid because the governor wouldn't authorize use of state funds to break up the illegal whiskey operation. Newspaper accounts reported that agents poured an estimated 1 million gallons of moonshine into the murky waters of the Chattahoochee River in a single day. The county sheriff was impeached and the mayor and the aldermen resigned "by popular demand." Whiskey was even found in the vault of the Phenix-Girard bank, held as collateral for outstanding loans. Hugo Black, then one of Martin's assistants and later a Supreme Court Justice, took part in the raid.

Federal authorities intervened in 1923, when U.S. government agents made their first effort to clean up Phenix City. They destroyed whiskey stills and confiscated illegal liquor from numerous bars and cheap dives. In 1931, a federal grand jury was empaneled and indicted several city officials for violating Prohibition laws. The police chief, his assistant, and another law officer were sent to prison. The city commission reacted by passing an ordinance legalizing beer sales in an attempt to discourage further raids.

In 1938, when the Ritz Cafe, a liquor house specializing in the lottery, collapsed under the weight of a huge crowd waiting for the daily lottery results, the presence of large-scale gambling became obvious. The Ritz was one of seven lotteries operating in Phenix City, some employing as many as a hundred "writers" who took bets on the daily numbers. Twenty-four people were killed and eighty-four injured. All of those killed and eighty of the injured were black. An estimated fifteen thousand people from both sides of the river crowded around the wrecked building; the incident is considered one of the Chattahoochee Valley's greatest disasters. A newspaper account of the accident lauded the rescue efforts by "men who put aside race differences and rose to the heights of valor and heroism." John Patterson, then a high school senior, watched as mangled bodies were pulled from the wrecked building. The city commission promised to investigate the existence of illegal lotteries. Predictably, it failed to deliver on its promise.[9]

In an effort to rationalize the existence of widespread crime, local authorities claimed that their "liberal" policies toward liquor and gambling were necessary because of the lack of revenue-producing industry and trade. City leaders rejected the argument that industry refused to locate there because of crime. The city went bankrupt during the Depression, incurring a $1.1 million debt, and was in the hands of a federal receiver until the debt was satisfied. In an attempt to generate income from the only commercial ventures in town—the liquor and gambling trade—the commissioners created a system of fines and forfeitures to raise money for the city treasury.

It worked this way. Certain types of businesses were specified as being in violation of city ordinances. Those who operated them were assessed a substantial fine, which they were expected to pay (through forfeiture of bonds). As long as the fines were paid, the business could operate. "We have licensed every kind of business that could be licensed and some that should not have been," Mayor Homer Cobb explained in a newspaper interview. "And our officers have been very diligent in making cases and collecting fines out of those businesses which could not be licensed. The citizens must either be tolerant and depend on fines, forfeitures and license fees from the rackets, or they must face a tax increase." The system, albeit as a form of legal extortion, seemed to work well and to the apparent satisfaction of the citizenry. By 1945, the city was collecting more than $228,000 a year in fines.[10]

The willingness of the city commission to "lie down with the devil" and accept vice as legitimate commerce, attracted still more sinister characters. Hoyt Shepherd, Jimmy Matthews, C. O. "Head" Revel, Clyde Yarborough, Godwin Davis Sr., plus an assortment of lesser lights, began methodically building an empire within the shelter of the city's protected environment. By the time World War II broke out and Fort Benning expanded its infantry training facilities, these men had fashioned a powerful political machine that not only regulated the flow of vice, but also controlled the local government through its complete dominance of the electoral process and the judicial system.

The city became a place where a highly vocal and powerful clique controlled business and political life. Without fear of prosecution they rigged the ballot box as well as jury selection to guarantee the results of city or state elections as well as criminal cases. A small group of tough, homegrown thugs attached themselves to the imported gangsters and intimidated civil authorities, the courts, and even some churches. Criminals held leadership positions in the chamber of commerce, on the school and hospital boards, and in numerous service organizations. Arch Ferrell, who chaired the Russell County Democratic Party in addition to being a leader of the gangster element, often boasted, apparently without irony, that Phenix City was "one of the cleanest little towns in America."

In addition to such perversions of justice, local law enforcement and city officials were members of the Ku Klux Klan. Locals remembered that the Klan held annual torch light parades through Phenix City to intimidate local blacks. Robed Klansmen walked or rode on the fenders of slowly moving cars; they were so easily recognizable under their sheets that people along the parade route called them by name. The parades always concluded with a raucous rally south of town at Ku Klux Hill, where a cross was burned in sight of the black community.

This was life in Phenix City, when Albert Patterson made his first bid for political office in 1946. He did so with the support of local crime bosses, but his relationship with the machine was a carefully measured blend of cooperation and caution. John Luttrell, a close friend and anti-crime activist, said: "Albert knew it was necessary to align himself with the machine, but he did it in a way where they never could completely control him."[11]

Local apathy, compounded by indifference from state and federal authorities, ensured that the machine's influence went unchallenged in the traditional southern politics of the river town. Albert Patterson fully understood those constraints when he decided to run for public office. Machine candidates were regularly elected in fraudulent primaries. Votes were bought for as little as three dollars and sheriff's deputies stationed themselves at the four polling places to mark ballots. The Russell County Commission repeatedly sent the same "select" group of people to serve on grand juries; some were laughingly referred to as "professional jurors." The voter registration board seldom purged its list of qualified voters. Many voters who had died or moved away remained on the voting rolls, and their ballots were cast by prostitutes, crap shooters, sheriff's deputies, and slot machine mechanics. Some Georgia residents voted regularly in Phenix City municipal elections. From 1942 to 1953 only one minister and one schoolteacher, symbols of respectability in the community, served on a Russell County jury. Of a population of more than forty thousand, only eighteen hundred names were in the jury box.[12]

The first Folsom administration did nothing to threaten the gamblers' hold on the town. There had not been a legal challenge to the city machine since the early 1930s, and there was little reason to believe state government under Folsom's successor, Gov. Gordon Persons, would enforce laws against crime and gambling. The nightly stream of soldiers across the Fourteenth Street and Dillingham Street bridges found plenty of lively entertainment, prostitutes, slot machines, and crap tables in Phenix City's gaming halls. By the time Albert Patterson finished his term in the Alabama Senate, the local underworld was riding the crest of unprecedented freedom, its establishments packed with eager patrons and taking in an estimated $100 million a year in illicit profits.

It was a world turned upside down, a place where good people were regarded as crackpots and gambling was an upright, respectable profession. It was the life and heritage of thousands of Phenix City Christians who, in 1950, knelt in a chain of prayer.

4
The RBA Challenges the Gangsters

The fifties was a period of prosperity for the nation, the best since World War II, and John Patterson's fledgling law career improved dramatically with the good times. He said his familiarity with Phenix City and its people proved to be an asset and he had little trouble acquiring clients with legal problems and the money to solve them. He regarded his work—even the bizarre cases—as opportunities to prove himself professionally. Within a year after being admitted to the bar, he had his first appeal before the Alabama State Supreme Court and the beginning of a respectable and lucrative law practice.

Then on June 25, 1950, like lightning out of a clear sky, Russian-equipped North Korean troops stormed across the 38th parallel and the United States became embroiled in its second military conflict in less than a decade. John Patterson and Joe Robertson were vacationing in Daytona Beach, Florida, the Sunday of the invasion. They reacted with the predictable anger of war veterans at the news of Communist aggression and agreed they should volunteer again for military service. John returned to his old haunts at Fort Benning while Joe went back into the air force.[1]

To say that Patterson was pleased by his return to military service would be an understatement. The army had been the scene of his earliest personal triumphs and he had not lost his passion for military adventure. When he started making arrangements to return to military service, Mary Joe Patterson believed it would ultimately lead to a major change for the family. She knew that John and his father were in constant disagreement over politics, and that they argued so much that she doubted at times if the partnership would survive. "I remembered how much John loved the army, so I thought I would probably be an officer's wife permanently," she said about his reenlistment.[2]

John Patterson, major now, never made it to Korea. Russia's complicity in the conflict generated the Red Scare, and America's military strategists and their European allies developed a policy of containment toward the Soviet Union. Patterson's artillery unit was sent to defend West Germany's eastern border where he became adjutant. The Fourth Division guarded the Fulda Gap, a long, broad valley through which the Soviet Union was expected to march if there was an invasion of Europe; the mission of the Fourth Division was to hold the enemy for three days between the Fulda Gap and the Rhine River. Patterson spent a year along the border, most of the time encamped in the forests, while his family lived in Gelnhausen. His forest venture was cut short when his superiors discovered he was an attorney and transferred him to the Judge Advocate General's Section at division headquarters in Frankfurt.

While Patterson savored the excitement of his military service, particularly the border duty, the new assignment also offered him more professional opportunity. "It meant the same kind of legal work I had been doing back home," he explained, "and I gained additional experience by trying court martial cases." Just as Mary Joe anticipated, he was seriously considering a military career. The idea was firm but not final in his mind, when he was made defense attorney in a highly publicized rape trial. An American Indian named Poorthunder on a drunken spree had raped a German girl, inflaming the local population.

The army wanted a quick trial and conviction to appease the Germans. Patterson objected to several violations of the defendant's right to a fair trial (the commanding general stacked the deck with court appointments). He became especially disturbed when he realized that the military hierarchy wanted little more than a token defense. Patterson prepared the case more thoroughly than usual and convinced a military panel to give Poorthunder a jail sentence rather than execute him. The verdict, a legal triumph for Patterson and his client, drew the ire of the commanding general who sent for him and gave him an old-fashioned dressing down. Disgusted by the army's disregard of justice, Patterson once again quashed the decision to remain in the army.

The Pattersons remained in Germany for almost three years. John worked, traveled around Europe, and became a father again. Barbara

Louise (Babel) was born in Frankfurt on May 19, 1953. During his second tour in the army he was more aware of his social and political ideals, which would stand him in good stead back home. A letter from his father a few months after his return to military duty, told of family news and mentioned the Russell Betterment Association (RBA), a newly formed organization that was successfully opposing the criminal regime in Phenix City. By return letter, John told his father that he was "glad something was finally being done in Phenix City," unaware of the intensity of the struggle that raged in his hometown.[3]

When John Patterson had left Phenix City, prayers to the Almighty for deliverance from evil had competed with brash, energetic honky-tonk music. By late October 1951, the season of prayer had turned to a more aggressive crime-fighting method. A small group of citizens emerged from the mainly apathetic population determined to turn their spiritual pleading into action. The group of self-appointed crime fighters, which never numbered more than ten, met in the second floor offices of Albert Patterson and organized the Russell Betterment Association, an antivice group that would challenge the racketeers where they were most vulnerable—legally.

The elder Patterson believed that a dedicated corporation, guided by careful legal advice, could apply enormous pressure on the gambling empire and eventually effect a cleanup. By all the rules of sanity and reason, it was foolhardy for any citizens' group to challenge thugs who held an indisputable advantage in money, power, muscle, and the willingness to savage their enemies. But Albert Patterson and the others were willing to accept the consequences. Just as an independent crime commission had cleaned up Chicago during the Al Capone era when criminals had corrupted local law enforcement, members of the RBA believed they would prevail because right was on their side. They considered themselves better than the criminal element that ruled Phenix City through fear and violence.

The men who assembled for the charter meeting of the RBA were country-tough and determined. Among them were Howard Pennington, a contract carpenter whom "the Devil himself couldn't scare"; Hugh Britton, who would serve as intelligence officer for the association; and Hugh Bentley, a wealthy sporting goods dealer who had battled crime in his hometown for almost a decade. Bentley had been part of several other groups that had fought the racketeers during the 1940s: The Christian

Layman's Association, the Good Government League, and the Citizen's Committee were among the more prominent. The strategy of the previous reform organizations had centered on challenging the Phenix City machine at the ballot box, where the gamblers held an undisputed edge. The underworld made sport of these cleanup efforts, quickly routing them by infiltrating and dividing the organization, a tactic they employed whenever the churches began to demand reform. Despite continual defeat, Bentley never abandoned his goal of a safe, clean city.

The formal partnership of Patterson and Bentley sounded the death knell for Phenix City's criminal empire. Both men were fearless and resourceful, and the underworld had been unsuccessful in influencing either of them. John Luttrell remembered the grim atmosphere at the charter meeting of the RBA in Patterson's office and Albert's stern warning about what lay ahead. "If anyone is getting into this organization for profit or self-glory," Patterson cautioned, ramming his cane loudly on the bare wood floor, "it will be written on their epitaph." Their objectives were clear: enforcement of the laws, fair elections, justice in the courts. Not one of these freedoms existed in Phenix City at that time. The RBA was essentially a citizens' crime commission. The members knew that the odds were against them, even if they managed to sustain a crusade. They also knew that those who opposed the local underworld did so at a great risk.[4]

The gambling interests, who took all reform efforts seriously, quickly organized opposition to the RBA. The presence of Albert Patterson alarmed them; his involvement added credibility to the crusaders' purpose. The underworld's first response was to spread rumors that the RBA was just another group of cranks, politically ambitious religious fanatics who wanted to gain power. For years, political leaders had discouraged citizens from "meddling" in city government. Politics, they said, was not the business of the general public. Albert Patterson said it was the "most damnable lie ever preached in Phenix City," but it kept the general population quiet and out of the power structure.

Initially, the RBA concentrated on gathering information that would incriminate elected officials and expose the city's lurid criminal life. Their strongest and most responsive public ally was the Columbus media, which regularly and with great pleasure, wrote about the shenanigans of its neighbor across the river. Tom Sellers, reporter for the *Columbus Ledger-Journal* cooperated with the RBA by attending association meetings, investigating leads, and generally giving credibility to the crusade with sensational front-page stories. Phenix City had a weekly paper, the *Herald*, which published an occasional denunciation of gambling or bootlegging, but the paper was never taken seriously by the townspeople or the racketeers. Reporters for the Columbus papers were beaten or their cars vandalized.[5]

The gambling interests received valuable help from a network of citizens who were sympathetic to the criminal empire. This highly vocal clique sparred with the RBA for several months, heaping scorn on their efforts. By January 1952, however, the mob decided it was time to flex its muscle. Hugh Bentley was nearing his home around midnight when a thunderous explosion shattered the brick structure. Miraculously no one was hurt, although Bentley's teenage son was blown out of his bed into a clump of bushes some thirty feet away. Gov. Gordon Persons came to Phenix City and offered a small reward for information leading to arrest of the guilty parties. He expressed dismay over the incident because of the negative publicity. The following Sunday, some Phenix City pastors preached sermons about "greater faith"; others declined to aid the crusade any further, saying they had members who were strongly opposed to the RBA. Within days, the crime-fighting association held a mass meeting at the courthouse and gained more support from a community traumatized by increasing violence.[6]

Initially the conflict had been little more than the back and forth of accusations and countercharges. As the RBA continued to gain community support, it pressed the city commissioners to close down the gaming establishments—and was surprised to get results. The bombing had created enough public pressure to require at least the appearance of an official response. More than three hundred slot machines were either seized or surrendered, and Hoyt Shepherd, Jimmy Matthews, and Godwin Davis were arrested. In reality, the gamblers feigned a quick cleanup, a scheme that often satisfied the public and the media.[7]

At a mass gathering held at the old county courthouse in Seale, a slightly inebriated Arch Ferrell, the Russell County district attorney, barged in and began haranguing RBA members. He challenged the stunned audience to "put up or shut up," daring them to bring impeachment charges against him. As the RBA ramped up its drive to rid the city of vice, Ferrell stepped forward as Phenix City's most vocal defender. Ray Jenkins, a *Columbus Ledger* reporter, described Ferrell as volatile, imperious, and surpassingly arrogant: "The prosecutor gave the impression that he wanted to run the county in an autocratic fashion." Soon after getting the district attorney's appointment through Albert Patterson's recommendation, he had aligned himself with the machine. Because the crime bosses needed his goodwill, Ferrell wielded tremendous influence with the underworld elements. Many people believed he was the brains behind the mob.[8]

For Albert Patterson the RBA's crusade offered him the leadership role he had been searching for. He was a deeply driven man, and in the rampant crime and corruption that was the hallmark of his adopted town, he had found the perfect antagonist for his social ideals. The Phenix City campaign would define him. After the bombing, Albert Patterson intensified RBA's challenge to the machine. He organized a women's auxiliary, telling the group that women could obtain information and do things that men couldn't. The ladies, who looked like a collection of prim schoolteachers, created a sensation with their sudden interest in government affairs. City commissioners squirmed and grew red-faced with anger when the women showed up at commission meetings, asking all kinds of troublesome questions. When the auxiliary discovered that more than two-thirds of all federal gaming licenses issued in the state were in Phenix City, city officials explained to the ladies that it was just people giving the town as their address.

Hilda Coulter and a delegation of RBA women went to Montgomery to see Governor Persons about the town's corrupt election process, carrying with them the list of gaming licenses with the names of appointed poll officials on it. The ladies waited all day to see the governor; when they were finally let in, he told them he didn't have the authority to do anything about the Phenix City situation. "The people of Phenix," Persons told them, "just want conditions like that and vote accordingly." The governor told them he believed in home rule, and they should go back home and educate the people. The women were not as innocent as they appeared; they knew that gambling money flowed regularly into the capital.[9]

When the governor refused to provide state support for their cause, the RBA looked to federal authorities for help. Hugh Bentley presented a huge amount of evidence related to crime and gambling in Russell County to a federal grand jury in Montgomery, yet the court turned a deaf ear, saying it was "unable to find any evidence of any organized criminal activities, or criminal syndication in existence anywhere in the Middle District of Alabama." The grand jury further insulted Bentley by commending all law enforcement agencies in the district, including Russell County sheriff Ralph Matthews, for their "splendid spirit of cooperation." Because of the influence of U.S. Attorney H. Burns Parker, the federal grand jury chose to ignore RBA's documented material. But they were correct in at least one aspect of their investigation. Local law enforcement was cooperative, but it was generally cooperating with the criminal element.[10]

When state and federal authorities refused to acknowledge the collected evidence of crime in Phenix City, Bentley and the others created novel ways of getting their message to the local populace. For example, a weekly radio program called *Timely Topics* broadcast public service information. The fifteen-minute program informed people of their rights and educated them about voting procedures. Supplementing the themes of patriotism and good government were stories of local interest, such as the time Arch Ferrell broke Jimmy Putnam's jaw in a courthouse brawl. Hilda Coulter, who wrote or moderated most of the programs, chided the two officials for their misconduct and related what transpired when Ferrell appeared before a judge to answer a disorderly conduct charge. The judge, anxious not to anger the district attorney, meekly asked: "What do you want me to do about it, Arch?" Albert Patterson mailed out copies of all the scripts to newspapers around the state.[11]

Those who opposed the crime bosses' regime in Phenix City paid for their defiance. RBA meetings were often interrupted by threatening phone calls or by the sound of some henchman's automobile engine and blaring horn. Members who owned businesses were boycotted: Coulter's floral business received fewer orders, even from churches; Howard Pennington didn't build as many houses; and Bentley's sporting goods store saw its sales plummet. But Albert Patterson was the real object of the mob's anger. Racketeers sent their lackeys to see if they could strike a deal with him, asking how much money it would take to get him to abandon the crusade. Patterson refused to bargain with them at any price. He was told that his law practice would be ruined, that they would see to it that he was removed from all appointed offices and committees, including those in his own church. If that doesn't stop you, the thugs told Albert to his face, "We'll kill you." Not long after the death threat, fuel oil was splashed around his law office and set on fire. Workmen in the building put out the blaze before it spread. Albert began routing his mail through Columbus when he realized that the contents of his post office box were being tampered with.

Around town, Patterson's daily routine included a barrage of heckling and insults by local toughs who cursed him as a "double-crossing son of a bitch." He laughed off the name-calling: "They think they own me because I worked for them. They needed a lawyer to defend them and they hired the best they could get. But they just bought my services. They did not buy me." Agnes Patterson began an unusual protective practice as the violence increased. After Albert and their younger sons were asleep, she would slip out of bed with her pillow and lie awake all night on the floor by the front door. Before dawn she would return quietly to her husband's side. Albert was not aware that his wife was going without sleep to protect her family.[12]

Opportunities for media coverage of the Phenix City conflict expanded when Albert Patterson won election as a delegate to the 1952 Democratic Convention in Chicago. Jack, his thirteen-year-old son, accompanied his father to help him with his clothes each day; Albert's battle wounds made it impossible for him to dress himself. Before leaving, Albert told the *Columbus Ledger* that he would lobby the convention for an anticrime plank in the party platform. Pledged to Tennessee senator Estes Kefauver, a leading presidential candidate going into the convention, Patterson was aware that once the convention convened Kefauver would call for the establishment of a National Crime Commission, independent of the Justice Department. Patterson mistrusted the Justice Department because the agency had consistently ignored crime in Phenix City. He had already assembled the legal documents to establish a State Crime Commission as another method of battling the local mob, as well as crime throughout Alabama. Patterson used his position as a convention delegate to focus more media attention on the mob. "The easy money boys," he explained to the *Ledger*, "just can't stand the light of pitiless publicity."

Patterson, who worked loyally on behalf of Alabama Democrats and Kefauver, was equally firm in his support of the national party. This became evident when Patterson took to the podium in support of Michigan senator Blair Moody's amendment that required delegates to assure the convention of their intention to support Democratic candidates. The amendment became necessary after several southern state delegations threatened to bolt because of the party's civil rights stance, the same regional battle that erupted at the Republican convention. Patterson's seconding speech for Moody's amendment was heard nationwide through radio coverage of the convention.[13]

When Adlai Stevenson, governor of Illinois, was drafted as the Democratic nominee for the party, it was another Patterson who took center stage. Lafayette Patterson, Albert's brother, professor of history and political science at Jacksonville (Ala.) State Teacher's College, and former three-term member of Congress before being gerrymandered out of his district because of his liberal political views, cast his one-half delegate-at-large vote for Stevenson. During his first term President Franklin Roosevelt had appointed Lafayette ambassador-at-large to promote the Agricultural Adjustment Administration (AAA). While traveling around the country Lafayette met Stevenson, then an attorney on the AAA staff (he also met future president Lyndon Johnson under similar circumstances). The *Montgomery Advertiser* chose not to report either Albert or Lafayette Patterson's role at the convention.[14] Stevenson later chose Alabama senator John Sparkman as his running mate to help balance the ticket and counter Eisenhower's popularity in the South.

John Patterson, unaware that his father and uncle were at the convention, was listening over Armed Forces Radio in the judge advocate general's office in Frankfurt, Germany. Surprised to hear his father speaking on the Moody amendment, Patterson remarked that he was proud of his family, especially his father. At the same time, he still resented Albert's political involvement, even in national politics.

The RBA garnered national publicity as a result of the heavy-handed tactics of the Phenix City machine during the 1952 elections. RBA members were acting as self-appointed poll watchers in front of a downtown polling place when Britton, Bentley, and Bentley's teenage son were attacked and beaten by a gang of thugs. The assault would have been passed off as another random act of violence if Tom Sellers and Ray Jenkins had not been on the scene for the *Ledger-Inquirer*. When both reporters were beaten because of their paper's support of the crusade, a photographer captured the assault on film. Pictures of the election-day brawl, along with the story of how a group of citizens were trying to have clean elections in their hometown, appeared in newspapers around the nation, a damning indictment of the infamous crime city. The mob's attempt to repress one of America's essential freedoms had drawn more attention to Phenix City than anything the RBA had done.

As the reign of terror continued to traumatize the town, City Commissioner A. L. Gullatt tried to assure the public and media that the rackets had been driven out of Phenix City.[15]

5
Albert Patterson Beats the Mob

The Phenix City mob stole the 1952 Democratic primary in Russell County. Stolen elections weren't unusual there, but this one attracted attention because the town's corrupt electoral system was being seriously challenged by the RBA. The underworld and its political allies were enraged and demonstrated it by striking out violently at those who dared to oppose them. The night before the election more than seven hundred supporters of the city's political machine gathered in the courthouse to hear officials denounce the RBA and the *Columbus Ledger*. County and city leaders assailed the "dirty, lying sheet," berated reporters covering the meeting, and ridiculed Patterson, Bentley, and the RBA for trying to change the town's ingrained criminal culture. Arch Ferrell, exhilarated by his role as chief spokesman and defender of the criminals, closed the rally by exhorting the cheering crowd: "Every time you put a ballot in that box, you are answering the *Columbus Ledger* and the RBA."[1]

The election took place as usual, but the aftermath was not the same. This time Albert Patterson thought he had amassed enough evidence to strike back: The RBA filed impeachment proceedings against Sheriff Ralph Matthews in the Alabama supreme court. The sheriff was charged with "willful neglect of duty." Twenty-four specifications pointed to sophisticated lottery systems, fifty-four gambling houses, and the failure of Matthews to prosecute known gamblers. The list of gambling sites included service stations, cafes, grocery stores, taxi companies, billiard parlors, the American Legion, and the Shrine Club. The case had more symbolic value than practical merit. Though impeaching Matthews was aimed at the heart of the Phenix City problem—law enforcement—impeaching him probably would not have had permanent results, anymore than removing the sheriff had in 1916. The matter was further complicated by the convoluted nature of the sheriff's office. Matthews was dominated by his chief deputy, Albert Fuller, a beefy, physically intimidating roughneck with brutal tendencies. The sheriff may have been the public representation of authority, but Fuller wielded the real power in the sheriff's office. He ran interference for the racketeers while controlling the prostitution business himself. Witnesses placed Fuller's patrol car near Hugh Bentley's home the night of the bombing.

The RBA retained Roberts H. Brown of Opelika to present their case before the Alabama supreme court. Initially, the mob tried to buy Brown off with a fifty thousand dollar bribe. Failing that, they torched the Brown home in the dead of night; he and his family barely escaped the burning structure. These cowardly acts of terrorism failed to dent the determination of the RBA. On June 8, 1953, after almost a year of waiting, a Fort Benning investigator began the proceedings by testifying that he witnessed open gambling in twenty-six establishments in Russell County, but gambling activities tended to subside around election time. Detailed drawings of gambling houses were submitted to the court, showing the location of gambling devices. Federal income tax records disclosed that Phenix City lotteries were reaping enormous profits. The RBA even produced a slot machine repairman who testified that he saw Matthews in one of the gambling houses. Howard Pennington told of seeing boxes placed in front of slot machines so that schoolchildren could gamble.

The defense presented slanted Russell County grand jury reports that gave the city high marks for good management, including the commendation of Sheriff Matthews "for his careful, diligent, conscientious attention to the duties of his office." They also offered records of the unique fines and forfeitures system, which referenced more than a thousand cases in less than two years, as evidence that crime no longer existed in Phenix City.

On the final day of the trial, the RBA's carefully prepared case was overwhelmed by a procession of character witnesses for the defense—forty in all—who praised the professional integrity of the sheriff. Not surprisingly, Russell County turned out a full complement of its elected officials—including the meat inspector—to laud Sheriff Matthews. In addition, Alabama's attorney general Silas Garrett, U.S. Attorney H. Burns Parker (on the day Parker testified there were 125 federal gaming licenses in Phenix City), the FBI agent assigned to eastern Alabama (he said the agency found no evidence of gambling), Chief State Criminal Investigator Joe Smelley, State Public Safety Director L. B. Sullivan, the state toxicologist, and the director of the state health department, all testified in support of Matthews and ridiculed the suggestion that open gambling existed in Phenix City.

The RBA was made to look like a collection of crackpots. The supreme court rendered a unanimous decision citing a "total and complete" lack of evidence of widespread gambling in Russell County. The court said, "we would be blind to realities if we did not acknowledge the unsavory reputation, justified or not we do not say, which Phenix City has acquired because of the alleged gambling operations there through years past." It was the court's opinion that crime had been miraculously eradicated from the wickedest city in the United States, and the RBA had merely been trying to repair the town's reputation. When the RBA had filed its impeachment charges against Matthews in July 1952, the sheriff predicted he "would be around a while longer." He was right.[2]

The power structure in Phenix City had succeeded once again in sidestepping civil reform, changing their behavior just long enough to retain control. By now they were adept at cover-ups and denials, at presenting a united front that refused to acknowledge that Phenix City was a corrupt community. The humiliating defeat at the impeachment hearings was a turning point for the RBA. Confident that their biggest asset was Albert Patterson and his political reputation, the group decided to take their message beyond the influence of the local mob. Patterson would campaign for attorney general as the "Man against Crime," with a public pledge to clean up Phenix City. Moving quickly, by late 1953 Patterson and RBA members suspended local activities and began mobilizing their hometown effort for a statewide political campaign.[3]

John Patterson returned to Alabama just as the attorney general's campaign was getting under way. He moved Mary Joe and their two children back into the same small basement apartment in his family's home on Pine Hill and returned to work with much the same expectations he had had before the Korean War—to get on with his legal career. Instead he found a siege-like atmosphere gripping Phenix City, with the community divided and challenged by an organization he knew only through occasional correspondence. He found, too, that his father stood prominently at the center of the controversy.

Their once-prosperous law practice had been laid waste by the racketeers. And all his father's committee and board appointments were gone, even those in the family church, just as the mobsters had threatened. His father had become immersed in the struggle and their law offices had become a political workroom. Politics, which John regarded as the most disagreeable intrusion in his life, now dominated the Patterson family. John was dismayed by the financial condition of the family law practice, but he was also perplexed about the role he was expected to play in his father's bid to become Alabama's next attorney general. Albert was as uncommunicative as ever. Thoroughly engrossed in the campaign, he did not say or do anything to address his son's concerns. John tried to generate some badly needed income, and on the weekends he campaigned for his father. He reasoned, as he had after graduating high school, that once the race was over, win or lose, he and his father would sit down and talk about the future of their law practice.[4]

Other than his own political reputation and the support of the RBA, Albert Patterson's chief campaign resource was Charles M. Meriwether, a Birmingham pharmaceutical company executive who had served as Patterson's chief adviser in the failed lieutenant governor's campaign. Initially, Patterson sought out the personable Meriwether for his help in heavily populated Jefferson County. When he learned of Meriwether's political connections, Albert wisely gave him a major role in the campaign. Meriwether's main interest was making money, which he did with adeptness, but his passion, as for many southern gentlemen, was politics. The son of a wealthy Tennessee cotton financier who had lost his fortune in the Depression, Meriwether earned a law degree from Cumberland Law School in Tennessee, where, by his own assessment, he "did as little as possible in the classroom," whiling away the one-year term in an aging brick dorm drinking corn whiskey and talking politics. "I was more or less interested in the combative nature of politics, the tactical intrigue, and how to get support for a candidate through our political system," he explained. Whatever Meriwether managed to retain from his Cumberland education—he failed the bar exam without regret—fueled this fascination.

Meriwether's first job was for an insurance company owned by Edward H. Crump, a shrewd, fiery-tongued political boss in Tennessee. The two years he spent in the insurance business with Crump were financially successful and further fueled his passion for politics. Tall, lanky, and likable, Meriwether had been polishing his political skills in a few Jefferson County races before he met Patterson in 1950. The attorney general race was an exciting experience for Meriwether; he believed he had the candidate and the cause—which seemed to him an unbeatable advantage.[5]

Meriwether's optimism was not supported by Alabama's ruling political hierarchy. Patterson had formidable opposition in candidates Lee "Red" Porter, a Gadsden attorney, and MacDonald Gallion, an assistant attorney general for the serving attorney general, Silas Garrett. Porter had a substantial lead; he had run a strong second to Garrett in the 1950 election and became a Garrett ally after the election. Rumor had it that Garrett would be named to a high position on Porter's staff if he won the election. Porter's standing in the race was further strengthened by the endorsement of Big Jim Folsom. Folsom, in a bid for a second term as governor, had named his favorites for the four top state constitutional offices—North Alabamians all—ignoring the risk of getting involved in other people's races. Porter, who had the advantage of extensive financial backing, had been carefully preparing for the race while Albert Patterson had been slugging it out with the Phenix City crowd. Not surprisingly, once Patterson announced for the attorney general's seat the Russell County machine quickly shifted its considerable resources to Porter.

Albert Patterson and his small group were not discouraged by the odds against them. They worked tirelessly as the primary approached. Failing to bring about civil reform in Phenix City, Albert Patterson took his anti-vice campaign across the state of Alabama, boldly claiming that if elected attorney general, he would personally clean up Phenix City. His speeches stressed his plan to fight organized crime and to establish a statewide crime commission, promised prompt opinions when needed on state legal matters, and proclaimed his support of home rule (a thorny issue in Alabama, then and now, with its power-centralizing constitution) and free and fair elections. He planned to radically change the traditional functions of the attorney general's office. Campaigning as the "Man against Crime" marked him as a crusader determined to rid the entire state of illegal activity.

Patterson lacked the means to gain widespread public support— organization, finances, and media coverage. Instead, he stumped for votes by car, with Howard Pennington driving. (Pennington quit his job and mortgaged his home to help finance the campaign.) And he walked the streets, with cane in hand, dragging his disabled right leg, day after weary day, the leg swollen so badly at times that Pennington was unable to get Patterson's special built-up shoe on in the mornings. He went wherever there were people; fire stations, hospital waiting rooms, restaurants, country stores, bus stations, and he persuaded his friends to hit the streets with him. He appointed a campaign manager at almost every stop and convinced them of the importance of what they were doing. Despite the growing controversy over school integration following the 1954 Supreme Court decision, Patterson sought the black vote with the promise to not "make the Negro a scapegoat," even though he supported segregation. He also said he would consider appointing a black to his office.[6]

Attracting voter interest in the attorney general's race was difficult because of the attention and curiosity focused on Folsom and the governor's race. Seemingly discarded by the electorate after his first term, Folsom campaigned to redeem himself, convincing Alabamians that he had repented of his misdeeds and reformed his embarrassing behavior. A field of six opponents, including a former governor, railed bitterly against the Folsom record, while Folsom admitted that he "stole" and acknowledged the corruption in his first administration. Although his campaign was more polished than it had been in the 1946 election, he stuck to his populist attitude that state services should be more widely available to the people and that this expansion would be financed through new taxes. Huge crowds flocked to hear him, even in the hometowns of his opponents, and he regaled his audiences with folksy humor that always ended with a familiar "Y'all Come!"[7]

The Phenix City racketeers lined up solidly for Folsom. Arch Ferrell served as Folsom's campaign manager for Russell County, and "voluntary" contributions were collected in the customary manner—by assessing the gambling establishments according to their volume of business. Ferrell coordinated campaign activities through Circuit Judge George C. Wallace of Barbour County, Folsom's South Alabama campaign manager. The racketeers were occupied on two fronts: returning the intemperate Folsom to the governor's office to protect themselves from state authorities and defeating the patently dangerous Albert Patterson. In the May primary, they concentrated on the governor's race because they were betting on Porter to defeat Patterson. The gamblers also laid down bets that Folsom would win without a runoff.

Results from the primary shocked the Phenix City underworld back to reality. Folsom won handily, but any cause for celebration was short-lived. Statewide returns put Albert Patterson firmly in the lead for attorney general, a lead that swelled to seventy thousand by official count. Porter edged out MacDonald Gallion for second place. For a few days it looked as if Gallion had beaten Porter for the runoff spot. Some newspapers proclaimed Gallion as a runoff candidate, and he was busy making plans for the campaign when a Folsom campaign manager called him and asked if he would go along with the governor if he were elected. The tone of the question angered Gallion, because it clearly meant "Can we influence you?" Gallion said no, he was going to be his own man and be fair to everyone. Subsequently, from the final seven to eight thousand votes counted, Gallion received only fifty-seven. Convinced that he had been muscled out in the final vote count by the Folsom/Porter faction, Gallion was ready to campaign for Patterson when Albert hobbled into his Montgomery office and offered Gallion the position of top assistant if Albert won the runoff and became attorney general.

Folsom's spectacular conquest of the gubernatorial nomination was of less importance to the racketeers since the unflinching Patterson was poised to capture the state's top law enforcement position. They moved quickly to close Patterson's considerable lead. Ferrell called Porter, an acquaintance at the University of Alabama Law School, and arranged a meeting at which he introduced Porter to gambling kingpins Hoyt Shepherd and Godwin Davis Sr. Ferrell explained their interest in Porter's candidacy with the frank explanation that a group in Phenix City was "bitter" against Patterson, who had "turned against them" after they helped elect him to the state senate and contributed to his lieutenant governor's campaign. Shepherd and Davis subsequently gave Porter twenty-five thousand dollars to use in his campaign against Patterson, the first of several contributions that Porter failed to list on his campaign disclosure forms.[8]

In the past, Phenix City's corrupt bosses had controlled the town without fear of opposition or legal consequences. The merchants of sin had achieved such success that they considered themselves invincible, immune from prosecution or even criticism. The attempt to subvert the electoral process was the beginning of a determined assault on Albert Patterson that would lead the underworld to self-annihilation. From this point on, whatever Ferrell and the gamblers did to steal the attorney general's nomination from Patterson, the violence and deceit they employed served only to hasten their own destruction.

The attorney general's race was the most hotly contested race in the runoff, attracting sustained media attention. Porter advertised heavily in the major newspapers and benefited considerably from the support of incumbent attorney general Si Garrett. Garrett was quoted as saying that he would be appointed special assistant attorney general to handle segregation and tidelands court cases for the state in a Porter administration. Patterson, without his family's knowledge, mortgaged his home to finance the runoff and went back to campaigning with Pennington.

By themselves, Porter and Patterson probably could not have produced enough interest for a spectacular contest, but the political and criminal alliance that opposed Patterson created enough fireworks to make the race an unrivaled political event. The gamblers went across the state in teams arranging and disarranging alliances to control the result of the runoff, often with Arch Ferrell along to do the negotiating. Albert Patterson saw his comfortable lead washing away because of the mob's whispering campaign, the abundance of campaign funds arrayed against him, and the tremendous political pressure the Folsom organization brought to bear on the race. Patterson and Porter had separate meetings with Folsom at his Cullman home, but the governor-nominate declined to take a personal hand in the runoff. "However," Folsom said, "if there is a runoff in which one of the candidates favors and the other opposes my program, you know what my friends will do." Folsom confided to friends that he couldn't see anybody from Phenix City being attorney general, even a former ally like Albert Patterson.[9]

Phenix City's contaminating reputation was hurting Patterson's election chances, and he himself was suspect because of his previous legal work for some of the town's best-known criminals. Newspapers noted these former links to the mob, and as suspicion of his probity spread Patterson grew depressed and became openly distraught, disappearing for days without telling anyone where he was going. During the final ten days of the campaign Charlie Meriwether had a hard time finding his candidate. Once, when he finally did locate Albert, he was in distant Colbert County in northwest Alabama, staying with relatives of his wife and doing what campaigning he could away from the daily exposure to the media.

With the runoff only days away, Meriwether was able to persuade Patterson to make a campaign speech over WBRC-Radio in Birmingham, one of the most widely listened to stations in Alabama. In his own characteristic southern drawl, Patterson used almost half his allotted time giving his family background, noting that his family had been some of the early settlers in Alabama and that both his grandfathers had served in the Confederate Army. He invested the remaining time in a relentless and persuasive attack on the "criminal octopus" that was reaching out into many parts of Alabama, inflicting great harm on children, education, and the business community. He told how the mob was using bombs and arson in reprisals against innocent citizens, revealing to his audience that on several occasions he had been threatened with murder. Patterson said he was "making a sacrifice" to run for attorney general, unknowingly foreshadowing his own death. Patterson said he was resolved to bring down the criminal empire in his hometown. He concluded the speech with the declaration that he had a "burning desire" to serve Alabama and pursue the rightness of his cause against the evildoers that reigned in Phenix City.

The June 1 Democratic primary was the closest race in Alabama politics in fifteen years. The *Dothan Eagle* wrote, "If ever a candidate had the works thrown at him, it was Mr. Patterson." Albert Patterson led early with Porter coming close in each county, but Porter could never fully close the gap. When the unofficial returns came in Porter was behind by a scant 1,454 votes. Garrett and Ferrell were frantic. Their campaign had fallen short, and they knew they would have to face the tenacious Patterson come inauguration day in January. But Garrett refused to give up. In a last desperate act he began phoning politicians, over fifty calls in two days, trying to steal enough votes in each county to turn the election to Porter. In the meantime, a dozen carloads of Phenix City hoods fanned out across the state, each carrying money to bribe election officials willing to change county returns. Alerted to what was happening, John Patterson chartered a small plane and made selected county by county stops around the state in an attempt to stop wholesale thievery. In the end the mob came up short. When the results were officially tabulated, Patterson had won by 854 votes out of 382,628 cast.[10]

With the official returns confirming his victory and the state media now attentive, Patterson vented his rage over the tactics of the opposition. "The attacks on me," he said in his first press statement, "were the most vicious ever heaped upon a candidate for public office in Alabama." He said the racketeers collected "a fantastic sum to fight me," and that "people sent from Phenix City tried to buy off my campaign managers in all parts of the state." The hostilities between the attorney general–elect and the Phenix City underworld were made public, and the man who intended to start pursuing his enemies come January made no secret of his intentions.

An editorial in the *Montgomery Advertiser* agreed with Albert Patterson's assessment of the race and congratulated him on the narrow victory, noting that Porter had benefited from heavy campaign contributions, the "hypnotic exertions" of Folsom, and "a crafty effort" by the gamblers of Patterson's hometown to disrupt his campaign. "Here's luck to the new attorney general and his collision with what throughout the first half of this century has been an immovable object." Patterson had the Phenix City mob dead in his sights and, once in office, he meant to make short work of the gambling empire. His wrath was focused more on Arch Ferrell than anyone else. Patterson knew the always contentious solicitor was the chief apologist for the underworld; he also made sure Ferrell understood that he was coming after him just as soon as he was sworn in.[11]

Albert spent less than fifteen thousand dollars on his campaign, eleven thousand of which came from mortgaging his home. It was a near miracle that he won the election. In the Patterson home, the election came and went without so much as a mention about the future of the Patterson law firm. John said he didn't know if his father planned to offer him a job in the attorney general's office or if he had fallen heir to the business. Just as he had been after graduation from high school John Patterson was left to make his plans alone. Now he determined to get away from Phenix City. "It was not a very attractive place to practice law, and the town didn't have the makings of a lucrative law career," John explained. He felt that run-of-the-mill cases like hurried divorces and real estate closings in an environment dominated by the local political machine had no long-term appeal. The future didn't hold much promise for John Patterson. He began looking around for something else to do with his life, perhaps another career.

Albert Patterson did not get a chance to fire his celebrated first salvos at the Phenix City underworld. Soon after the runoff, with Patterson's nomination secure, an assassination plot was being masterminded to prevent him from taking office. Chief Deputy Albert Fuller ordered two black men, safecrackers in his burglary ring, to kill Patterson. The two men reluctantly agreed to do the job, but no specific plans were made. Fuller looked around town for a murder weapon that couldn't be traced and found a .38-caliber pistol mounted on a .45 frame. Fuller obtained the gun from Johnny Benefield (referred to as "the professor" because he taught safecracking) who had stolen it from a residence in Milledgeville, Georgia. Fuller gave the gun to the would-be-assassins and told them they would be notified when to kill Patterson. A few days later, the burglars got cold feet about the murder plot, pawned the pistol at the Bridge Grocery, and left town.[12]

In the meantime, two events pulled back the curtain on the fraud committed by the Phenix City machine in the Democratic primary and set in motion events that led to Albert Patterson's assassination. First, two Russell County members of the Alabama House of Representatives, also in disfavor with the racketeers, were defeated in the May runoff. The men contested the election results and the Alabama Democratic Executive Committee conducted lengthy hearings in the Russell County courthouse, finding evidence of graft, vote buying, and intimidation at the polls by local election officials. The state party leadership announced that no fair elections could be held in Russell County and voided the results of the May runoff. For the first time, the public, with the help of the media, was allowed to examine the corrupt political process that protected the racketeers. For decades, Phenix City had defended itself by refusing to publicly acknowledge widespread crime and the strong-arm political machine that controlled the underworld and the community through civil terrorism. Such claims were no longer tenable.

The other event was cataclysmic for the town, setting off a chain of events that wreaked havoc with the underworld. Fred Bodeker, a Birmingham private investigator hired by Ben Ray, chairman of the State Democratic Executive Committee, uncovered evidence that in their frenzied efforts to fix the runoff, Si Garrett and Arch Ferrell convinced Lamar Reid, chairman of the Jefferson County Democratic Executive Committee, to alter the returns by manufacturing some six hundred votes for Lee Porter. State senator Neil Metcalf of Geneva County was present during the vote switch. When the fraud was made public and the Jefferson County grand jury began investigating, Porter and Reid testified that they knew about the fix. For the first time, the gambling empire was facing potential destruction.

The voter fraud investigation was heartily endorsed by Folsom's opponents who had complained in the primary about Folsom's shady campaign practices. Jimmy Faulkner of Mobile, considered a top contender for governor, believed that Folsom's organization, all of them seasoned politicians, had stolen fifty thousand to a hundred thousand votes from his opponents to carry the gubernatorial election without a runoff. The technique used most often was the "misdirection" of votes by transposing the counts of candidates, which did not affect the total number of ballots cast. Folsom poll watchers would also get vote tallies in one area and phone their friends in other parts of the state to tell them what kind of lead was needed out of their box.

The Folsom camp, alarmed at the possibility that the probe could do serious damage to the incoming administration, and aware that John Patterson and the private investigator Fred Bodeker were scouring the state gathering information on the case, appealed to Albert Patterson, through Folsom, to use his influence to stop the grand jury inquiries. Patterson telephoned his friend and campaign supporter Birmingham attorney Albert A. Rosenthal and asked if the grand jury probe could be stopped. "Hell no!" Rosenthal exploded. Albert Patterson told him that was all right with him; he was merely asking as he had promised. Aware of widespread election fraud, Albert Patterson had begun to gather incriminating information to contest the election should he lose. Eddie George, editor of the *Geneva County News,* sent Patterson detailed information about how the E. C. "Bud" Boswell machine in Geneva County had changed the runoff votes to Porter's favor. "This sort of thing has been going on for 30 years," George explained. In a letter dated June 18, 1954, Patterson said he thought he understood the extent of crime in Alabama, however, "We really need to take stock of what is going on in our state."[13]

The possibility of exposure was eroding the customary arrogance of the Phenix City underworld. On Sunday, June 13, Garrett called an early morning meeting of Ferrell, Shepherd, Jimmy Matthews, Sheriff Ralph Matthews, and an assortment of henchmen, who gathered in the grand jury room of the Russell County courthouse. They discussed what to do with Patterson and agreed on testimony they would give the Birmingham grand jury. The meeting broke up about midmorning. That afternoon, Hugh Bentley gave a victory party for RBA members, campaign workers, and friends of Albert Patterson. Albert spoke to the gathering, thanking them for their loyalty. At the end he paused and in a somber tone told them, "I don't believe I will live to hold office." The statement hushed the gathering, and, later, as people began leaving Albert hugged his sister, Mae, longer and tighter than he normally did, telling her in a voice almost breaking with emotion that he loved her.[14]

Events of the following week made a shambles of the embattled criminal empire. The Democratic Executive Committee hearings in Phenix City continued to uncover still more details of political corruption, while a grim-faced Albert Patterson observed the proceedings every day from the front row. Away from the hearings, Patterson was telling mob leaders and criminal types face to face that he was coming after them. In the meantime, the Birmingham grand jury was unraveling the sensational maneuvering of the vote-stealing case, with suspicion pointing directly at Garrett and Ferrell and the Phenix City underworld. Albert told Pennington and others in the RBA that his chances of being sworn in as attorney general were about a hundred to one.

On Friday, June 18, the grand jury grilled Attorney General Si Garrett in an exhausting ten-hour session that left Garrett visibly shaken as he left the courtroom. That afternoon he checked into the Redmont Hotel in Birmingham and began telephoning around the state. Albert Patterson was in Montgomery that day. He attended a hearing at the Montgomery County courthouse, paid an advertising bill, and went by the state supreme court building to visit friends. On Monday, he was to appear before the Jefferson County grand jury and testify about the illegal money from Phenix City that had been funneled into Lee Porter's campaign.

J. B. Brassell, one of the Lee and Russell County representatives "diselected" by the Phenix City machine, was also in Montgomery on Friday. He went to the governor's office and insisted that raids be made on Phenix City that night to support his voting-fraud case before the state Democratic Executive Committee. The visit prompted a call from the capitol to Albert Fuller in Phenix City informing him that a political figure was in the governor's office demanding raids. The caller failed to identify the political figure, and Fuller, assuming it was Albert Patterson, spread the word around. A raid would have meant even more sensational newspaper headlines at a time when the underworld was suffering under two galling investigations.

In the course of telephoning around the state, Garrett hastily developed an alibi by improvising a dinner party in his hotel room. Hurriedly he gathered a number of guests from the hotel lobby, mainly young men who had gone to law school together at Alabama, and ordered drinks and steaks for everyone as he continued to work the phone. Meanwhile, Ferrell telephoned Garrett at the hotel and Frank Long, a confidant of Garrett, answered, handing the receiver to Garrett. They talked, and soon afterward, Albert Fuller, aware that his would-be assassins had pawned the stolen weapon, hurried off to the Bridge Grocery and got the .38 pistol out of hock. A little after nine, Garrett called the courthouse again and was told by Ferrell and Fuller that Albert Patterson was alone in his office, the light clearly visible less than a block away. With Garrett holding the line and the dinner party in full swing, the stage was set for Patterson's murder.

Fuller and Ferrell made one last attempt to reason with the unwavering Patterson, before acting on their fears and silencing him for good. Albert Fuller met Patterson as he was leaving his office and attempted to talk him out of testifying before the Birmingham grand jury, making a final offer of thirty thousand dollars for his silence. The two men were arguing as Patterson, cane in hand, limped toward his car parked in the nearby alley, where Arch Ferrell, Patterson's bitter enemy, lurked in the shadows of the building.[15]

A block away at the county courthouse, Quinnie Kelley, a janitor, was sitting on the east steps of the building in the humid summer air. A little after nine o'clock he had watched Ferrell leave the courthouse and walk up the street toward the Coulter Building. Minutes later, he heard shots and the sound of a car accelerating loudly, its tires squealing down Fourteenth Street. Looking up he saw a man running toward the courthouse, his head back and his arms churning the hot, night air. It was Arch Ferrell.[16]

6
Assassins Make a Politician of John Patterson

John Patterson said he was reading in bed when a neighbor rushed over to tell him and Mary Joe there had been trouble at the office. They had owned a modest frame house in Phenix City for some three years, renting it out for income while in Germany, but that day they had moved to Columbus. The phone had not yet been connected. John was halfway through a book, *Scottsboro Boys*, when around 9:30 p.m. the neighbor arrived. Patterson remembers that a feeling of dread swept over him. With all the uproar and the atmosphere of menace in the city, he felt that something had gone badly wrong. Marking the page, he laid the book aside. He never finished it. The neighbor insisted on driving him to the law office.

When John Patterson arrived downtown, he had to make his way through a throng of people crowding the street in front of the Coulter Building. He saw his father's car, the door open with the oak cane still inside, and a dark, thick circle of blood that had pooled on the sidewalk. Someone volunteered to drive him to Cobb Memorial Hospital emergency room where the body of his father lay. Standing in the room talking in hushed tones were a nervous and visibly shaken Arch Ferrell, Sheriff Matthews, Albert Fuller, and others—virulent enemies of his father. Grief and anger welled up inside John Patterson and his first thought was of revenge. "I wanted to lash out furiously at the group of men huddled at the opposite end of the emergency room," Patterson remembered. "But I managed to control my emotions. I thought it best to not say anything to them." Carefully, he removed the personal effects from his father's pockets: a billfold with no money, some loose change, car keys, and the

Phi Beta Kappa key that usually dangled from his father's vest. The next hours were a blur of hands clasping his, condolences, and words of sympathy. Late evening television and radio programs were interrupted to break the news of Albert Patterson's assassination to a stunned Alabama. That was how Albert's and Agnes's kin across the state found out about the murder.

Around midnight Governor Persons arrived at the Patterson home on Pine Hill and promised a thoroughly shaken Agnes Patterson that he was going to do something about the Phenix City problem. The family felt reassured by the governor's new determination and personal intervention, a long-standing objective of the RBA. When John finally lay down fully clothed across his father's bed in the early hours of the next morning, he remembered that it was Albert Fuller who had driven him from the hospital to his parent's home. Also, in the dead of night he recalled, with vivid clarity, the remark Fuller made during the brief ride: "When we get the man that did it, John, I'll bring him to you." He thought it was an awkward, curious thing for Fuller to say.[1]

There was an immediate clamor for John Patterson to replace his father as attorney general–elect. Almost with the rising of the next sun, the idea came as a natural, spontaneous demand of Alabama's citizens that Albert Patterson's son take up his father's crusade against crime. Shortly before noon, Charles Meriwether drove down from Birmingham to visit with the grief-stricken and devastated Patterson family. When Meriwether asked about John, Agnes Patterson led him through the house to a small bedroom. He sat quietly in a rocking chair, totally composed in contrast to the rest of the family. It was the first time they had met. "John," Meriwether said, "there's talk around Birmingham about having you appointed to your father's position." Patterson answered quietly. "There's been talk around here about it also." "Shall I get to work on it?" Meriwether asked. Patterson agreed.[2]

Charles Meriwether and Albert Rosenthal set about getting John Patterson his father's nomination for attorney general, lobbying members of the Alabama Democratic Executive Committee for the appointment. John, while acquiescing to the move, had more immediate concerns and felt almost helpless in addressing them during the first days following the assassination. The press arrived from all over, following him about town, making the family feel caged by the constant attention and the insensitive demands of reporters. John moved into his father's office and attempted to launch an independent investigation. He believed state and local officials "wouldn't lift a finger to solve the murder." Although he had never been a member of the RBA, even harboring resentment toward the organization, there was a wordless transfer of leadership, and people looked to him to assume the lead in the investigation. RBA members brushed aside John Patterson's aversion to politics and insisted that he assume his father's role in the organization.

Taking stock of his situation, Patterson realized that the law firm had virtually no income. He was responsible for his father's unpaid bills, and there was little money to support either of the Patterson families. He was broke, deluged with visitors, besieged by the media, and trying to make time to find his father's murderers. Help came when Jack Miller, former fighter pilot and friend of the family, joined the firm. Together they generated some income despite the chaotic circumstances. They set about to pay off Albert's campaign debts, more than fifteen thousand dollars. Some creditors, including a printing company in Montgomery, refused to accept money. Joe Robertson, Patterson's confidential friend since university days, arrived early the morning after the murder. A captain in the Alabama National Guard, his Birmingham unit assigned him to stay with Patterson as long as he was needed. For the next nine years, Robertson was Patterson's most trusted ally.

For the first time since its inauspicious beginning, Phenix City was silent, its gaudy honky-tonks quiet, its corrupt government in retreat. The quietness and civil order came about in response to a personally delivered ultimatum from Governor Persons, who sent in seventy-five battle-equipped National Guardsmen under the command of Gen. Walter J. "Crack" Hanna. Fort Benning declared the town off limits to military personnel. Across the state, citizens called for action and laid blame for the murder at the feet of a badly compromised state government. An editorial in the *Huntsville Times* said, "It will be the eternal shame and disgrace of Alabama if the state government does not move on all fronts not only to catch and punish Albert Patterson's murderer, but also to bring to [the] bar the ringmaster behind him." The *Dothan Eagle* laid the blame on state government officials, stating that the blood of Patterson "is on the hands of Alabama governors and attorneys general who have refused or failed to use the power of their offices to stamp out organized crime in Russell County."[3]

The governor had the most impact when he called a halt to criminal activities. "This is the end of the line," Persons told Arch Ferrell, Albert Fuller, and Sheriff Matthews in the Russell County courthouse when he delivered the ultimatum. "There'll be no more gambling, no more rowdiness in the night clubs." The governor's remarks made front page news in papers across the state and nation. General Hanna, who overheard the heated exchange between Persons, Ferrell, Fuller, and Matthews, told those close to the investigation, including Patterson, that the governor also told the three men sternly that they had been warned about murder.[4]

Persons, not known for an aggressive response to crime, took immediate executive action to shut down Phenix City's gambling empire. His personal attention and the presence of the guardsmen brought the full weight of the governor's office to bear on the problem of violence and corruption in the city. While Persons's stance signaled the end of the state's tacit acceptance of wrongdoing in Phenix City, the stunned and angry local population was left to cope with the shock that permeated the city. Churches again began all-night prayer meetings, and a steady stream of worshipers, including the bereaved Patterson family, met and prayed and drew strength from their common grief. Ray Jenkins, the reporter for the Columbus newspaper who had been present at so many Phenix City crises, noted that the town was quiet and introspective.[5]

Phenix City, however, was still fearful, for the criminals remained free to walk the streets and the murder investigation moved forward slowly. Attorney General Garrett, who refused to comply with the governor's request for a special grand jury and prosecutor, agreed to let Arch Ferrell handle the case for Russell County. Patterson publicly called it a "sloppy job" of criminal investigation. Dismayed by the way the case was being handled, John flew to Washington to see FBI director J. Edgar Hoover, assuming that the Phenix City problem had received enough national attention to warrant federal interest. Hoover declined to see him; too busy, a lesser official said, and Patterson was told that the bureau didn't get involved in local matters. Patterson returned to Alabama, disappointed but wiser. He repeated the FBI official's remarks to the reporters who thronged Phenix City. He also told the media, "Some of the people doing the investigating have the most to gain. They are afraid that if the murderer is caught, he will implicate somebody else. This thing is big. It's tied to the vote fraud." The increasingly outspoken Patterson was among the first to recognize the unsavory combination of Garrett-Ferrell-Fuller, identifying them as suspects because of evidence that he and the RBA were developing.[6]

Even as he demanded an impartial investigation, Patterson reported that the Phenix City underworld was circulating rumors and gossip about both father and son to conceal the motive for the murder. Straitlaced, churchgoing Albert was rumored to have had numerous extramarital affairs, and Albert Fuller told state authorities that John killed his father because both were sexually involved with John's eighteen-year-old secretary. The young woman was picked up and questioned intensely for more than ten hours and followed clumsily by state investigators for days.

Meanwhile, pressure for John Patterson to seek his father's nomination became a mandate from the people, which caused John considerable personal conflict. And he remained discouraged by the circumstances of his law practice. "[Phenix City] was really not a promising field for a lawyer in the first place. Everything was fixed: juries, grand juries, law enforcement officers, the works. Everybody was making deals. There was no practice at all for a criminal lawyer, although the town was saturated with crime of every variety." While John was willing, even eager, to start a new career, he didn't relish the thought of getting into politics. He wasn't sure it was the right thing to do, and he was subject to feelings of inadequacy because of his lack of extensive legal experience.

In the end John concluded that the only way the Phenix City problem could be resolved was for the community to have an advocate in the state attorney general's office, the same conclusion his father had reached in his campaign against crime. "Until my father was killed," Patterson explained, "I had no political ambitions. I'd like to have the job because I don't think anyone else would do it as conscientiously as I would. I pledge myself to carry out my father's program against crime in the state of Alabama." He was even willing to campaign as an independent candidate, but when he was assured of official party support by the Democrats, he accepted their nomination. Patterson said he wanted revenge on the corrupt political system that allowed and then condoned the murder of his father. "I saw the nomination as an opportunity to get the mob and those politically connected to it," he explained. Once the decision was made he adopted his father's platform: clean elections, stamping out organized crime wherever it existed in Alabama, and the provision of a prompt attorney general's opinion service for city and county governments. Whether he liked it or not, John Patterson was now a politician.[7]

In the meantime, the seemingly impenetrable system that held the gambling empire together for decades was being picked apart. The Birmingham grand jury brought Si Garrett back for a second time and questioned him extensively about his involvement in election fraud. Afterward, he left the state for a "rest" in a Texas mental hospital. In Garrett's absence, Bernard Sykes, the first assistant attorney general, assumed the chief investigator's role for the state. Sykes, who was the opposite of the unstable and tainted Garrett, removed Arch Ferrell from office and launched a drive to find evidence in the Albert Patterson murder. At the same time, the Alabama supreme court replaced Judge J. B. Hicks with Judge Walter B. Jones, one of Alabama's leading jurists. A new list of Phenix City jurors was assembled that impaneled the city's first honest grand jury in decades, and Sykes had his investigative process in place. Si Garrett's sudden withdrawal had opened the door for justice.

The most spectacular assault on Phenix City corruption was Governor Persons's decision to grant the National Guard full control of the town by declaring martial law. It was a drastic move and Persons was initially reluctant to make it. General Hanna repeatedly asked the governor for authority to replace local law enforcement. Patterson supported his request. Armed with growing evidence from the Birmingham grand jury and aided by front-page stories in the Ledger, he claimed that the only way to clean up the crime-ridden town was by military control. In the sweltering afternoon heat of July 22, Patterson received a phone call from Governor Persons, asking him to go to the window and describe what he saw. John, with Joe Robertson at his side, stood by the open second story window of his father's law office and witnessed a historic event. A large force of Alabama National Guard supply trucks, jeeps, and troop carriers rolled into the main business district of the city; then the military fanned out to take control of the Russell County courthouse. Phenix City had been occupied.[8]

John Patterson experienced tremendous relief as the state guard seized control of the town. The occupation lifted the fear from local residents and allowed unprecedented freedom for discussion of the corruption that had intimidated much of the population. Ledger reporters Tom Sellers and Ray Jenkins found people who were willing to talk to reporters, and for the first time previously secret county and city records were made public.

The sudden and dramatic imposition of military law and order was an uncomfortable change for the Phenix City crowd. Almost overnight whores, pimps, and criminal enforcers stole quietly away, although some went no farther than across the river to Columbus. Remnants of the corrupt crowd and the local population who remained sympathetic and supportive of the semisecret organization continued to be defiant, but they were powerless with the military in control. Si Garrett, from his self-imposed exile in Texas, would venture no closer than Mississippi, where he secluded himself in a motor lodge for three days, calling Ferrell, relatives, and friends.

Albert Fuller still swaggered around town, gun on hip, arrogantly claiming that "there won't be nothing to it. In a few days it'll be over and forgotten." But Arch Ferrell's actions revealed the truth about how the burden of guilt weighed on the principal suspects. As the finger of suspicion began to point inexorably at Ferrell and Fuller, Arch Ferrell began to get publicly drunk. Three days after the Patterson murder, state investigators observed him drinking for several hours at the CoCo Club; they followed him when Si Garrett took him to the Ralston Hotel in Columbus. After the National Guard takeover, Maj. Ray Acton, military mayor of the city, was standing in front of city hall late one night when a military car drove up with a thoroughly intoxicated Ferrell; he was under arrest for drunk driving. Sensing an opportunity to get information from a chief suspect, Acton had the military police take Ferrell to his office where he sprawled across the couch, ranting loudly about making a statement to the press. Acton phoned General Hanna who came to the courthouse and slipped into an adjoining room to witness the interrogation.

Acton spoke cautiously with the drunken Ferrell, trying to lead him to the Patterson murder, but even drunk Ferrell was cagey and elusive. He sneered and made faces at Acton, cursing and insulting him repeatedly, aware that the major was trying to obtain a confession. At one point, Ferrell rose from the couch, lit a cigarette, and staggered over to Acton. Standing almost nose to nose with the major, Ferrell stared fixedly at him, occasionally glancing down at the .45 pistol strapped to the major's gun belt.

Acton said Ferrell rocked back and forth, seemingly near collapse. Then Ferrell offered to make a deal if his wife and family were not subject to questions from the investigators. "On that premise I'll make a deal with you," Ferrell said. "I'm no damn fool. I know what people are thinking. If you will promise there will not be any more investigating, and no one will come to my house questioning my wife and daughter, you can take that goddamn big gun and blow my head off." Acton, taken back by the outburst, told Ferrell that he was not an executioner. Ferrell wobbled drunkenly back to the couch and sat precariously on the edge. He sat there quietly for several minutes smoking as the room grew still. Then suddenly Ferrell began to whimper softly; slipping off the couch to his knees, he crawled to Acton, and clasped his arms tightly around the major's legs. He began to cry and begged Acton to shoot him. Acton and a lieutenant in the room were stunned by Ferrell's behavior. They interpreted it as the uncontrollable plea of a deeply troubled soul.

Major Acton walked out of the room to relieve the tension, leaving Ferrell sobbing, to find the entire company of news media waiting in the courtroom. In the three-hour period that Ferrell was being questioned, word had gone out that the solicitor was in custody. Acton picked three reporters from the crowd to talk with Ferrell, one of whom was Hugh Sparrow of the *Birmingham News*. Sparrow immediately asked Ferrell about Albert Fuller, since Fuller had told investigators that Ferrell was the brains of the Phenix City political machine, hoping Ferrell would react to the accusation. Ferrell rose and faced Sparrow and said, "Hugh, I love the man," and began spelling the word L-O-V-E cheerleader-style, waving his arms wildly. All the time he was cheering, his body was folding forward in exaggerated slowness, until he landed headfirst on the wooden floor, cutting his face.

After Acton and the lieutenant cleaned the blood off him, Ferrell made his statement to the press: "I no longer believe in the church; I no longer believe in religion; I no longer believe in Jesus Christ. I'm an infidel and I want it on the front page of every goddamn newspaper in Alabama tomorrow." The press failed to report Ferrell's conversion to infidelity, publishing, instead, a photo of the drunken, disheveled solicitor being led away to jail with a comment that "his statements were incoherent and inconsequential." Pelham Ferrell, Arch's brother, got him out of jail the next morning.[9]

The city's criminal element was unable to resurrect itself as it had in the past. Hanna, Sykes, Acton, Judge Jones, and their supporters and allies provided justice, fair elections, and law enforcement. The goals of the

Russell Betterment Association had been achieved. Judge Jones and the grand jury remained in session for more than four months, tried 144 defendants, returned 753 indictments, and cited the local underworld as a "diabolical enterprise." Justice had been made possible by the military occupation led by Hanna. Guardsmen were both cheered and cursed by the locals. Hanna took the press with him on the around-the-clock raids on nightclubs, whorehouses, and gambling establishments still trying to operate.

Hugh Bentley received more than two hundred green plastic recording disks from a secret "phantom wire tapper." The disks were recordings of Hoyt Shepherd's personal telephone conversations over a period of several years. (It later emerged that the wiretapper thought Shepherd was having an affair with his wife.) As the recordings became public, newspaper headlines printed the truth about fixed juries and the corruption of public officials, including many in Columbus, and details of murder, burglary, narcotic trafficking, and gambling operations, some as far away as Florida and Maryland. The wiretaps revealed that much of the crime originated with or was influenced by Shepherd. The public was shown just how extensive his influence was when Shepherd was heard to say on one recording, "We got the word from the governor's secretary, 'go ahead and run your damn politics like you want and don't worry about no one over here'."[10]

For the most part, citizens of Phenix City were supportive of the cleanup. Their willingness to serve in minor but critical civic offices displaced mob lackeys, further weakening the political machine. Reporters and investigators probed the city's dark side, while Patterson and the still aggressive RBA conducted their independent investigation of the Patterson murder.

The newly appointed sheriff, Lamar Murphy, not state authorities, provided the first major break in the case when he located an eyewitness to the murder. Murphy found Johnny Frank Griffin, who saw Fuller and Albert Patterson walking together toward Patterson's car, their conversation loud and heated while the chief deputy shook his head as if he were saying "no." Griffin had continued down the street until he heard shots. Returning to the parking lot, he saw Fuller and Ferrell by the car as Patterson stumbled toward the street, clutching his throat and groaning "like he was trying to say something and couldn't." Griffin testified before the grand jury. He was stabbed later that same afternoon and died in the hospital. John Patterson told the press that the stabbing was "a fantastic coincidence that could only happen in Phenix City." Privately he told everyone that Griffin had been murdered outright to keep him from testifying.

Other witnesses turned up: A cab driver who saw Albert Fuller dart out of the alley and jump into a waiting car and a part-time jailer who witnessed the murder but who fled the country to keep from being killed. The star witness, Cecil Padgett, was another Murphy coup. Padgett was standing by his car directly in front of the parking lot when he heard at least three shots. He turned and saw Fuller and a man in a light-colored suit and hat, whom he believed to be Arch Ferrell, standing beside Patterson's car. Fearful that Padgett would meet the same fate as Griffin, Patterson and Murphy did not announce their find, not even to state investigators because of the known connection between the underworld and many state officials.[11]

At about the same time that mounting evidence was implicating Ferrell in the murder, Jefferson County prosecutor Emmett Perry charged Arch Ferrell, Si Garrett, and Lamar Reid with fraudulently changing votes in the June primary. All three had given testimony before the Jefferson County grand jury. Garrett's loud, blustery manner had failed to impress the jurors. Reid provided the details of the vote fix when he reported Garrett's rationale: "Patterson's crowd has stolen the election, Lamar. We've got to steal it back." Garrett went on to tell the young, naive Reid that Patterson was "the biggest crook to ever walk the face of the state. Why, can you imagine what it'd be like with him as attorney general," he asked Reid. "That Phenix City crowd would be walking in and out of his office carrying bags of money out in the open." Remarkably, Garrett and Ferrell apparently convinced Reid that Albert Patterson was the head of the gambling operation in Phenix City and that making the six-hundred vote change would be the "right way to get rid of the Phenix City gamblers." The switch was made at the Redmont Hotel. By coincidence, the night clerk at the Redmont Hotel was Roy Cole, Albert Patterson's brother-in-law. Doubling as a waiter, Cole served drinks and watched as threes under Porter's name were altered to eights and ones became sixes.[12]

An investigation by the Jefferson County Democratic Executive Committee two days prior to Patterson's assassination had identified the irregularities and restored the switched six hundred votes. Lamar Reid, the same party official who had illegally changed the vote, then certified the corrected returns. On June 22, Lucille Smith, Albert Patterson's secretary, sent Jefferson County Democratic Party election official William Brannon Patterson's response to the vote recount together with a note explaining it was the final letter he signed before leaving the office on the night he was killed. In the letter, Albert Patterson said he was happy that the committee had taken a stand on the matter. "I would not want a single vote that was not honestly cast for me," he explained.

The Alabama Democratic Executive Committee voided the May 1954 primary because of the evidence of fraud, an unprecedented move in state politics. They also made appointments to vacated offices and replaced Sheriff Ralph Matthews with Lamar Murphy. Other than in his military service, Murphy had no law enforcement experience, but he was respected because of his character and physical courage. He had once bodily removed Albert Fuller from a downtown polling place when Fuller tried to intimidate RBA members monitoring the election. On the day Murphy received his commission as sheriff from Governor Persons, General Hanna drove Murphy and the disgraced Matthews to Montgomery in a National Guard car. No one spoke during the two-hour trip, either going or returning.[13]

In November 1954, Phenix City held its first free elections in decades, perhaps even in the town's history. Ray Acton placed armed guards beside each ballot box and personally rode from polling place to polling place during election hours, inspecting the voting site each time. That night he took the ballot boxes, five shiny, galvanized metal trash cans, to the main courtroom, placed them in the middle of the room with floodlights fixed on them and surrounded by armed guardsmen. In a last desperate attempt to control the outcome, local officials asked that the ballots be placed in the city's safe overnight. Acton refused.[14]

The question of who would take Albert Patterson's place as attorney general was played out on the stage of state politics. The symbol of the son picking up his father's fallen standard to continue the battle against crime was reinforced by Patterson's active search for his father's killers and his public statements recalling his father's crusade. Charles Meriwether sensed the public mood and took the initiative in securing Patterson's nomination for attorney general. He had help from Ralph Smith, a classmate from the university, and Roy Smith, a Phenix City attorney, both members of the state Democratic Executive Committee. The effort also received support from the committee chairman, Ben Ray, a longtime friend of the Patterson family. Folsom forces on the state committee did not welcome the appointment of young Patterson. They had campaigned hard against his father—sometimes surreptitiously—and still preferred that Lee Porter be part of the incoming administration. Folsom supporters criticized widespread efforts to draft Patterson because of his age, thirty-two, and his inexperience: the same reasons John was initially reluctant to accept the nomination.

The executive committee met in Birmingham a week after the murder, with Patterson supporters still unsure of the nomination despite overwhelming public support. The committee could name a candidate without a primary election. The power of appointment by the Democratic Party was evident when Folsom insisted that A. W. Todd, who was not the runner-up in the Democratic primary, be named agriculture commissioner when the party's nominee died following the primary. But Folsom was not inclined to give Patterson the attorney general nomination outright, despite public sentiment. Fuller Kimbrell, Folsom's designated finance director, and Barbour County circuit judge George C. Wallace advocated a special statewide election to decide the issue. Wallace, according to Meriwether, had favored naming Patterson to the position but accepted the administration position on the special election. There were strong indications that Porter might enter a special election.

About an hour before the committee convened at Birmingham's Redmont Hotel, leaders from both sides met in Charles Pinkston's room in an attempt to reach a compromise. Pinkston, Fuller Kimbrell, and George Wallace represented Folsom; Roy Smith, Ralph Smith, and Meriwether spoke for Patterson. Roy Smith, who had taken the younger Patterson under his wing, vouched for his ability to be an effective attorney general and made the strong argument that the public wanted him to succeed his father. The Folsom camp remained adamant about Patterson not getting the nomination outright, but after heated discussion they agreed not to interfere with a special election.

Meriwether said Pinkston and Kimbrell warned Wallace, who they knew was positioning himself for an eventual run for governor, that Patterson could change the state's political picture: "If we do this," Pinkston said, "he'll run for governor four years from now and he might beat you."

Wallace replied, "He's qualified for the job and the people want him to have it. He ought to have it, so let's go ahead and give him the job. Don't worry about me. I'll take care of myself."[15]

The committee, following the wishes of the Folsom administration, set July 27 for the special election and July 1 as the deadline for qualifying. After several statements warning against "handpicked" candidates, the fifty members present voted unanimously for the special primary. Patterson believed that the Folsom forces prolonged the nomination as long as they could "in hopes that some unexpected, dramatic occurrence would give Porter another chance at it." The committee also passed a resolution expressing its sorrow at "the passing of so noble a man" as Albert Patterson.

Patterson and Meriwether sat in the back of the hotel ballroom and watched the proceedings, which included an unsuccessful appeal by Arch Ferrell to retain his seat on the committee. As soon as the meeting adjourned, Patterson and his supporters filed his qualifying papers amid heavy media attention. The RBA paid the two hundred dollar qualifying fee. Afterward, Patterson told newsmen, "If elected to the office, I will strive to be the best attorney general Alabama ever had. It is my intention to serve all of the people to the best of my ability." The statement was simple and not at all original, but he had been in politics exactly one week. Patterson was still stunned by the process that had uprooted him from a stable life and thrust him into public life.

After Patterson qualified, MacDonald Gallion announced that he would not run for the office again, saying, "I've got better sense than to run sideways into a roaring train." Patterson fulfilled his father's promise to Gallion by naming the Montgomery attorney as the first assistant in the attorney general's office. Porter, the erstwhile darling of the Folsom organization and the Phenix City machine, decided against qualifying, thereby conceding the nomination to Patterson. There were considerable political risks for anyone who qualified against Patterson because of the emotional public reaction that almost willed the office to him. If the Folsom forces had been so greedy as to put up another candidate and had succeeded in engineering his nomination, Patterson could still have qualified as an independent for the November general election. And he would have probably won.

When it became certain that John Patterson would be the attorney general nominee, Governor Persons invited him to the governor's man-

sion for lunch—just the two of them. The governor wanted him to accept an appointment as special assistant attorney general in charge of the
Patterson murder case, which would allow him to immediately head the
investigation. The job carried an eighteen thousand dollar annual salary,
an attractive offer considering that his financial position was not strong
and he now had to care for his widowed mother. But Patterson was reluctant to take the position because he had serious reservations about working with state investigators.

He was well aware of the state's long-standing complicity with regard
to Phenix City crime figures and feared they would wreck his efforts to
find and prosecute the killers. The chief investigator, Joe Smelley, had
testified on behalf of Sheriff Ralph Matthews at his impeachment trial.
"Also, I didn't want to be branded a witch-hunter because of my close
ties to the case and be discredited as an investigator," he explained. Until
he took office in January, he preferred to work independently with RBA
members rather than risk having his work crippled by the state. RBA operatives didn't trust state officials either. So John declined the governor's
offer, angering Persons, and said publicly he had "too many pressing problems," which included closing out the family law firm.[16]

John Patterson did not mislead the public when he spoke of problems with
the law firm. He and Jack Miller devoted most of their time to complet-
ing Albert Patterson's cases where the fees had been collected. The first
month they practiced together, they split a profit of fifteen dollars. To
economize, John sold his small frame house in Columbus and moved his
family back into the basement apartment at his mother's home. His father's murder and the resulting media attention were also imposing personal adjustments. He resented giving up the freedom to come and go as
he pleased, but John was learning to assume the affable personality of a
southern politician, a difficult role for him.

With the nomination came requests for speeches and personal appearances, which he accepted as a way of drawing public attention to
the Phenix City cleanup. "We don't have any government in my town,"
he told a Dothan audience during the investigation. "The citizens have
no protection other than what they provide themselves. People never answer the door after dark without a gun in their hand." For months, Patterson referred to Phenix City in his speeches as "Crime and Politics,
Inc." In his speeches, he took every opportunity to cast public suspicion

at the new governor: "I can as attorney general achieve only what [Governor] Folsom . . . will allow me to achieve. The vultures are still hanging around Phenix City. The racketeers thrived in Phenix City during the last Folsom administration, in spite of the citizens' appeal to state officials for help."[17]

By fall, many of the problems in Patterson's life were being resolved. "By then, I had finished my father's cases and turned the law firm over to Jack Miller," Patterson said. In the November general election, he overwhelmed token Republican opposition and an obscure write-in candidate to become, at age thirty-three, the youngest attorney general in the state's history. Public sentiment about the Phenix City tragedy was effectively demonstrated at the ballot box, with Patterson drawing more votes than Folsom or Senator John Sparkman. Allied Artists sent John a script to review for a movie about Phenix City, which he found oddly gratifying. The nation could now see in local theaters the conditions that had caused his family so much grief.

The Phenix City crowd did not let John Patterson continue his father's campaign without interference. "The gambling crowd hired detectives in an attempt to find something incriminating to embarrass me," Patterson explained, "and brought in a skilled wiretapper from New Jersey." John began carrying a .45-caliber pistol, sometimes stuffed inside a brown paper sack, as he walked about town. Phenix City remained under martial rule for the remainder of Governor Persons's term while the state pursued its case in the Patterson murder.

In early December, Arch Ferrell, Albert Fuller, and Si Garrett were indicted for the murder of Albert Patterson. The decision to indict the trio was based on the testimony of a secret witness that Lamar Murphy had located. It took eight days to present the evidence to the Russell County grand jury. Fuller and Ferrell were arrested; Garrett, still in a Texas mental hospital, was served a fugitive warrant of arrest. The indictments were identical, charging that each man had "unlawfully and with malice aforethought killed Albert L. Patterson by shooting him with a gun or pistol against the peace and dignity of the State of Alabama." A front-page story in the *Ledger* observed Ferrell at the arraignment proceedings and noted that "his usual smile was gone from his pale face." Albert Fuller had laughed when State Investigator Claude Prier questioned him about the murder, confident that Phenix City's once powerful influence over state government was still protecting the local criminal organization. It wasn't. Fuller was not laughing when Prier went to arrest him and took him into custody. The Albert Patterson assassination and his son's ascension to his place as the top law enforcement officer in the state was the top news story in Alabama for 1954.[18]

John Patterson, even as he made preparations to assume the attorney general's position, was busy gathering evidence to prosecute his father's killers.

7
Trying His Father's Murderers

The passage from private to public life was not as difficult for John Patterson as he had anticipated. His dramatic election to the state's top law enforcement office quieted the restlessness that had troubled him since returning from Germany. Politics definitely was not his first career choice, but circumstances made it a heady and agreeable move, and one made with a large measure of idealism.

In the beginning, Big Jim Folsom and his administration were cordial to the new attorney general. Patterson said Fuller Kimbrell assured him that, in spite of their opposition to his nomination, the new administration would support him. Folsom made a sincere effort to begin his second term on a note of harmony, aware of the suspicions aimed at his administration in the 1954 Democratic primary and of the embarrassment his uproarious behavior had caused many Alabamians during his first term. Without mentioning Phenix City or the Pattersons, Folsom told his inaugural audience that he would keep gangsters out of Alabama and enforce criminal laws "as never before." The inaugural festivities were the most lavish Alabama had ever seen. The parade stretched for almost three miles, with black soldiers and black bands mixed in the parade, breaking a tradition of relegating them to the very end of the procession. There was a "Big Inaugural Sing" in the state coliseum with gospel groups and country recording stars, and parties all over Montgomery were primed with free liquor from distilleries wanting to do business with the state. Folsom insisted on holding two inaugural balls, one for whites and one for blacks. Folsom and administration officials attended both events. "When I was your governor before, such a thing was unheard of," he reminded the large throng of blacks assembled at Alabama State University. "The way for you to achieve progress in your community is to vote your convictions—and whatever your convictions, vote—we are all Alabamians, your vote counts just as much as my vote."[1]

John Patterson was sworn into office on the morning of January 18, 1955. Chief Justice Ed Livingston, the state jurist who had found a "total and complete" lack of evidence of corruption in Phenix City in Sheriff Ralph Matthews's impeachment trial, administered the oath in supreme court chambers packed with media, family, and Albert Patterson's campaign supporters. A twenty-five-car "John Patterson Motorcade" drove over from Phenix City to participate. In a strained voice, John acknowledged that he owed the office to his father. The ceremony was emotional, with the memory of Albert Patterson clearly on everyone's mind. John promised to carry out his father's promise: a safe, clean town for the good citizens of Phenix City. Later that afternoon, John and Mary Joe Patterson attended the inaugural parade in the winter chill but remained apart from the nightlong celebrations that swirled around the new administration. They spent the night at home with the children while Montgomery toasted the new governor.

The Pattersons' move to Montgomery had its financial drawbacks. "We had had a difficult time building any kind of financial security during the short time we had been home from Germany," Patterson explained. "I spent virtually all of my time closing out my father's legal cases." In late 1954, when it came time to leave the basement apartment on Pine Hill, they were broke and in debt. Joe Robertson, a house guest since the assassination, lent them money for the move to Montgomery and helped the family settle into a rented three-bedroom house in Cloverdale, the upper-middle-class section of the city.

Mary Joe Patterson complemented her husband's new political adventure. She displayed a hearty and open enthusiasm for new people and circumstances and understood the importance of her role at social functions. She was an active partner in John's developing ambitions. "I entertained guests, announced or otherwise, and kept the spare bedroom ready at all times," she recalled. With her daily routine centered on her family, she was seen socially with her husband when necessary but never harbored any real desire to be a part of Montgomery's social structure built around state politics. Mary Joe said she was not comfortable with how the wives of elected officials were constantly watched and talked about in the capital—and not all the talk was complimentary. Tiring of the attention that at times approached rudeness, many of the wives of elected officials began gathering among themselves for their own social time.[2]

The first day John Patterson reported for work, he had to ask the janitor of the supreme court building where his offices were located. "Why upstairs, boss," the surprised janitor answered. "The first two weeks I was attorney general," he said, "I literally shut myself off in the office, reading everything I could find about attorney general responsibilities." (He also found a collection of books and pamphlets on mental illness that Si Garrett had left behind in his hasty departure from the state.) MacDonald Gallion, who had spent the previous four years as an assistant attorney general, helped organize the office and saw to it that Patterson understood what was expected of him. There were eighteen assistant attorneys and another ten assigned to other state agencies who reported to Patterson. One of the valued assistants was Owen Bridges, a law school classmate of John's who had sent Albert Patterson confidential memos about events in Si Garrett's office during the primary campaign. Ralph Smith of Guntersville and Noel Baker of Opelika served as trusted assistants, as well as Ted Rinehart, a New Jersey native and friend of Patterson from his service in Germany. Bernard Sykes, who distinguished himself during the Phenix City cleanup, was named head of the criminal division. Sykes and Gallion's initial assignment were the Fuller-Ferrell cases.[3]

Patterson's first responsibility was self-imposed: to legally avenge his father's murder. He wanted to prosecute Albert Fuller and Arch Ferrell himself but was convinced that his presence in the case would be a distraction. Gallion and Birmingham prosecutor Cecil Deason agreed it was best for Patterson to keep a low profile during the trials and not be seen in the courtroom. "No one wanted to create a situation that would cause even the slightest amount of sympathy for the defendants," Gallion explained. "We thought it best if John stayed in the background." The defense did not believe that Fuller and Ferrell would receive a fair trial in Phenix City. So, following a change in venue to Jefferson County circuit court, Patterson and Robertson set up offices on an entire floor of the Essex House.

Albert Fuller, who was tried first, was represented by highly respected Birmingham criminal attorney Roderick Beddow Sr. Cecil Deason and Emmett Perry handled the prosecution for Jefferson County, while Judge J. Russell McElroy presided over both trials. The Fuller trial turned into the longest jury trial in Alabama history—twenty-six days. Judge McElroy's spacious, high-ceilinged courtroom was packed with spectators; the press sat inside the court well. Ray Jenkins of the *Columbus Ledger* reported the trials nearly verbatim. The paper had won the Pulitzer Prize in the Journalism for Public Service category that year for its coverage of the Phenix City story.

Beddow was a formidable opponent. Aiding the defense were the remnants of the Phenix City machine, which worked effectively behind the scenes to frustrate the state's efforts. Patterson and Sheriff Lamar Murphy said they had a "devil of a time" getting credible witnesses. Many told of being harassed; some even lost their jobs because Beddow would not agree to release them after hearing their testimony. Beddow was particularly hostile to RBA members.

The evidence against Fuller was overwhelming. Witnesses placed him with Ferrell in front of the Coulter Building minutes before the murder, and one man said he saw Fuller walking around the corner of the building with his arm around Patterson. The most damaging testimony came from Cecil Padgett, the surprise witness that the attorney general's office sprang on the trial at the last minute. Padgett said he saw Fuller and Ferrell "against" Patterson's car when the shots were fired. Quinnie Kelley, the illiterate but unshakable Russell County courthouse janitor, described how Arch Ferrell came running toward the courthouse: "He weren't losing no time." Beddow's only defense was to discredit state witnesses, some of whom reflected the disreputable nature of the town: in trouble with the law, involved with shady enterprises and vulnerable to ethical scrutiny. Beddow spent most of a week on Fuller's "impregnable alibi," wherein former Sheriff Ralph Matthews tried to convince the jury that Fuller was in the jail office with six other people including a state ABC Board agent at the time of the shooting.

Remarkably, some of the state's top law enforcement officials came to Fuller's aid. J. F. Brawner, chief of the Drivers License Division; Alabama Highway Patrol officers C. W. Hall and George Wallace (Wallace was identified in the Phenix City cleanup as the courier who delivered a black satchel of money to the capital every month); Joe Smelley, chief state investigator; L. B. Sullivan and Ben and W. L. Allen, criminal investigators for the state—in all over fifty witnesses stood before the court and defended Albert Fuller, who told the judge and jury that he received one-third of the money from the Phenix City slot machine racket and was paid off regularly by a prostitution ring. When the defense rested, the jury deliberated for almost seven hours before returning a guilty verdict. The former deputy sheriff was convicted of first-degree murder and sentenced to life imprisonment. Ray Jenkins said that throughout the trial, Fuller maintained the same slightly ingratiating smile, even when he was escorted to jail, as if he were still trying to win the confidence of his "betters."[4]

While Fuller was being tried, Arch Ferrell was in the same courthouse defending himself in the Jefferson County voter fraud case. Lamar Reid turned state's evidence (as did Lee Porter) and told how Ferrell and Garrett altered the vote totals. Reid's testimony made headlines across the state when he told the court that Folsom was going to close the "transaction" in Geneva County, where some twenty-five hundred votes were suspected of being switched. Ferrell's defense was so weak that before the trial he offered to plead guilty if Emmett Perry would recommend a fine without imprisonment. To everyone's surprise, including Ferrell and his lawyer, the jury acquitted Ferrell because jurors said prosecutors failed to prove that Ferrell engineered the vote-switching scheme. After the acquittal, Ferrell walked down the corridor of the courthouse, his arrogance temporarily restored, and, spotting the reporter Jenkins, taunted, "You look sick, fella. You look sick as hell."

Ferrell did not have time to savor the small victory. In mid-April, he was called to trial for the murder of Albert L. Patterson. George Rodgers, Drew Redden, and Pelham Ferrell defended Ferrell, with the assistance of Beddow's legal team. Many of the same witnesses who appeared in the successful prosecution of Fuller were called to testify against Ferrell. Between them, the defense and prosecution called some four hundred witnesses, including a frail, black-clad Mrs. Albert Patterson, who calmly described the final day of her husband's life.

The state had ample evidence against Ferrell, from witnesses who placed Ferrell at the scene of the crime to the telling testimony of law enforcement officers who received telephone threats from Ferrell "to stop investigating the Patterson murder or we're going to kill you.'" Sheriff Lamar Murphy also received drunken telephone threats from Ferrell. One witness told how Ferrell "rubbed the right side" of Patterson's car, the side where he was seen standing at the time of the murder, obliterating his fingerprints. (Fuller's prints were found on the left side.) Ferrell was further implicated by a statement he made at a meeting of Alabama solicitors. He told the gathering that he and Garrett would see to it that Albert Patterson "never becomes attorney general." Lamar Reid, testifying a second time against Ferrell, related how he was told not to worry about switching votes, that "the incoming governor" wanted the vote changes to defeat Albert Patterson.[5]

When the thirty-eight-year-old Ferrell took the stand, he was taut and spoke in crisp tones, his eyes darting around the courtroom. The newspapers carried a full text of his testimony, an account that was little more than a monotonous invention bearing scant resemblance to the evidence. For example, Ferrell testified that he was not aware of any unusual activity that evening—not the sirens or the noise of the large crowd at Patterson's office—even though he was well within sight and sound of it all. Nevertheless, the case against Ferrell was not as solid as Fuller's had been. Cecil Padgett could only identify the other assailant in the alley as Ferrell "in my best judgment." One of the material points in Ferrell's defense was the contention that he had been talking to Garrett by long distance and produced telephone records to substantiate that. The jury foreman from the Fuller trial sat in on the second trial and told reporters midway through the testimony that the case against Ferrell was not as "firm" as it had been against Fuller. Apparently, the jury agreed. They deliberated almost fourteen hours over a two-day period before reaching a verdict. Reporters seated near Ferrell said his emotionally charged body literally jerked and pulsated as the court waited for the jury to return to the courtroom.

The jury foreman read the verdict, "not guilty," to the dismay of the state's prosecutors, many of whom had been gathering evidence for more than a year. Ferrell had escaped conviction a second time. He stood unremorseful before the media and declared that the jury had "confirmed his innocence." It was a bitter blow to John Patterson who had relentlessly pursued his father's killers. Moments after hearing the verdict, Arch Ferrell was smiling and enjoying the congratulations of his brother, Pelham, when John Patterson strode into the courtroom, his anger suppressed as it had been the night at the hospital when he stood over his father's lifeless body. Ferrell stopped smiling when he saw Patterson; his face resumed its impassivity and his body stiffened. Patterson refused public comment on the Ferrell verdict until the next day, and then he would only say, "A man is never acquitted at the bar of his own conscience."[6]

Former attorney general Si Garrett, who remained in Texas for many years, never came to trial for the murder of Albert Patterson. Garrett returned to Alabama briefly in 1955, still under psychiatric care and still asserting his innocence: "I am in every respect ready to meet my accusers or those individuals responsible for my indictment." But the state never could prosecute him because of his mental condition and kept the case open until his death in 1967. Albert Fuller served his sentence at Kilby Prison in Montgomery; appeals for a new trial kept the Patterson murder in the news for another two years. Fuller, who was paroled after ten years, maintained his innocence until his death in 1969.

Despite having been acquitted in two trials, Arch Ferrell was an emotionally distraught man. People who saw him on a regular basis believed he was suffering from great mental anguish. Russell County sheriff Lamar Murphy arrested Ferrell almost weekly for alcohol-related offenses. This went on for almost a year until one night Murphy received a call to go to Ferrell's home. He found the place in shambles: Eggs had been thrown on the walls; the furniture was broken; and Ferrell had beaten his wife and run his children off. Ferrell, who was seeing monkeys everywhere, had bitten his brother Pelham's hand severely. He was armed with a .357 magnum pistol and a Winchester riot gun. Murphy asked Seth Floyd to commit Ferrell to Bryce Mental Hospital in Tuscaloosa for psychiatric treatment, but the family would not agree to seek help. This behavior continued until one night in 1965, when Ferrell went to Sheriff Murphy's home in tears and asked for his forgiveness. Ferrell hugged Lamar Murphy and his wife, Joyce, and told them he wanted to reform. Murphy forgave Ferrell, took him to the local chapter of Alcoholics Anonymous, and helped him begin rehabilitation. Ferrell, disbarred after the trials, eventually got back his license to practice.[7]

John Patterson's first year in office was half spent by the end of the Fuller-Ferrell trials. In those early months, he was reluctant to give much attention to the great groundswell of public support that surrounded him, because he could ill afford distraction. Occasionally, Patterson and Joe Robertson would visit Charles Meriwether and they would talk, sometimes into the morning hours, about John's increasing popularity and how people were already talking about his succeeding Folsom. "By the end of the trials, Charlie and Joe and I began to spend more time to listening to what people were saying about running for governor," said Patterson. "We agreed that it was best to bide our time before making a decision."

Just as he was beginning to test the waters with a few speaking tours around the state, Patterson received an invaluable boost to his career when the film *Phenix City Story* was released nationally in late 1955. Produced by Allied Artists and billed as a "full-length documentary picture" of the "sin days" of Phenix City, the black-and-white picture was filmed on location using many local people (Ma Beachie played herself) and real honky-tonks and dives. An attempt were made to be as authentic as possible. John McIntire, who played the elder Patterson, visited the Patterson home and selected some of Albert's suits for his wardrobe; he even wore Albert's built-up right shoe, and several scenes were shot in the Patterson law offices. RBA leaders Hugh Bentley and Hugh Britton also had roles in the movie.

Though the film was faithful to the broad issues at play in Phenix City, it was badly skewed by Hollywood writers who took considerable liberties with the historical record. In one scene, a group of gangsters tossed a black child (actually a dummy) from a speeding car onto the Patterson lawn, something that did not happen. After the assassination, the story changed focus to John's character (played by Richard Kiley) and the shift of leadership. At that point, the picture blended fact and fiction and exploited the misery of the town. Some of the scenes were sensationalized, such as wild fights and violent confrontations with local toughs. Many of the local people who attended the premiere at the Palace Theater in Phenix City were disappointed in aspects of the picture. Others didn't like the movie at all and thought it was a poor representation of their city. Ray Jenkins, who knew the story as a journalist, said "as a piece of docuhistory it was atrocious." The overblown heroics attributed to John Patterson offended RBA members who had fought the criminal element with Albert Patterson; they resented the picture presenting John as the hero of the cleanup.[8]

Regardless of local reactions, the *Phenix City Story* became a very effective communications tool for Patterson. It helped raise the level of public awareness of crime and reinforced the popular call for law and order in Alabama. And fair or not, it made a folk hero out of John Patterson. His larger-than-life exploits, heretofore told only in newspapers, unfolded in storybook fashion on the screen and Patterson became real to a curious, admiring public. Authenticity didn't matter. None of this passed unnoticed by either Meriwether or Patterson. "The movie was taken at face value by the public," Meriwether explained. "People thought the story was completely authentic, so it became the bible about Phenix City."[9]

Public interest manifested itself in a continual stream of speaking engagements, which Patterson accepted, emphasizing the dangers of crime. He would sometimes produce an official voter list for his audience and declare that one-third of the names on it were fictitious. His appeal was broad enough that he was invited to speak at a variety of civic and social organizations, but he seemed especially popular with the religious denominations interested in the fact that the RBA had been largely sustained by Phenix City churches. Realizing this emotional link to Alabama churches, rural and urban, Patterson attended a number of summer revival meetings across the state, where often he sang in the choir.[10]

"Public indifference breeds crime." This was John Patterson's message and he carried it up and down the state of Alabama. His appearance was an advertisement for decency and good government. News accounts described him as impeccably dressed in conservative business suits and his manner when meeting people as comfortable. Often he was heralded as "Alabama's Fearless Attorney General," and the media reported on his visits and speeches throughout the state. All of it—speeches, media interest, sensational murder trials, the movie, and the romanticized story of the vanquished sin city—generated public attention for Patterson.

At the same time, Patterson was developing a distinct following— nonpartisan, staunchly loyal, average citizens—who saw in him something they believed was needed in Alabama to move the state out of its backward past into the twentieth century. They wrote him letters and he answered every one of them, filing the correspondence away for future use. With every speech and each passing day, the file grew larger.[11]

8
Bankrupting the Loan Sharks

By the fall of 1955 John Patterson was on solid ground in the attorney general's office and had the support of the people. His first clash with Governor Folsom came with the appointment of state legal counsel for such matters as acquiring property for the highway department. Patterson made the appointments, all of them colleagues in the legal profession, and sent them to the governor's office for approval. To his surprise, Folsom returned the list unsigned. Disturbed that not a single name had been approved, Patterson went to see the governor who told him bluntly, "My friends have just as much merit as your friends." They compromised by each selecting a lawyer in turn until the list of appointments was complete. John Patterson would find many ways to differ with Folsom during the four years they held office—but cronyism was not one of them.

The weekend before the fall elections, Patterson made a surprise visit to Phenix City when a rump group of the old political machine attempted to replace Sheriff Lamar Murphy and other cleanup officials. This was the first general election since the town had been reformed and Patterson believed having an honest election and retaining the incorruptible Murphy were critical. The attorney general made himself visible around town, even barging in on a clandestine meeting of the "old crowd" at their seedy campaign headquarters. "On election day, I moved the entire Montgomery staff into town and monitored the voting," Patterson said. He stationed himself on the east steps of the Russell County courthouse, conspicuously visible during polling hours. Murphy won, along with a slate of honest officeholders, and some townspeople groused publicly that Patterson "frightened the people away."[1]

About the same time, a series of unconnected events gave Patterson a rare judicial opportunity. Over a period of several months, a number of citizens asked him and his staff to do something about the small-loan system that operated in Alabama. For decades, small-loan companies had preyed on the economic difficulties of Alabama's large pauper class, impoverished people black and white, by charging exorbitant interest on small sums of money lent to sharecroppers and industrial workers. It was a highly profitable, largely unregulated industry that could thrive only in a repressive society. The foreclosure and seizure process against those who could not pay was a profitable business, since items put up as security were often worth many times the value of the loan.

This financial activity could be measured in some rather astounding facts. Alabama, with little more than 1 percent of the nation's population, claimed more wage-earner bankruptcies than all the rest of the United States and its territories combined. More than two-thirds of those driven into bankruptcy had debts with two or more loan sharks. The practice was ignored by public officials, and Birmingham, Montgomery, and Mobile were the bankruptcy capitals of the nation. The system achieved such enormous proportions because there was no other choice for low-income families but to seek out the loan sharks; they could not borrow money from banks and there were no legitimate loan companies operating in the state. The year Patterson took office, there were more short-term loan companies in Alabama—more than two thousand—than any other state in the nation. Mobile County alone had more loan companies than the entire state of New York.[2]

The Alabama attorney general became involved when attorneys representing legitimate loan companies approached Patterson about the small-loan problem. W. H. Sadler Jr., who was retained by Beneficial Management Corporation, had been a friend of Albert Patterson and had worked extensively in his campaign with the understanding that Albert would investigate the issue after his planned Phenix City cleanup. Sadler's law firm assigned a capable young attorney, Goodloe Rutland, to work with the attorney general's office and draw up a remedial small-loan law that would foster a climate in which a reputable firm could make loans and collect debts. Douglas Arant, an attorney representing Household Finance Company, told Patterson that Household wanted to do business in Alabama but the company couldn't operate profitably without breaking state usury laws, which set the maximum interest rate at 8 percent annually. "Sadler and Arant suggested that the attorney general enforce Alabama laws with an exactness that would put legal pressure on the small-loan industry," Patterson said. "That would be easy to do since the loan companies were generally ignoring the state laws." Earlier in the year, attempts to pass more strenuous regulatory legislation had been defeated because the political arm of state loan companies, Alabama Finance Institute, kept the bill bottled up in committee.

Despite public outcry and legislative efforts to correct the problem, Alabama loan sharks continued to operate openly without adjusting their exorbitant rates. Alabama's usury laws, written a year before the state joined the union in 1819, had been continually amended to favor loan sharks. In 1945, the state legislature created a haven for loan sharks by passing the Harris Act, which contained the unusual clause that charging interest at a rate in excess of 8 percent per annum was illegal—but it was not a criminal offense. This fantastic loophole allowed loan sharks to continue charging up to 5,000 percent interest; while the law benefited existing companies, the low maximum legal interest rate kept legitimate loan companies out of Alabama.[3]

Patterson launched his first attack in the courts. The biggest stumbling block was the Harris Act, which held that the unjust system was illegal but not a crime. Discovering a similar case in North Dakota where a thriving small-loan industry was shut down by declaring it a public nuisance, Patterson decided to use the same tactic to sidestep the Harris Act.

Convinced by Arant and Sadler that the "best way to get rid of a bad law was to enforce it to the letter," Patterson assigned Noel Baker and Robert Bradley to work with Goodloe Rutland on Montgomery's loan shark problem. The three-man team set out to make a landmark case by finding the most extreme example of small-loan extortion in the capital. Examining bankruptcy petitions, they determined that Tide Finance Company, a thriving operation in the downtown business district, had the most cases on record. Noel Baker discovered quickly that it was going to be impossible to build a solid case against Tide Finance because black customers of the firm did not trust white officials.

Rutland came up with the idea of getting an influential black leader to intervene on their behalf. Consulting his brother's maid, Mary Owens, about the most important black man in the city, he was told that Pluey Blair, whom she referred to as "the bronze mayor of Montgomery," would be their best bet. Blair owned a dry cleaning business and was the chief potentate of Black Masons and Shriners in North America. (White-controlled Masonic Lodges in twelve southern states did not recognize black lodges—and some black lodges took a similar position with regard to whites.) Blair had an excellent education and genteel manners. He was cordial but cautious when approached by Rutland. Blair's first move was to investigate the investigators and determine if they had legitimate reasons to question impoverished blacks about their financial dealings. He then agreed to meet with Patterson and help persuade reluctant blacks to appear in court against the moneylenders. He led the three men into Montgomery's sprawling black district where they quickly obtained enough witnesses and affidavits to incriminate Tide. By late September, Patterson was ready to go to court and bring the loan shark problem under public scrutiny.[4]

Patterson took his case to Montgomery circuit court and senior judge Walter B. Jones, the man who had presided over the Phenix City trials. Patterson and Jones had become fast friends during the cleanup; after John moved to Montgomery they would while away an occasional late evening over a bottle of scotch. A member of Alabama's aristocracy, Jones was the son of former Alabama governor Thomas Goode Jones. He had been an outstanding jurist for more than thirty-five years and president of the state bar association. A sturdy defender of states' rights, Jones was one of Patterson's allies and a definite advantage in any legal battle.[5]

Jones impounded Tide Finance records and ordered its owners to appear in court to defend themselves against the charge of operating a public nuisance. For two days, scores of poor blacks ("some of them positively ignorant," Jones later remarked) told how, pressed by financial need, they had borrowed money from Tide, who then charged up to 700 percent interest for sums as small as ten dollars. These were people who did not fully understand their legal rights and were easily exploited by devious loan officers. Blacks reported being threatened and intimidated by bill collectors who sometimes came en masse, demanding payment in the dead of the night. Some 70 percent of the witnesses were debtors who had been taken to court and had garnishments made against them by three or four loan companies. In the face of overwhelming evidence, Tide was unable to make a viable defense of its practices.

Judge Jones issued a ten-page decree charging Tide Finance with continuous and intentional exacting of "unconscionable rates of interest" in small loans. The case became an instant news sensation, and Judge Jones had made another major impact on the state. The attorney general with the legal resources of his office and support from concerned citizens had scored heavily against a deeply entrenched system that abused Alabama's poor, black and white. It was the first action against loan sharks in Alabama's history. Patterson called Judge Jones's decree a tremendous victory for the state and advised small-loan officials to take the decision seriously. "I can assure all of them that we do not plan to stop this drive."[6]

The appeal process kept him from taking any action against the loan industry until the Tide case was resolved in the courts. When the Tide appeal decision was handed down by the Alabama supreme court it affirmed Patterson's public nuisance theory. The victory, a headline event across the state, did not actually help Patterson in his effort to shut down the loan sharks. He would have to take them on one at a time, an endless process that could take decades, considering the large number of small-loan companies operating in the state.[7]

Meanwhile, the loan sharks resorted to other tactics to bilk people and became more creative with their loan agreements. They set up new companies and sold inflated insurance policies to pad loan payments. One company required its clients to pay twenty-five dollars for a cheap bottle of vitamins with each loan. Moving forward with the legal battle against loan companies, Patterson launched an ambitious attack on the loan industry in Calhoun County, a moderately populated county in northeast Alabama. Patterson looked to Calhoun because of Guy Sparks, a young lawyer he knew from law school. Sparks, who had roomed down the hall from Patterson at Mrs. Cummings's boarding house in Tuscaloosa, was known for his brashness and arrogance. "I took great care to develop a friendship with Guy because I admired his exceptional intelligence," Patterson said about Sparks. "I also discovered that in a crisis he was absolutely fearless." While the Tide case was making its way through the litigation process, Sparks and Patterson discussed the loan shark problem in Calhoun County. Sparks assured him that Circuit Judge Leslie C. Longshore had the will and determination to issue an injunction, provided the attorney general's office could come up with valid affidavits as evidence.[8]

It took Sparks (whom Patterson appointed special assistant attorney general), Noel Baker, and Robert Bradley less than a month to secure enough evidence to make their case. Sparks wasn't faced with the same

hurdle Patterson had to clear in Montgomery. He was a close ally of Anniston's black leadership, who helped him quickly obtain sworn statements from loan-shark victims. Patterson appeared before Judge Longshore in a closed hearing, armed with the supreme court ruling on the
Tide case, and got a temporary injunction against forty-one people doing
business at thirty locations in Calhoun County—every small-loan operation in the county. Patterson told the *Anniston Star* that "this was the
first time in the United States that an injunction has been sought against
a group of loan companies and their operators." He convinced local authorities that the Tide case should be broadened to include more loan
sharks because the industry had rallied to defend itself against state prosecution. The approach was a gamble on his part, one without precedent.
Essentially, Patterson wanted to develop small-loan laws in the courts because the legislature would not bring the system to heel. The Alabama supreme court upheld the mass injunction and small-loan operators across
the state began to marshal their forces in the Alabama legislature. A dramatic showdown was in the making, but it would not take place until after
John Patterson had been elected governor.[9]

This battle against the loan sharks had increased Patterson's political
credibility. Early in his term he had walked in the long shadow of Albert
Patterson and fulfilled his father's campaign promises. The loan shark
crusade gave him his first genuine public attention as attorney general as
people saw him successfully confront another corrupt and powerful element in the state.

Patterson also provided the state with a chuckle during the small-
loan litigation. Only days after enforcing the sweeping injunction against
Calhoun County loan sharks, a Phenix City small-loan company, Investors, Inc., was fined for making loans without a state license, collecting charges exceeding the legal interest, and selling insurance on loans.
Patterson was identified as one of the twenty-eight stockholders in the
company, along with Lamar Murphy; his former law partner Jack Miller;
and an impressive list of city and county officials. Each stockholder had
bought into the company, managed by RBA supporter Jack Gunter, for a
modest three hundred dollar investment. The company was started with
the idea of organizing a bank since Phenix City had only one. However,
as money accumulated from the investors and it was clear the bank would
not be capitalized right away, Gunter decided to lend out the accumulated capital and let the money work for the group. The problem was that

Gunter failed to comply with state legal requirements before he opened for business.

The revelation would not seriously damage Patterson's law-and-order reputation, though it gave his growing list of political enemies an opportunity to point to his questionable financial investments at the same time he was leading a crusade against Alabama's predatory loan shark industry. The deposed Phenix City crowd, and Folsomites in particular, delighted in the blunder. They laughed even harder when the newspapers reported that Patterson said he "thought it was a bank."[10]

9

Playing Cops and Robbers
with the Folsomites

Patterson's crusade against extortionists preying on Alabama's poor brought him even more public attention and became another popular subject for his now heavy schedule of appearances around the state. Events had fashioned a larger place for John Patterson in people's imagination and they begin touting him for bigger things. Within a year of his becoming attorney general, people turned out in impressive numbers to see this living link to the martyred Albert Patterson. And they began encouraging him to run for governor. "The name of John Patterson is a byword both in the cities and in the branch heads," the widely read *Montgomery Advertiser* editorialized. "The people feel that new blood is needed for the governor's office and they feel that a young, honest man might deliver this state from the tax and spend trend." Patterson listened to the talk and read the newspapers and every few weeks met with Charlie Meriwether to discuss developments. Meriwether advised him to remain aloof to the public's call and delay a decision until the timing was right.[1]

Patterson did not have to go searching for his next legal project. By the time he completed his court cases against the loan sharks, his office was flooded with calls and letters. Patterson and his staff had to sift through them to select their next campaign. "Bootlegging and small-time gambling were the most common complaints," Patterson observed, "and people would invariably compare their problem to Phenix City." In the eyes of the public he had become a watchdog attorney general, and people wrote letters or sent delegations to ask for help with local problems. During this period Patterson and his staff began to notice that many reports dealt with actions of the Folsom administration: someone unqualified got a job with the state, or some expensive or unnecessary equipment had been bought by the state, or the state was paving roads for the convenience of local officials. Their curiosity piqued, Patterson and his assistants begin concentrating their investigations on the activities of the Folsom administration.

Folsom's first administration was but a foreshadowing of things to come when he and his friends took control of state government again in 1955. By the end of Folsom's first term, newspapers and state political leaders had grown indignant at the open corruption of the administration. Folsom appointees to the Pardon and Parole Board, the prison system, Alabama State Docks, the Highway Department, and the Alcoholic Beverage Control Board had thoroughly disgraced themselves. Some were under indictment; others had been removed from office. But the average Alabama voter seemed more amused than alarmed by Folsom's behavior.

Big Jim drank himself into a stupor in public, sprawled headlong across courthouse lawns, sired illegitimate offspring, and had a paternity suit brought against him. He gleefully committed almost every conceivable social and moral transgression in a Bible Belt state and still he failed to incur the wrath of the people. People close to Folsom believed he was able to act outrageously yet escape public censure because of his charisma and size. At six feet eight inches tall with size sixteen shoes, Folsom resembled a carnival sideshow, and he enjoyed giving his supporters a few thrills by thumbing his nose at convention. The Alabama author William Bradford Huie derisively referred to him as "the Guckenheimer Kid, multiplying his kind behind every barn door." But for many of Alabama's citizens he was simply good political fun.[2]

From the outset of the second administration, Folsom immersed himself in the many and varied luxuries of the governor's office. He fished in the Gulf on the state yacht and took his family and friends on out-of-state football trips aboard National Guard planes, always at state expense. He abused the governor's mansion fund, and friends said he started his drinking bouts early in the morning—as soon as he rose from bed. Legislators hurried to the governor's mansion to see him early because they knew he would be drunk by breakfast. Folsom ate so little during these drunken binges that he was given vitamin injections.

He did little administrative work on behalf of the "common man" who snickered at his antics, leaving the state government to his political appointees and a cast of supporters who accommodated his indulgences.

The reporter Bob Ingram described the governor's behavior at a party celebrating Folsom's fiftieth birthday: "Folsom became angry at his wife's insistence that he cut the cake, and grabbed a ceremonial sword off of the dining room wall and like a pirate of old, began slashing the cake, sending chunks flying around the room." Later, Ingram said, the governor stood on an ottoman and led the gathering in singing spirituals from a Broadman Hymnal; he sang "Amazing Grace" twelve times.[3]

John Patterson couldn't have had a better backdrop as the state's chief law enforcement officer. Folsom's sottishness and revelry coupled with the irresponsibility of some administration cronies made a stark contrast to Patterson's stance as Alabama's advocate of clean government. Folsom pals and appointees committed startling mistakes in their government positions. Rumors of corruption filtered into the attorney general's office from virtually every corner of the state, from illegal purchases and contracts to cronies getting questionable appointments to state positions.

One source of information about wrongdoings in the administration came from Patterson's friendship with Hugh Sparrow, veteran investigative reporter for the *Birmingham News*. Sparrow was considered something of a sleuth in the statehouse, spending days looking through financial records and contractual dealings of the state government. He didn't ask for information from state employees; he checked the public records himself and knew how to retrieve the information. (State employees referred to him as "old possum eyes.") "I made a private agreement with Sparrow, that he would share his findings with the attorney general's office for a scoop on any legal action taken against the administration," Patterson explained.

In addition to Sparrow, Patterson received considerable information from Ralph Eagerton Sr, chief examiner for the Department of Public Accounts. Eagerton had more than one hundred auditors and accountants responsible for examining state and county agencies every two years, making him the prime source of information about state operations. Eagerton and Folsom had been political enemies since the governor's first administration, when legislative forces hostile to Folsom created Eagerton's position in an attempt to halt the loose management of state finances. Eagerton found an ally in Patterson and started sending him suspicious audit information.

Patterson established another source of information, this one inside the finance department, when a state employee walked into his office with a document pointing to illegal activities. He offered to watch for questionable contracts as long as he remained anonymous. The employee said he would alert the attorney general's office and tell them where the evidence could be found. "The employee would let us in the building at night and show us where the documents were," Patterson said. "Sometimes he would bring them to us. We made copies of the contracts and returned them to the finance office before it opened the next day. We didn't want someone to miss them and get wind of what we were doing and suspect our contact in the department." The arrangement remained in place throughout Patterson's term as attorney general, with Joe Robertson and Noel Baker helping in the night work. The state employee never once asked for or received benefit from this arrangement, and his identity has not been revealed.[4]

Patterson's surveillance system, along with Judge Walter Jones's inclination to grant Patterson injunctions almost at will, concentrated investigative power in the attorney general's office. Patterson's predecessors had failed to exercise the full authority of the attorney general's office. Si Garrett had been indicted for murder, and previous administrations had used the office as an opinion service or to process the state's routine legal business. MacDonald Gallion remembered that the office would provide opinions for state courts but was not inclined to get involved in controversial issues. Under Patterson, the attorney general's approach to issues of law and order was being redefined.

This new approach led Patterson to obtain firm evidence that the state was letting highway work outside of the competitive bid system. Purloined documents from capitol offices revealed that the state finance department was obtaining bids on minor building projects but was awarding multimillion-dollar highway resurfacing work to friends of the administration through private arrangements. Patterson wanted to correct this shortcoming in the bid law through the courts, the same way he had approached the small-loan problem. Armed with copies of illegal contracts Patterson went to Judge Jones and got injunctions against several asphalt companies doing business with the state. One of them, Glencoe Paving Company, had been formed soon after Folsom's election. The company sold eighty thousand tons of resurfacing material to the state its first year in business, giving Cecil Folsom, the governor's brother, a fifty-cents-a-ton commission on all state sales. The administration was so shaken by the court challenge to their "spend without bidding" arrangement, that Finance Director Fuller Kimbrell ordered all fifty firms supplying road repair material to the state to halt shipments. Apprehensive and unsure about Patterson's next move, the Folsom camp looked around anxiously for some way to resolve the problem so they could get on with state business.

Folsom's advisers decided they needed a test case to get the private contracts issue before the state supreme court and supported Glencoe Paving's mandamus proceedings to force the state comptroller to pay their resurfacing bill. Patterson advised against payment because the work had been performed in violation of state law, which required a competitive bid. Glencoe Paving appealed to the Alabama supreme court. The administration contended that the roadwork was repair and therefore exempt from the bid process under a law passed during Folsom's first term. Glencoe charged that Patterson's motives were political. The supreme court agreed with the administration and ordered full payment, seriously damaging Patterson's legal battle with the Folsom crowd and its patronage system. Folsom then paid Glencoe Paving's attorneys fee out of his "emergency fund."[5]

Patterson's effort to end favoritism in the highway department was dead in the water. He urged the legislature to correct the loophole that enabled the contract abuses: "The door is now wide open and the major amount of highway work now being done in the state has been let to friends and associates of the administration at any price they want to negotiate, without regard to cost." Folsom said that the governor had "vast responsibilities" in the expenditure of all state monies. "In politics," he quipped, "all the money your friends spend is legal, and all the money your enemies spend is illegal."

The supreme court ruling cut short Patterson's effort to take the administration to task for improper spending. However, the series of injunctions and the Glencoe Paving case did succeed in informing the public that Folsom and his friends were using state resources to secure favors for political associates. Ralph Eagerton's department of public accounts did a study that compared prices paid by the state of Alabama to prices paid by states with effective competitive bid laws and found that Alabama was paying 20 to 30 percent more. State deposits went to banks run by Folsom cronies; heavy equipment was purchased from companies owned by Folsom's friends; private roads were paved by the state highway department; liquor companies paid kickbacks to state liquor agents; and Folsom intimates profited handsomely in real estate from advance information on new federal Interstate highway routes through the state. While Folsom didn't appear to have personally profited from the deals (other than a steady supply of liquor), even a small portion of the graft and corruption would have guaranteed the governor a life of financial security upon leaving office. A close supporter said, "Folsom got himself surrounded by crooks." Furthermore, not once did Folsom have any problem with the IRS.[6]

Despite the setback with the highway contracts litigation, the attorney general's office continued to pursue its new approach to law and order. Expanding an investigation into the Conservation Department, Patterson began to delve into the dealings of its director W. H. (Bill) Drinkard, a Cullman County mortician who had served as Folsom's finance director in his first term. Drinkard was responsible for the state's park and forest lands. On the basis of Judge Jones's earlier rulings, state auditors declared illegal all jobs and services performed by private companies without competitive bids. Using that criteria, Bill Drinkard was held personally responsible for illegally spending $709,487. Patterson was unsuccessful at recovering the money, but he linked Drinkard to other scandals in the state parks system. Folsom decided to close several state parks because a lack of maintenance had allowed them to fall into deplorable condition. After the closings, contracts were let, without bid, to administration favorites for timber cutting at three state parks. The contracts were discovered through Patterson's mole in the finance department. The three timber companies completely devastated stretches of state park lands, allowing winter rains to erode the soil and prompting a national parks official to remark that he had never seen logging operations as destructive as those in Alabama. Patterson informed the public of the environmental damage and waste by taking Hugh Sparrow on a personal tour of Little Mountain State Park near Guntersville.

Drinkard ignored calls for environmental considerations in the logging contracts, even from the TVA, and displayed little concern that the public knew about the devastation in state parks. All Drinkard's actions, which included hiring Folsom kin, were undertaken with Folsom's full knowledge and support. Patterson obtained a series of injunctions from Judge Jones to halt the wanton waste of public assets and temporarily halted the timber cutting. The most effective deterrent, however, was the press, which applied enough public pressure that Folsom intervened to stop the ruin of the public parks and forests. Drinkard, Folsom, and Fuller Kimbrell, the key Folsom administration aide for patronage, were soundly criticized in the state press, and the stories undermined public support for the administration. Indignant state legislators toured the parks in four-wheel drive Jeeps and planted pine seedlings; state funds were appropriated to help repair the vast timber cutting damage.[7]

Patterson wasn't finished with Drinkard. When state supreme court rulings upheld administration abuses, Patterson continued to pry into the affairs of the conservation department while the Folsom administration cried foul and denounced Patterson's political ambitions. The source inside the finance department alerted him to still more evidence of wrongdoing and Patterson continued his legal assault against corruption. "By then," Patterson explained, "we had an assembly-line process going. We would select the next project, go down the street to Judge Jones's court and get an injunction, and turn the information over to Hugh Sparrow for the next day's headlines in the *Birmingham News*." Other state media would then follow up on the story. Soon other reporters were either bringing evidence to the attorney general's office or notifying Patterson of suspicious dealings in the capital. Patterson had the support and confidence of the state press during a period when it was increasingly antagonistic toward Alabama political leaders.

The final round between the governor and the attorney general was fought in Mobile, where the state had entered into long-term leases for property that the highway department had created by dredging and filling along the Mobile causeway. When Patterson's office examined the lease for the causeway property, they found that Folsom and Drinkard had let for $150 state land that was valued at $100,000. The dredging costs alone topped $31,000. The lessee was Peggy Finch, a Drinkard intimate, according to newspaper reports. Patterson immediately obtained a decree of cancellation from Judge Jones, setting aside the lease arrangement. Charging constructive fraud, he claimed that the lease amounted to a giveaway of state property. "If the governor can do this, he can give away the capitol." The lease ran for fifty years with renewable rights for another forty. Folsom remained silent. Drinkard said it was not his policy as conservation director to try and make money for the state because Alabama was not in the real estate business. The state appealed the cancella-

tion decree and the Alabama supreme court held for the conservation director using the rationale that the department had full power to buy and
sell property. The court stated that the evidence "was insufficient to show
fraud, corruption or bad faith," even though the state had rented other
parcels on the causeway to oil companies for far greater amounts. Once
again the state supreme court had upheld administration excesses.[8]

Patterson and his staff rebounded quickly with the revelation that Folsom and Drinkard had illegally leased 2,739 acres of state park land on
the Gulf of Mexico to a private corporation. The property included 1.27
miles of beach property. While a fair market value for the state property
was over $3 million, the lease called for a nominal payment of $25,000
and 4 percent of any income received by the lessee, Tri-State Corporation, a front for unknown investors. Tri-State had already cut the timber
off the park land by the time the attorney general's staff discovered the
lease. The company was virtually free to do as it wished with the property for the life of the ninety-year lease.

However, Tri-State made a serious error when it financed the construction of a ten-unit motel with an $80,000 loan through the Small Busi-
ness Administration (SBA). Patterson avoided another losing confrontation in the Alabama supreme court, which had consistently ruled in
favor of the administration, by encouraging the U.S. Justice Department
to intervene on behalf of the SBA. The presence of federal authorities
meant the case would be transferred to Judge Frank M. Johnson's court
in Montgomery. Patterson said, "I believed that we could get a fair hearing in Judge Johnson's court."

When Johnson heard the Justice Department's argument on behalf
of the SBA, with Alabama's attorney general admitting to the allega-
tions against the state, Johnson voided the lease and returned the property to the Conservation Department. He also ruled that the state had to
pay the SBA for Tri-State's outstanding loan for the motel. Repayment of
the loan was unimportant compared to the near loss of a long stretch of
beach property in the resort town of Gulf Shores that the state later developed into a multibillion-dollar industry.[9]

Throughout the legal maneuvers and public criticism, Folsom remained
civil to Patterson and received the attorney general cordially whenever
state business required them to confer. Furthermore, Folsom spoke re-
spectfully of Albert and Agnes Patterson, often asking John about his

widowed mother. Only once did the governor approach the subject of their public problems when Folsom jokingly accused Patterson of suffering from "injuctivitis."

Injunctions, court action, and ongoing revelations about widespread corruption in state government dealt solid blows to Folsom and his administration. The Folsom circle had eagerly embraced state jobs and state revenue following Big Jim's landslide victory, treating the state as their private endowment. The spoils system had worked well for Folsom and his friends during the first term, and it was taken for granted that it would again be open season after the governor redeemed himself with the electorate in the '54 campaign. But they had not reckoned on the drama of Phenix City and the subsequent demand for clean government or that the attorney general office's would change its long-standing practices and make law enforcement a top priority.[10]

Patterson made five highly publicized moves against illegal spending by the Folsom administration, all of them top news stories in Alabama in 1956. While he was often unsuccessful in his attempts to rein in administration spending, the court actions were successful in casting a pall of suspicion that eroded public support for Folsom. Folsom's losses were Patterson's political gains. In spite of unfavorable supreme court rulings, Patterson received accolades from an admiring state press. "Press and Public Applaud Patterson's Crackdown," read a *Birmingham News* headline. "Patterson Shields Treasury from the Marauders," said the *Montgomery Advertiser*. The *Advertiser* commented that it was a "fine and courageous thing Attorney General John Patterson is doing in taking legal steps to shed more light on the matter of state contracts and state expenditures of public funds." The excesses of the Folsom administration were added to the loan shark fight and the Phenix City story as recurring themes in Patterson's speeches as he spoke of "Building a Better Alabama."

The Alabama Junior Chamber of Commerce honored Patterson as one of its "Four Outstanding Men in Alabama" for 1956 and nominated him for the prestigious national honor. In January 1957, John Patterson was named, along with acclaimed missionary-physician Tom Dooley and Olympic star Bob Richards, as one of the "Ten Outstanding Young Men of America." It was an honor that gained the young attorney general still more respect and focused national attention on his fight against corruption.

Patterson was thirty-five now, wiser and more experienced after two years as attorney general, and the foremost state official championing clean government. "Ever since open contempt for law and bald-faced thievery began to make themselves evident in the second Folsom Administration," the *Selma Times-Journal* proclaimed in an editorial, "citizens of Alabama have been yearning for a political Moses. . . . If John Patterson proves himself that Moses . . . he automatically would become a governorship candidate hard to beat." Heeding Meriwether's advice, Patterson brushed aside the talk of higher office, publicly at least, and refused to talk state politics to the press.[11]

10
Patterson Sets His Sights on Integration

The next phase of John Patterson's political adventures would not provide him with the excitement of investigating Folsom's blunders, although the headlines would be more sensational. The South was facing a controversial issue—integration—a topic Patterson said he had been too busy to address during his first two years as attorney general. Before his career was over, however, he would be embroiled in emerging racial changes that would affect the entire South.

Patterson had become attorney general not through serving the state's political system, which meant the ruling Democratic Party, but because a family tragedy had thrust him into the center of Alabama politics. He was quite aware that the state's power brokers did not want him in office. He later explained: "I looked at my presence in state government as the will of the people because of the great public pressure that was placed on the political system, and I meant to be loyal to them." Having benefited from this turn of events, he did not feel constrained by conventional political considerations; he felt free to chart his own course without answering to special interest groups, even the dominant Alabama Democratic Party. Now, the will of the people—the white voters—centered on the question of integration. Loyalty to the people prompted Patterson to defend the South's traditional segregation practices. That sense of loyalty would prove to have a lasting effect on his political career.

The beginning of John Patterson's political career and the modern civil rights movement occurred only weeks apart in 1954. The *Brown v. Board of Education* decision that struck down "separate but equal" public education, which was handed down during his father's tense runoff campaign, was not fully understood by the general public when John took office. Like many others, Patterson said the decision meant nothing to him when it became law. Phenix City, with its long list of moral shortcomings, didn't have a history of racial conflict, in part because of the high-profile Klan, which intimidated opponents of segregation in the same way the gamblers cowed their foes. Patterson was just another small-town lawyer with the customary social attitudes of southern conservatives. Alabama remained calm during the first months after the Brown decision. Since the court order did not directly involve the state, Governor Persons did not call a special session of the legislature to address the debate over public education. The only acknowledgment that Folsom made about the decision was a jocular remark during the '54 campaign that he would not force Negro children to go to school with whites.[1]

When Patterson took office in January 1955, there was a lot of outraged posturing and harsh rhetoric by public officials around the nation, particularly in Virginia. The most noticeable opposition in Alabama came from members of the legislature who stumbled all over themselves trying to take the most aggressive position against integration. Folsom, who openly supported blacks and wanted his second administration to have the largest road construction program in the state's history, became frustrated with segregationists in the legislature who introduced an avalanche of bills in defense of Alabama's dual school systems. The bills and resolutions were silly, self-serving efforts by legislators to defy the U.S. Supreme Court decision, causing Folsom to publicly taunt lawmakers for showboating over the issue. One of the more imaginative legislative creations was submitted by Sen. Sam Engelhardt of Macon County in the Black Belt (so named because of its rich soil, but coincidentally the area in the state with the highest proportion of African Americans), the home of famed Tuskegee Institute. Engelhardt, who owned sixty-five hundred acres of farmland, was by far one of the county's wealthiest citizens.

A gruff, square-jawed man, Engelhardt often stated that the reason he was in politics was to keep Macon County from being governed by blacks. His contribution to the pile of segregation bills was the School Placement Bill, where students would be assigned to schools on the basis of school faculty and facilities, the student's ability, psychological stability, home life and morals, social environment, and other highly subjective factors. Frustrated by Engelhardt's tactics, which were stalling his highway program, Folsom knew how to get the senator's support. He told Engelhardt that he would get a new board of registrars and "register every damn nigger in the county." Engelhardt quickly released the highway legislation.[2]

During the early period of racial unrest, Patterson avoided official involvement in the South's integration troubles. He was busy with the seemingly inexhaustible judicial opportunities of the attorney general's office. Patterson said that what he did know about the gathering political storm he didn't like, but he knew enough about contention and strife to remain apart from the crisis until it was absolutely necessary. In December 1955, just blocks from Patterson's office, Rosa Parks refused a bus driver's order to give up her seat to a white passenger and was subsequently arrested for violating Montgomery's segregation laws. E. D. Nixon, a friend of Parks, helped her make bail and called an impromptu boycott of the city's bus system. Eventually the boycott was supported by the efforts of the Montgomery Improvement Association, with Martin Luther King Jr. as its president. King, new to the city, was selected to lead the boycott because the cause needed an educated, articulate spokesman. Nixon, an energetic sleeping car porter, helped plan and implement the boycott before stepping aside in deference to King. Fred Gray, who attended church with the Nixons, said E. D. Nixon was highly respected in his community because of his longtime efforts to obtain for blacks the same rights as other Americans—particularly the right to vote. Nixon's organizational abilities provided critical leadership for the new civil rights cause. Response to the boycott overwhelmed even King, who said he hoped to have 60 percent black participation. Churches provided their vehicles; black taxi companies ferried African Americans to and from their jobs; and people walked when they could have ridden virtually empty city buses.

The boycott called attention to Montgomery's racial flaws, and the city became the topic of critical scrutiny by out-of-state media as the nation and the world lent its moral support to those who were demanding better treatment in public accommodations. The crisis could have been easily avoided according to the historian J. Mills Thornton III. He contends that black demands were simple and direct and not at all threatening to the local power structure: courtesy from bus drivers; the hiring of black drivers for predominately black routes; and a seating arrangement that did not designate special sections on the bus for each race. There was support within the city government to accommodate the requests without changing existing segregation laws. But in the end officials refused the requests, saying that blacks "would go about boasting of a victory that they had won over the white people." Unable to get a few minor concessions from city leaders, blacks became more aggressive and began to push for total abolition of the city's segregation system.[3]

Patterson said he was reluctant to get involved in the integration issue when it burst into life in the capital, maintaining that he mostly "sat in the gallery and watched." His only venture into the matter came when he filed a motion on behalf of the state Public Service Commission to dismiss a federal suit seeking to declare Alabama's travel laws unconstitutional. He argued the traditional states' rights position that it really wasn't the concern of the federal courts, that such a case should be heard first in state court. When the movement began solidifying its support and was the lead story on national news, Patterson said he attached more importance to the boycott than he did the Brown decision. In Alabama, the Brown school case did not get the kind of grassroots participation from the black community that the Montgomery bus boycott did.[4]

After more than a year, the boycott ended when the U.S. Supreme Court upheld the decision of a special three-man U.S. district court that declared Alabama's segregation laws unconstitutional. Blacks gained much more from the boycott than they first expected, and Martin Luther King emerged as the leading spokesperson for the rising civil rights movement. Montgomery city officials had not called on the governor or the attorney general for advice or legal support, and Folsom and Patterson treated the boycott as a local matter. The events precipitated by Rosa Parks developed into a major defining event for civil rights, not because of the extent of black demands or because of pressure by the state to end the boycott, but because of the stubborn insistence of local authorities that segregation laws had to be upheld at all cost. The all-or-nothing attitude would characterize southern white leaders when they faced the campaigns for school and social integration.

The bus boycott also fostered racist rage, foreshadowing the southern white emotional response to the integration of blacks into society. During the early months of the boycott, membership in the newly organized White Citizens Council increased dramatically; in one month membership in the Montgomery group doubled from six thousand to twelve thousand. Even without encouragement from the state's political leaders, the white population began to rise up in opposition to the Brown decision and displayed open hostility to blacks in the city. The homes of Nixon and King were bombed, and carloads of armed whites made nightly tours through the black community, shouting threats and obscenities. With the Klan an active force in Alabama since Reconstruction, violence was predictable.

At one point during the boycott, after a particularly frustrating meeting with members of the black community, Montgomery mayor William A. Gayle attacked black leaders for "saying one thing to a white man and another to a Negro." Gayle called them a "group of Negro radicals" whose only goal was to stir up racial strife. Declaring that white people were firm in their convictions, the mayor said whites didn't care whether blacks ever rode a bus again. The statement got an overwhelmingly positive response from the city's white population. The city hall switchboard was swamped with calls, hundreds of telegrams flooded the mayor's office, and citizens came by Gayle's office to shake his hand. City officials were amazed by the avalanche of approval, and whatever remnants of moderation still existed in Montgomery at that point quieted considerably as local politicians rushed to associate themselves with the mayor's popular stand.

The response of an angry white population angered blacks. Both camps became increasingly hostile, more vocal, and more militant. Race-baiting was raised to an art, and politicians in Alabama realized that to win white votes they had to come out strongly in defense of segregation. The lesson that was not lost on Alabama's ambitious attorney general and his political mentor Charlie Meriwether.[5]

In spite of having a front row seat for the developing civil rights movement, John Patterson said his views on *Brown v. Board of Education* did not originate in Alabama. In the summer of 1955 he attended a national state attorneys general conference in New Hampshire at which the Brown decision dominated all other topics among southern representatives. This was Patterson's first exposure to the legal issues surrounding integration and he gave close attention to how his counterparts were addressing them. During the meeting he developed a relationship with Virginia attorney general Lindsay Almond, a silver-maned image of the southern gentleman. Almond's views on school integration would greatly influence Patterson. Almond knew of Patterson from the Phenix City cleanup and found the nation's youngest attorney general to his liking. Virginia was the first southern state to confront integration in public education, and Almond developed a strategy for the state's massive resistance effort. Virginia threatened to close public schools and adopt a private school system rather than integrate. Almond promised Virginians a "fight to the finish."

Patterson went to Virginia several times during early 1956 to consult with Almond and even joined him as a witness in some court cases.

Almond ran for governor on the strength of his anti-integration battles, and he invited Patterson to join him in the final days of the campaign. Patterson heard Almond tell the voters, "I have fought with my back to the wall in an effort to save the public school system of Virginia from destruction." Almond won the election, and Patterson took home copies of his speeches and literature, as well as the excitement of the campaign. Until that time, Patterson had seen himself as a racial moderate; now he was being swayed by the idea of resisting forced integration and federal intervention in state matters. The rhetoric of defiance became more noticeable in his speeches. He did not call for militant resistance, but he said enough to let his audience know he was prepared to defend racial segregation of Alabama schools if the state was threatened by litigation.[6]

While the bus boycott was going on in Montgomery, another racially charged situation took place at the University of Alabama. On February 3, 1956, Autherine Lucy was admitted to the school after a three-year court fight between the university and the NAACP. The incident would further harden racial attitudes in Alabama.

The night Lucy was admitted to the university, a crowd of students set off firecrackers, sang "Dixie," and marched through the women's dormitory area. Though it was termed a riot, observers on the scene said it looked more like a panty raid. However, resistance gradually increased until a few nights later a riot did indeed occur. Lucy was suspended because university officials claimed they feared for her safety.

The University of Alabama reflected a traditional southern conservative philosophy. Much of that conservatism could be traced to the board of trustees—a staid, self-perpetuating group of white men who did not welcome change. Patterson said he anticipated being called into the litigation over integration of the school and was prepared to assist the university in defending itself, but the trustees did not request help from the attorney general or the governor.

With trouble brewing in Tuscaloosa, Folsom went on a fishing and drinking binge in Florida. He knew nothing about the mobs in Tuscaloosa until he heard a radio news broadcast and phoned university officials from a country store in South Alabama. Then Folsom's only action was to send a few highway patrolmen to help university police restore order. The governor said he had not taken more drastic action because the trouble did not seem serious: "It is perfectly normal for all races not to be overly fond of each other." The issue ended when Lucy's legal team committed a legal blunder by alleging that members of the board of trustees were conspirators in the demonstrations that led to her suspension. With the NAACP unable to prove the charge, the university asked for her permanent expulsion and the federal judge ruled it was justified.

Governor Folsom lashed out against the NAACP and "outside agitators" for causing turmoil at the university; students participating in the demonstrations were expelled, suspended, or otherwise disciplined. The Alabama legislature went into a frenzy. One resolution ordered Lucy to appear before them to determine whether the NAACP was controlled by communists, while another called for federal funds to resettle southern Negroes in the North and West "where they are wanted." The Montgomery bus boycott and actions of the NAACP, while uniting Alabama blacks in their efforts to gain equality, inflamed a hostile and determined opposition.[7]

Any hope for racial moderation was gone, and hard-line segregationists turned their attention to the relatively liberal Folsom. The governor had made a significant political blunder while Harlem congressman Adam Clayton Powell was visiting Montgomery for a black voter registration rally. He was invited to the governor's mansion where he talked with Folsom over drinks. Afterward, with Folsom's permission, Powell spoke about his conversation with the governor at a rally and later to the press. He said he had scotch and soda with the governor, a statement that alienated not only the segregationists but also the prohibitionists, who regarded public liquor consumption in the governor's mansion as an affront. (Folsom was later quoted as saying, "They say I drank Scotch and soda with Adam Clayton Powell. That's a lie. Anybody who knows me knows I don't drink Scotch.") Folsom further accommodated Powell by lending him the state limousine and Winston Craig, his personal driver. Throughout Alabama and even in neighboring states whites were enraged by Folsom's blatant disregard of southern racial conventions. The Adam Clayton Powell incident caused enormous political damage to Folsom.

If there was a redeeming feature in Jim Folsom's politics, it had to be his liberal attitude toward blacks. He repeatedly suggested that race had been used to blind poor whites to their common economic interests with blacks. During the 1954 primary, he had argued for a bond issue with a large part of the money raised going to black schools: "We'll take the Negro schools out of the barns and shotgun shacks and put them in buildings."

Folsom's fall from grace with the electorate was strikingly evident when the 1956 Democratic primary elected committeemen for the Democratic National Party. Folsom was opposed by Charles McKay, a member of the state legislature who had introduced a resolution in the House that declared the Brown decision "null and void." McKay made the campaign a referendum on race by attacking Folsom as a "friend of the Negro and the NAACP and the host of Adam Clayton Powell, the whiskey-drinking Negro congressman from Harlem." McKay's main support came from the increasing ballot strength of the White Citizens Councils throughout the state. Voters used the 1956 primary to express their anger over the bus boycott, the Powell meeting, and integration in general: the vote was McKay, 232,751; Folsom, 79,644. The governor was embarrassed that his opponent won majorities in sixty-four of sixty-seven counties only two years after his big gubernatorial win. After that primary, every politician in the state understood that preserving segregation, especially in schools, was a paramount consideration for political success.[8]

John Patterson saw racial extremism sweep Alabama. The response to the Montgomery bus boycott proved that getting tough with blacks was popular. The open support by many whites for aggressive opposition to an attempt to integrate the University of Alabama revealed the depth of racial hostility. And the furor caused by Folsom's meeting with Powell demonstrated that even symbolic accommodation between the races was a serious political mistake.

"Everyone in politics at the time understood what was on the minds of the people," Patterson remembered. After seeing how racial issues energized Alabama voters, he realized the benefit of opposing integration. Patterson responded to a new challenge and liked the high stakes and excitement of leading what white southerners regarded as a battle between good and evil.

Others realized it too. George Wallace knew that, despite Patterson's meteoric rise in state politics, race would be the issue in the people's mind come the primary elections of spring 1958. Joe Azbell, political reporter for the *Montgomery Advertiser*, was very nearly prophetic when he wrote: "There seems to be a new political climate emerging in Alabama that may have a vast and profound importance in the future selection of all political office-holders. It doesn't mean the White Citizens Council will control the voting populace but it does mean that the next governor of Alabama probably will be a man who takes a firm stand on behalf of the white people."[9]

Politicians with an eye on state races were maneuvering themselves into the "correct" stand on the integration issue. John Patterson knew that if he were to continue as a people's advocate, he, too, would have to take the popular position.

11
The Montgomery Bus Boycott
Changes Alabama Forever

John Patterson does not recall exactly when he realized that he had found the perfect antagonist. It was probably during his visits with Lindsay Almond in Virginia that he recognized that the NAACP was the devil incarnate in the mind of the white South—and a worthy opponent. During the legal battles in Virginia, he saw boldness in the black organization that he admired as it made shambles of that state's massive resistance strategy. Almond had attempted to stop the NAACP and its Legal Defense and Education Fund from undertaking litigation to integrate schools by attempting to use against them a series of barratry and champerty acts that made it unlawful for any organization to encourage lawsuits in which they were not a party. As the NAACP easily outmaneuvered Almond, Patterson understood the futility of getting into a court fight with the NAACP; if the highly capable and more experienced Almond could not blunt the NAACP's integration effort in Virginia, it would be useless for him to take them on in Alabama.

That lesson was amplified by a confidential meeting that Patterson attended with a group of constitutional lawyers in Birmingham in mid-1956. Birmingham attorney Joe Johnston had called the meeting of senior officials and attorneys from Alabama, Georgia, Tennessee, and Mississippi to discuss each state's integration strategy. Patterson, Gordon Madison, and Albert Boutwell attended on behalf of Alabama. Griffin Bell represented Gov. Ernest Vandiver of Georgia.

The attorneys gathered around Johnston's conference table had a wary eye cast northward to Virginia, sure that the battle for integrated schools would soon reach the Deep South and overwhelm its passive resistance to integration. Patterson and the others wanted to be ready when the time came to go to court and defend Alabama's education laws. The group hoped to develop a common strategy so the four Deep South states could present a solid front. Not surprisingly, the consensus at the meeting was a recognition of eventual defeat. "We all knew that school integration was inevitable," Patterson explains. "There was just no way the states could preserve segregation as a way of life. It was the law of the land that had been reinforced too many times in the federal courts." With the courts ruling for integration, the group reluctantly decided they had no legal grounds to maintain their states' segregation policies.

Patterson reports however that the opinion expressed around the table was that they were obligated to fight a delaying action on behalf of the South's white population. "We believed, to a man, that time would help resolve the enormous resistance to an integrated society and lessen the probability of violent resistance," Patterson explains. The group further agreed that to gain time they would take a nonconfrontational approach and avoid litigation with the U.S. Justice Department and the NAACP because the states would lose. One of the delaying tactics proposed by the lawyers was to decentralize the power of school boards so that each system would be autonomous. The shift of power would require a multiplicity of suits to integrate individual schools or local school systems, rather than having the entire state legally overwhelmed by the Justice Department in a single court order. The meeting gave Alabama's legal officers a comprehensive strategy—although a losing one—to approach the coming integration battle.

Not long after the meeting, sensing that the NAACP was about to recruit complainants to file suits against the state, Patterson went ahead with a plan conceived by his staff to stop the organization from initiating integration suits in Alabama. On June 1, he went to his reliable ally, Judge Walter B. Jones, seeking an injunction to stop NAACP activity in the state. Judge Jones granted the injunction.[1]

The idea was not original with Alabama. Months earlier, Louisiana attempted to remove the NAACP under an old state anti–Ku Klux Klan law that required such groups to file membership lists. Patterson based his legal argument in part on a New York precedent that outlawed the Klan because it violated similar statutes. His case charged that the NAACP was a foreign (out-of-state) corporation, organized in the state of New York, that engaged in business in Alabama without complying with state law. A 1940 Alabama statute required all "foreign corporations" to file a copy of its certification of incorporation or charter with the secretary of state, designate an authorized agent for service of process, and pay a ten dollar fee. An investigation by Patterson's staff revealed that the NAACP had failed to file the proper registration papers or pay the fee. Patterson charged that the organization had been in violation of state law since 1918 and that the NAACP regional office in Birmingham was therefore illegal.

Nor was this Alabama's first strike against the NAACP. Earlier, Alabama had been one of many Deep South states to adopt measures to curb or suppress NAACP activities. Legislation was passed that required the association to pay fees and licenses and tried to force them to disclose membership records, contributions, and other organizational data. During the period following the Brown decision, the state legislature threw all kinds of restrictive and regulatory conditions at the NAACP. Officials of the organization admitted that conditions in Alabama, Georgia, Florida, Mississippi, and North and South Carolina were "particularly discouraging." In each of these states, official resistance was beginning to stiffen over time rather than weaken, and the attitude of the white population encouraged the prosegregation position of its constitutional officers.

Patterson's move against the NAACP, however, hurt the organization more than the petulant reaction of southern legislatures. Taking a law-and-order approach, Patterson charged that the association was involved in activities that resulted in breaches of the peace. To support his contention that the NAACP was fomenting trouble in Alabama, he produced evidence that the organization had engaged in "organizing, supporting and financing" the Montgomery bus boycott and "employed or otherwise paid money" to Autherine Lucy to enroll at the University of Alabama to test its admissions policy. Patterson asked Judge Jones to bar the NAACP from conducting further business in Alabama, dissolve all state chapters, and enjoin it from maintaining offices in the state. At the time the NAACP had some thirteen thousand members in forty chapters throughout the state.[2]

W. C. Patton, NAACP executive secretary for the Alabama region, didn't know about the injunction until James Kilpatrick from the Associated Press phoned his office in the Brown-Marx Building in Birmingham. "Did you know that the NAACP has been enjoined from doing business in Alabama?" Kilpatrick asked. Patton, puzzled, replied that he didn't.

Within an hour Patton was no longer puzzled. A deputy sheriff with a reporter in tow served a temporary injunction, an ex parte restraining order, barring the association from conducting business in the state of Alabama and forbidding it from taking the necessary steps to qualify legally under state law. Patton accepted the papers but refused to turn over association records to the deputy as ordered by the injunction.

Patton then notified Gordon Rodgers, an Anniston dentist and the state NAACP president, about the court order. Rodgers said he immediately left for Birmingham and the two men surreptitiously moved the records to what they described as a "junky business place" in the vicinity of the state offices. Then they called New York headquarters with the news of the attorney general's action. It would be eight years before the NAACP was able to operate in the state again.

In New York, Roy Wilkins was baffled by the injunction; discussion at a quickly called staff meeting showed that a great deal was at stake. Suppose Judge Jones issued a permanent injunction. Could regional activities still be directed from the Birmingham office? When NAACP leaders emerged from the meeting, Thurgood Marshall defined the organization's immediate strategy this way: "We'll just go along. They can't provoke us. They can't slow anything down. We'll just keep moving along." The national chairman of the association described Jones's injunction as "a direct violation of the American tradition and constitutional principle of freedom of association." NAACP leaders were not sure what would happen in Alabama because up to that point no state had been able to keep them from operating.

Patterson was prepared for the worst when he moved against the NAACP. "I anticipated a great cry of protest and a lot of complicated legal maneuvering, maybe even intervention by federal agencies," Patterson said. "Instead, I was surprised by the quiet and completely legal style of answering the complaint." NAACP attorneys Arthur Shores and Robert Carter simply filed motions to dissolve Jones's temporary injunction, claiming it was inappropriate. Patterson countered by filing a discovery motion against the association for failing to comply with the court order; he wanted the NAACP charter, membership lists, names of contributors, bank statements, canceled checks, and all correspondence dealing with the Montgomery bus boycott and the Autherine Lucy episode. Patterson wanted the financial records to determine the extent of NAACP involvement in integration efforts, which he would make public.

Judge Jones issued the subpoena while Shores and Carter insisted that state corporation laws did not apply to the association and that the attorney general was just trying to harass the association. Jones condemned the "brazen defiance" of his writ and promptly found the NAACP in contempt of court and levied a one hundred thousand dollar fine.

Roy Wilkins refused to make public the membership lists to Alabama authorities. NAACP members in Selma had been subjected to personal threats and violence when a similar list was revealed. The refusal to produce the records meant the NAACP was barred from further activity in Alabama until it cleared itself of contempt and the injunction and fine were lifted. A single exception was made to the NAACP's refusal to reveal the contents of its membership list. Arthur Shores informed the court that one of the attorney general's relatives was a member of the association. A stunned John Patterson listened as Shores revealed that former congressman Lafayette Patterson, who had served in the U.S. Congress as a Democrat from 1928 to 1933, was a member of the Alabama NAACP. Embarrassed by the revelation, Patterson called his uncle to ask about Shores's claim. Lafayette, a pre–New Deal liberal, admitted that he had been a member of the NAACP for many years.[3]

John Patterson went to the U.S. Supreme Court four times in an effort to evade or overturn its direct rulings. Each trip through the courts cost the NAACP some eighteen thousand dollars. During the eight years the NAACP was barred from doing business in Alabama, any association activity was almost certain to bring a contempt action by the state. "The NAACP is an irresponsible, radical, and highly dangerous organization, which has done more than any other agency to bring about racial friction," Patterson told a Talladega audience. Patton, Rodgers, and other NAACP leaders were watched closely by state authorities. When the Reverend Fred Shuttlesworth of Birmingham and other black leaders organized the Alabama Christian Movement for Human Rights to continue registering black voters, Patterson accused them of being a front for the NAACP. He tried to exert additional pressure on the association by going to New York and talking with the Lord and Lord law firm about suing the national NAACP organization for the hundred thousand dollar contempt fine. "They turned me down, as I expected, but word of the visit eventually found its way to association headquarters and Wilkins."

Patterson's strategy in restricting NAACP operations was copied in Texas, Arkansas, Georgia, and Virginia. There were efforts within the black community to resume activities under other guises. Ministerial groups were especially active in voter registration in an effort to offset the barred NAACP leadership. The Alabama State Coordinating Association for Registration and Voting spent much of its existence under legal attack by Patterson as the NAACP's alter ego. It became difficult for black groups to replace the money, connections, expertise, and prestige when the national NAACP was separated from the state.

With Patterson temporarily holding the NAACP at bay in Alabama, many southern attorneys general continued their attacks on the association. Eugene Cook of Georgia, Bruce Bennett of Arkansas, and John Ben Shepherd of Texas attacked the NAACP in a similar fashion. Cook wrote a book entitled *The Ugly Truth about the NAACP* and stumped the South making speeches castigating the Supreme Court and the NAACP. Shepherd, with Patterson's courtroom assistance, attempted to have the NAACP removed from Texas. Years later when the Supreme Court finally ruled for the NAACP, the court made reference to the association's role in representing the constitutional rights of black people in Alabama, which in the court's opinion was sufficient reason for it to operate in the state. The court also upheld withholding membership lists, noting that "on past occasions revelation of the identity of its rank-and-file members has exposed these members to economic reprisals, loss of employment, threat of physical coercion, and other manifestations of public hostility." The court found that the NAACP was a different kind of organization not subject to customary state restraint. But in the mid-1950s John Patterson's efforts had found favor with segregationists and had increased support for his rising ambition. His strategy elevated him to the front rank of white supremacists in Alabama, where public sentiment indicated he must be if he was to be a serious contender for governor.[4]

At the same time that Patterson was challenging the NAACP's role in school integration, Sam Engelhardt, one of Patterson's most vigorous supporters, was generating a startling bit of resistance down in Macon County. Engelhardt had continued the plan previously thwarted by Folsom to gerrymander the Tuskegee city boundaries to retain white control. He believed that a gerrymander would survive in court because traditionally federal courts did not interfere with a state's internal political boundaries. In May 1957 Engelhardt introduced a bill in the Alabama legislature, passed without debate, that would change the shape of Tuskegee from a perfect square to a twenty-eight-sided figure that resembled, according to some observers, a stylized seahorse. Later black attorney Fred Gray challenged Engelhardt's gerrymandering before the U.S. Supreme Court; when Gray showed the court the strangely shaped map, Justice Felix Frankfurter asked about the location of Tuskegee Institute, and Gray explained that "Tuskegee Institute is not on the city map." What remained was the town square, streets with a majority of white residents, and long narrow stretches along Tuskegee's primary roads where whites lived—but not the back roads and byways populated by blacks.

Predictably, Engelhardt's invention created a furor. Blacks in Tuskegee responded quickly to the ploy. Many of those fortunate enough to register to vote were associated with Tuskegee Institute, the education community for blacks founded by Booker T. Washington in 1881. Charles G. Gomillion, a history professor for almost thirty years, had for years led efforts to register black voters. In the early 1940s Gomillion organized the Tuskegee Civic Association (TCA) to improve community life and obtain equal opportunities in public education for blacks. Engelhardt's move to eliminate black influence prompted Gomillion to call a mass meeting at a local church and announce that TCA would lead a "selective buying" campaign. Avoiding the use of the word "boycott," he encouraged Macon County blacks to "trade with your friends." Regardless of its name, it was a boycott and a decidedly effective one. Virtually all Tuskegee blacks stopped buying at white businesses and those seen shopping in a downtown store were ridiculed. Engelhardt responded by charging that "goon squads" of institute students were enforcing the boycott; he retaliated with a proposal that Macon County be carved up into five parts and annexed with neighboring counties.[5]

Patterson immediately saw political advantage in the boycott. His opportunity came when one of the affected store owners, B. D. "Bunny" Cohn, appealed to the attorney general for legal relief. Patterson went to Tuskegee with a complement of attorneys: Noel Baker, Ted Rinehart, MacDonald Gallion, Bob Bradley, and investigator Joe Malone.

"What we found was the downtown section, Confederate Square, filled with blacks milling around, passing out handbills, and discouraging other blacks from trading with white merchants," Patterson said. A boycott was a violation of state law, and for several days Patterson interviewed merchants and witnesses in the courthouse before going to the local county judge to ask for a search warrant at TCA headquarters. Patterson took his team of attorneys to a building located at the entrance of the institute and was greeted by a smiling and polite Gomillion. The Tuskegee professor cordially showed them around the rooms, opening cabinets and doors that revealed little more than scraps of paper and a few flyers. Patterson asked for the membership list and was told that the association didn't keep one. Gomillion said the association kept up with their members by issuing identification cards, an answer Patterson was forced to accept. Anticipating just such harassment, the TCA had stopped keeping a membership roll months earlier.

Patterson announced to the public that the raid was "aimed at uncovering evidence of violation of our state laws, and evidence of subversive activities . . . designed to create disorder, strife, and destruction of our government." A few days later Gallion made his own raid on TCA's empty offices, then he went on the radio and warned blacks not to participate in the boycott, promising protection for anyone who wanted to trade with white merchants. The raids received considerable media coverage, allowing Patterson to continue appearing as a strong segregationist with the governor's race only months away. He told the press that civil rights activists were exploiting ignorant blacks so they could "buy expensive cars, silk suits, and pay for expensive trips."[6]

When Patterson went to the local circuit court for the hearing on the injunction he sought, he faced a courtroom filled with blacks and he stood virtually alone, save for Bunny Cohn. Arthur Shores called Patterson to testify and asked him why he pursued the NAACP and TCA but never the Ku Klux Klan. "I carry out the duties of my office to the best of my ability without regard to race, creed, or color," he said defensively. Was it true, Shores asked, that Patterson was already running for a higher state office? Patterson responded that if it were true he certainly would not announce it from the witness chair. Judge Will Walton denied the request for an injunction, ruling that blacks had a right to trade where they pleased. Fred Gray, one of the attorneys in the case, believed that Judge Walton was the only state judge with the courage to rule in favor of the TCA.

Though Patterson failed to stop the boycott in Tuskegee, his actions did achieve two purposes: they played well to white voters and they kept his name in the papers. Shortly after the Tuskegee incident he took advantage of another opportunity to emphasize his opposition to integration when he testified in Washington against a proposed civil rights bill. The 1957 legislation was quite weak and did little to protect voting rights, nonetheless it was the first civil rights legislation that Congress had passed in eighty-two years. It drew the usual heated response from southern states. Activist blacks and liberals saw it as a sell-out. White southerners saw it as federal intrusion and they crowded the hearing room to oppose it.

The legislation reflected the Eisenhower administration's moderate-to-conservative attitude toward the race issue and its reluctance to confront head-on the problem of racial inequality. President Eisenhower refused Martin Luther King's invitation to make a major speech on civil rights in the South, and U.S. attorney general Herbert Brownell declined a request to hold a conference with southern blacks. The Brown decision had created such a national furor that the president remarked he was "very much worried" about widespread disturbances; he urged Americans not to regard the school integration issue as one that might divide the nation. In Eisenhower's State of the Union speech that year, he asked Americans "to approach these integration problems with calm and reason, with mutual understanding and good will."[7]

The administration's bill basically called for a Civil Rights Commission to investigate violations of the law, a new civil rights division in the Justice Department, new laws to protect voting rights, and provisions for civil damage suits. "Extremists on either hand will not be satisfied by them," Herbert Brownell said when he urged enactment of the legislation. Certainly southerners were vehemently opposed, and hearings on the bill had to be extended to accommodate those who wanted to appear before the congressional committee to indignantly express their opposition. Representatives from the former Confederacy, including many state attorneys general, insisted that they be given an opportunity to speak against the civil rights package. It was a chance for southern conservatives to appear in an important national forum and grab a few headlines back home, a point that was not lost on committee members.

Patterson, Gallion, and Sam Engelhardt were scheduled to speak for Alabama, but before they could appear, Judge George C. Wallace of Barbour County asked to appear before the committee. Wallace's egotism openly irritated members of the committee, who questioned him pointedly about his threats to cite FBI agents for contempt when they came into his district to investigate voting irregularities for the Justice Department. Wallace, who was from largely rural Barbour County, just south of Phenix City, and therefore isolated from the mainstream of the integration conflict, had found it to his advantage to bluster about people and events outside his jurisdiction. It was a harmless game that Wallace played to stay in the news and portray himself as someone who dared defy federal authorities. He was caught off guard when the hearings focused on his publicity stunts.

Terming Wallace's statements "intemperate" and "inflammatory," members of the committee charged the rural Alabama judge with irresponsibility in a way that made him ill at ease in front of the media. Wallace said he was sorry they felt as they did, but he was going to "protect" his circuit against interference by the Justice Department. The Wallace testimony went back to Alabama in big front-page splashes, giving him the kind of exposure that his appearance was designed to obtain. It also foreshadowed Wallace's willingness to indulge in confrontations that he had little chance of winning just for the publicity. Recognizing the Wallace appearance as an effort to puff himself up, one House member wondered aloud "why some of the other men who are planning to run for governor next time didn't come up?"[8]

Two days later, Patterson, teaming with other state attorneys, challenged the proposed federal laws as a way to force racial integration on the South, noting that the pending bills were strongly backed by the NAACP. He told the committee that the NAACP had violated the corporation laws of Alabama and other states and was encouraging its people to do likewise by refusing to pay legitimate fees or to obey orders of the state courts. Registering his "bitter opposition" to the pending proposals, he expressed the belief that a vote for the bills would be a vote to reduce the states to a status of counties so far as police powers were concerned. The 1957 civil rights legislation did pass, and by a wide margin, due to Lyndon Johnson's efforts, and the Democrats reaped major gains among blacks and liberals. Southern conservatives went home frustrated by their continuing string of losses, but still committed to preserving segregation.[9]

The highly publicized actions that John Patterson took against the NAACP and the Tuskegee Civic Association as well as his opposition of the Civil Rights Act served his political purpose. He was in the forefront of the public debate on the integration issue in Alabama, proclaiming himself dead set against a federal system that he knew would eventually win. By now he had a list of sixteen thousand people who wanted him to run for governor, many of them without a grain of political savvy, but who were willing to give their time and a few dollars to help someone who fought against crime in Phenix City, corruption in state government, and "forced integration" of their schools. Charlie Meriwether had crisscrossed the state for two years talking and listening; he was convinced by the enthusiasm of the people that his candidate should run for governor. And he had seen and heard enough to believe that Patterson would win.[10]

12
Nobody but the People

By 1958 a number of candidates were primed for the campaign for Alabama's top government office, and they had thoroughly prepared themselves on the emotional issues affecting the state. The corrupt, though often uproarious, Folsom administration, along with the beginning of the modern civil rights movement, had the electorate in a surly mood. Wearied and angered by Folsom's numerous personal and political weaknesses and desperately concerned about the future of the state's segregated society, Alabamians took particular interest in the Democratic Party's spring primary, where nomination was synonymous with election.

People wanted change—both symbolic and substantive. The historian Bill Barnard said the state was experiencing an economic recession in a decade of national affluence, and Alabamians were expecting and wanting relief from their government. The voters turned from Folsom, no longer amused by his rusticity and coarse mannerisms, and looked for state leadership that would give them a share of the nation's prosperity. They also wanted the new governor, whoever he might be, to maintain segregation and defy federal intervention in the public schools. Segregation was a very personal and emotional issue with the white adult population of Alabama. It did not take a political wizard to recognize that this would be a dominant theme in the upcoming campaign. Alabama was about to embark on its most vitriolic, race-baiting election in a century.[1]

A large field of candidates began marshaling their forces several months before the May 6 primary. The most prominent was Jimmy Faulkner from Bay Minette, a wealthy, resourceful businessman with extensive legislative experience. Faulkner ran second in the suspect 1954 gubernatorial race. He was well organized, with a large staff and a substantial war chest; from the outset of the campaign Faulkner appeared to have the best shot at becoming Alabama's next governor.

Predictably, the person most likely to challenge Faulkner was George Wallace of Barbour County. Wallace's political ambitions were legendary, dating back to the days when he was a sixteen-year-old page in the Alabama legislature. For years he had prepared his political base by building support in county courthouses across the state and by forging friendships with elected officials in every one of them. Locals remember that he spent most of his judgeship lounging on a bench in front of the decaying Barbour County courthouse, talking politics, waving at passersby, and greeting courthouse visitors.

When Faulkner ran in 1954, Wallace had agreed not to get involved in the race but then served as Folsom's South Alabama campaign chairman. That broken promise would come back to haunt Wallace before the election was over. His ambition was further threatened by his relationship with Folsom, now in intense disfavor with the voters. During Folsom's first term, Wallace, a freshman legislator, had followed the governor with loyal affection, regularly accompanying Folsom on jaunts around the state. He even convinced Folsom to appoint him to the board of trustees at Tuskegee Institute, from which Alabama's small black vote was traditionally orchestrated. Theirs was a master-disciple relationship, according to a former Folsom aide. "Everything that boy learned, he learned at the feet of Folsom," he said. "He even got to where he'd mispronounce things like Folsom, like saying 'I-dee-ho' and things like that."[2]

Before the campaign Wallace moved to sever ties with the governor. Troubled by the Adam Clayton Powell furor, he looked for an excuse to break with Folsom and secure his own political career. The issue he chose was little more than a petty political appointment back in Barbour County, but Wallace played it to the hilt, walking up and down the hall outside Folsom's capitol office talking loud enough to passersby that Folsom could hear him. That night he did the same thing for the benefit of legislators at the Jeff Davis Hotel. The break, however clumsily contrived, failed to accomplish the purpose, as Wallace would discover with great disappointment once he got on the speaking platform with other candidates.[3]

Behind Faulkner and Wallace came a long string of dark horses, novelty candidates, and more than one good ol' boy running for governor on a lark. Legitimate contenders were Patterson, George Hawkins, Laurie Battle, C. C. "Jack" Owen, and A. W. Todd, with Patterson clearly ahead because of the media attention he was getting. Hawkins, Folsom's floor leader in the legislature, benefited from a forty thousand dollar contribution from a group of administration cronies. Battle had respectable credentials as a former congressman from Birmingham, and Owen was president of the Alabama Public Service Commission. Todd had been named commissioner of agriculture by the State Democratic Committee (with Folsom's blessing) at the same time Patterson became attorney general.

Another seven candidates had little or no chance of winning: Karl Harrison once served in the state legislature; Montgomery jeweler Shearen Elebash graduated from Choate and Yale; William Dodd, a millwright from Bessemer, ran on a bet with fellow workers; the Reverend Billy Walker was a Southern Baptist preacher; Winston Gullatte owned an insurance agency in Selma and lived in a huge antebellum mansion; John Crommelin was a former navy admiral who retired after leaking secret documents to the national press. The campaign had comedic relief in the perennial candidate Ralph "Shorty" Price, also from Barbour County, who was proud of the fact that he was even shorter than Wallace.

Described as a man of kindly demeanor, Faulkner started his campaign early by holding "home folks" parties and rallies around the state. Although blessed with instant name recognition, Faulkner found it difficult to generate excitement about his candidacy, even losing many of his county chairmen from the previous race. Nonetheless, Faulkner thought his chances of success were excellent. "I couldn't see anyone on the horizon who could give me serious competition," he said. "I thought all I had to do was to sit back and wait."[4]

While Faulkner was confidently biding his time, Wallace felt the governor's office was within his grasp, the office he had coveted most of his life. He prepared a network of political allies and managed to maneuver himself into attention-getting issues, taking whatever position he thought would improve his name recognition. Because of his strong support in the county courthouse system, Wallace had the unfailing assistance of Alabama's League of Municipalities, the powerful organization of local government leaders. He also had the services of Grover Hall Jr., editor of the *Montgomery Advertiser*, the most widely read forum of political opinion in the state. Hall obtained permission from his publisher to support Wallace, whom he had befriended during Wallace's first term in the statehouse. Hall admired Wallace and saw in him the incarnation of the next great southern politician.[5]

Patterson was suspicious of the *Advertiser* and outright disdainful of editor Grover Hall. His attitude harked back to Phenix City when the Russell Betterment Association had appealed for newspaper pressure and investigative reporting of the Persons administration's lack of interest in a cleanup. Unlike the two large Birmingham papers and the *Columbus Ledger*, the *Advertiser* had failed to help in exposing the Phenix City problem. As the RBA was trying to effect change, the gossip around town was that the underworld annually bought twenty-five hundred paid for but undelivered subscriptions to the *Advertiser*.

The paper's silence about Phenix City first caused Patterson to mistrust the *Advertiser*'s editor, but it was Hall's actions during the murder trials that clinched his feelings. Hall assigned himself to Albert Patterson's murder trials rather than sending a staff reporter, an unusual decision for a paper of its size. During the Fuller and Ferrell trials, Hall hung around the prosecutor's table criticizing the state case. Patterson said, "He made frequent comments to people in the courtroom, expressing doubt about Fuller's and Ferrell's guilt. It was discouraging for our team." Later Patterson obtained copies of correspondence between Hall and Avon Fuller, wife of convicted murderer Albert Fuller. The letters revealed a relationship of surprising familiarity and contained references to visits by Hall during the trials to Avon in Phenix City and to Albert in Kilby Prison. During the gubernatorial campaign Patterson did not know about these letters, but he did know that the editor of the most influential political paper in the state was solidly in the Wallace camp. And he knew his paper had looked the other way while gangsters reigned in Phenix City.[6]

Patterson waited as late as he could to announce his candidacy. He kept postponing the announcement, saying one week that they were going to announce the next week. "Flirting with the press," according to Meriwether. Suspense maximized already favorable publicity and increased interest in his candidacy even in the far reaches of rural Alabama. Much to the dismay of candidates already on the campaign trail, they were often asked by voters if Patterson was going to run. According to Patterson and Meriwether the reason for the delay was a lack of funds. They didn't have the money to campaign, so they strung the press and public along before finally committing to the race.

Patterson had attempted without success to devise a financial solution for his campaign months earlier. In early 1958, Bruce Henderson, an influential Black Belt farmer-politician, set up a series of meetings for Patterson with a group of Birmingham industrialists—"Big Mules" in the Folsom vernacular. Patterson naively thought if he could sell them his ideas about good government, they would fund his campaign (he asked for $250,000) and he would have cleared a major hurdle. "My pitch was, if you finance me, I can win and I will not have the commitments which would be troublesome, and the governor's office could be run by the book." Patterson was astonished by their lack of interest in good government, and neither Henderson nor he heard anything more from the executives. Patterson decided he would have to raise money the hard way, a few dollars at a time.

Finally on January 28 Patterson called a press conference at the attorney general's office and officially declared his candidacy for governor of Alabama. He made a brief one-page statement on issues that he thought people were the most interested in: no "mixing" of the races; education; old-age pensions; an end to graft and corruption; and again the race issue by reference to his battle with the NAACP. His campaign approach was based on two strategies. He had made his name as attorney general by opposing the misdeeds of the Folsom administration, and he was not reluctant to attack them on the issues of graft and corruption. The same logic applied to segregation; he stressed his effort to keep the NAACP from operating in Alabama. The week of Patterson's announcement, southern newspapers published lead stories about a wave of stabbings, assaults, and rapes in racially mixed New York schools, especially Brooklyn. The stories of racial violence validated the South's worst fears about integrated schools, and newspaper editorials challenged Eisenhower to send in troops to restore order as he had in Little Rock. Patterson's timing couldn't have been better to remind Alabama voters that he had resisted the very agency that was helping integrate the nation's schools.[7]

Almost unnoticed in the packed news conference was a middle-aged cameraman filming the announcement. Roy Marcato, a freelance photojournalist from Birmingham had been hired by Meriwether the previous year to work for the campaign. The son of an Italian marble craftsman, Marcato wasn't paid a salary but depended on Meriwether for expense money every week or so to keep his family housed and fed. Marcato and Jim Atkins, later a news director at a Birmingham television station, organized South Newsreels, then a pioneer political advertising service for television. The two journalists were in the experimental stage with their news service when they signed on with Patterson, mainly at their own expense. After the news conference, Marcato did what he had been doing for months under Meriwether's guidance. He drove around the state peddling the press conference as a news story. There were few television stations then operating in Alabama—in Mobile, Montgomery, Birmingham, Florence, and Huntsville—so Marcato was able to provide film to them regularly.

Lacking sophistication in film journalism, stations often showed—as authentic news—film of Patterson that Marcato had edited for the campaign. Almost weekly, Patterson filmed 30- to 60-second campaign spots in a private home in Tuskegee and submitted them to Alabama television stations as news. They were little more than Patterson advertisements about crime fighting, corruption in state government, and the always reliable segregation issue. Patterson explained that at this relatively early stage of southern television "there were few trained reporters, and news directors were not generally selective with political material. Most of them simply needed film for the news hour." By employing Marcato's skills and media contacts, when Patterson announced he was running for governor, he had already established a highly reliable system of getting on the evening news.[8]

Patterson's campaign strategy revolved around the extensive name files he had developed from the great outpouring of public sympathy following his father's assassination and the public's response to his work as attorney general. For more than three years Patterson had carefully cultivated political support through frequent correspondence with those who wrote him or came by his office. From these files Patterson also drew a county-by-county appraisal of his support that Charlie Meriwether used during his campaign travel. The files told them that his strongest support was in the rural areas and on the edges of the state's growing urban areas.

In addition to Meriwether's ongoing work with potential supporters, some of the first campaign-building was done by Maurice Patterson, John's younger brother. With much the same handsome appearance and easy, likable manner of John, Maurice resigned a successful sales position in Atlanta and moved to Montgomery to work full time on the campaign.

He and his wife lived in one side of a duplex apartment in Montgomery; the other side served as campaign headquarters. He received no salary because the campaign didn't have the funds to pay him.

For months prior to the campaign, Maurice would set out by car on Monday morning armed with a list of names and return, usually on Friday afternoon, to discuss his findings. He lived off the land, taking his meals wherever he happened to be at the time, staying overnight with supporters, often people he met that day. Working mainly in rural areas, he was astounded by the reception he received on behalf of his brother. Maurice would drive back to Montgomery and tell John what people were saying about him and the campaign support they could count on. "He would act real surprised when I would talk about what I had heard, grin a little, and say, 'Sure 'nuff!'"

Whatever campaign organization Patterson and Meriwether were able to muster was in place for the kickoff rally at New Site in Tallapoosa County. Their local campaign organizations were typically committees that were coordinated from the home of appointed chairmen. Many campaign workers were small-town businessmen but rarely prominent community leaders. Lawyers generally ignored Patterson, and his campaign organizers tended to avoid them anyway. A few law school friends joined him early and gave Patterson some badly needed financial support. Albert Rosenthal of Birmingham, Albert Patterson's 1954 campaign coordinator, provided leadership by introducing John to his father's strongest supporters.[9]

With few exceptions, the Patterson organization was made up of white, unseasoned political novices, people who were usually ignored by the traditional political system. For reasons personal and unique to each of them, they were extremely loyal and devoted to Patterson, more so than customary political activists.

The New Site High School auditorium was packed for the first rally, as the campaign introduced the only luxury Patterson could afford—a country band. Rebe Gosdin and the Sunny Valley Boys were retained at the handsome salary of seven hundred dollars per week to help turn out crowds in rural areas. That night the large crowd whooped it up while the band played country music and home folks predicted victory for their candidate. Patterson's speech that night, the prototype of more than five hundred he would eventually make, was known as the "Bucket Speech."

It compared state government to an old rusty water bucket that leaked tax dollars. The heart of the speech was a proposal that, if the holes in the leaky water bucket were stopped up the state would have enough money to operate without raising taxes. It was imagery that rural people understood, and Patterson said he learned to give varying abbreviated forms of the original speech, sometimes as short as five minutes. It was the same speech he gave the entire campaign.[10]

Patterson's campaign style matched the serious tone of his speeches. He talked personally and simply to his audiences. He dressed conservatively in dark suits and ties and wore a dress hat most of the time. Compared to the lumbering Folsom who always seemed to be in disarray, John Patterson looked like someone who would not embarrass the state. The Bucket Speech contained a something-for-everyone list that Patterson was convinced people wanted in Montgomery: segregation, law and order, good government, old-age pensions, health programs, education, agriculture and industry, highway and road improvement, state docks and inland waterways, and a "fair deal" for labor. The Patterson concept reflected the concerns that he had learned as a boy in rural Tallapoosa County: people who had nothing looked to the government that had everything, and in Alabama people were looking to Montgomery for help.

Segregation and the war on crime were strong identity issues for him. *The Phenix City Story*, however inaccurate, still played to large audiences in state theaters, keeping fresh the image of a dashing, rugged Patterson in a life-and-death struggle with the underworld. Arch Ferrell's ongoing legal troubles and Albert Fuller's appeals kept the assassination prominently in the news. With the addition of segregation as a hot campaign issue, Patterson was seemingly without peer. Stressing his fight with the NAACP and his personal intervention in the Tuskegee boycott (without dwelling on the lack of success at Tuskegee), Patterson engaged the troubled emotions of people feeling the cutting edge of the immense changes impending in the South.

Patterson's legal war against corruption in the Folsom administration made him the foremost advocate of good government. Folsom and his pals had created the perfect environment for Patterson's enterprising style of law enforcement. When the governor's race opened in early spring, many of the cases Patterson had brought against the administration were still in the appeals process and getting front page attention by the press, especially the loan shark litigation. The major issues that Patterson initiated seemed to have a life of their own, adding to the Patterson mystique. Everything Patterson did was news.

Considering the enthusiastic response to his candidacy and the extensive media coverage, Patterson did not think it was necessary to make any specific campaign promises. Nevertheless he made one that stirred interest and criticism alike. In past elections, he said, "Folsom had made a lot of hay out of the old folks and mailbox road issues," so Patterson decided to make old-age pensions an issue. He promised to double them. Alabama's one hundred thousand pensioners were receiving about thirty-eight dollars a month from the state, well below the national average. "I doubled the going rate to keep other candidates from raising the ante during the campaign," Patterson explained. His opponents cried foul, saying that Patterson was misleading old folks by telling them he could pay seventy-five dollar pensions. Publicly he estimated that the state was wasting more than one-fourth of its economic resources. He couldn't prove this, but with the reputation of the Folsom administration he didn't have to. The voters believed him.[11]

Wallace and Faulkner kicked off their campaigns with large televised rallies. Wallace hired Minnie Pearl, a leading country entertainer. Faulkner decided to appeal to voters through gospel singing with the Blackwood Brothers Quartet and the Chuck Wagon Gang. After the kickoff rally at New Site, Patterson and Meriwether didn't have the funds to move their campaign about the state. Stalling for time, they held several night rallies until they could keep a regular schedule like other candidates. After a hugely successful rally at Phenix City, one that turned out a record crowd and ten thousand dollars in contributions, Patterson finally had the money to start meeting the people.

The Patterson team hit the campaign trail. Meals were meager, often no more than cheese, crackers, and a soft drink at some crossroads general store, and workdays were long. But the people who made up the team were young, energetic, and enthusiastic. They made up to a dozen campaign stops each day with their flatbed trailer and an oversized campaign sign; the hillbilly band got the crowds in a clapping, foot-stomping mood. When the band launched into its rollicking rendition of their theme song, "Wabash Cannonball," Patterson made his way to the trailer for his campaign speech. The audiences were white, mostly rustic folks in work clothes and overalls, with an interest in political entertainment. He gave "the speech" and recognized some of the locals that Maurice would note for him in the advance work. Before the development of large television markets such campaign stops were the best way to reach people in sparsely populated Alabama. Some candidates treated their crowds to fried fish, fried chicken, or barbecue. Patterson said they were proud to have a band.[12]

But there was an element to the Patterson campaign that neither he nor the other candidates could have predicted and no one could manufacture—emotion. The memory of Albert Patterson, the martyred crusader, was still fresh for Alabamians, so strong that people were still offering condolences. "After making a speech," Patterson said, "I would be surrounded by people, men wanting to shake hands, women crying, and folks stuffing money into my pockets." It was a scene played over and over again in virtually every small town, village, and crossroad community in the state. Sometimes John's mother was driven to campaign stops by an elderly gentleman from Phenix City, where she told first-person stories about her late husband's crusade against crime and asked people to "vote for my boy." It was not uncommon for one of the other candidates to arrive in a town that Patterson had just left and find people standing around crying and wiping their eyes.

Patterson knew that Phenix City was his trump card and he played it in every speech. "I don't want to ever have to live again in a town where I have to carry a pistol downtown when I go to work or where I have to worry about somebody poking dynamite up under my house where my wife and children are sleeping." He would reach deep into the emotions of his audience by turning to one side and lifting both hands as if he were reaching for something: "Every time I pull a law book out of the shelves of my office and open it up, I get [soot] on my hands from where the gangsters tried to burn me and my daddy out." The remark often brought tears to many in the audience.[13]

In the initial stages of the campaign, many state political experts weren't able identify the intangible but powerful force that permeated the Patterson campaign. It was Hubert Baughm, editor of *South* magazine, who identified it for what is was, emotional support. An early admirer of Albert Patterson, Baughm put his magazine prominently behind John Patterson almost as soon as he became attorney general, giving him such preferential treatment that Folsom referred to it as the *Patterson Pravda*.

In late 1957, Baughm conducted a poll on the upcoming governor's race to test Patterson's strength. Political polling, like political television advertising, was an unsophisticated and little-used device. The magazine mailed out ten thousand penny postcards listing eleven prospective candidates to a broad sample of voters in all sixty-seven counties. Secretly, Baughm perforated cards sent to a select group of political activists to gauge their opinion of Patterson. About 43 percent responded, giving Patterson 1,316 votes or 30 percent with George Wallace a distant second at 582 votes. Although the poll was unscientific and generally discounted by other candidates because of the magazine's unabashed support for Patterson, it did indicate a critical point that escaped Alabama's political hierarchy—John Patterson was extremely popular in Alabama.[14]

The first primary, with a record field of fourteen candidates, turned into a carnival. Gubernatorial candidates were bumping into each other at almost every turn, even hurrying into town after other candidates had left to "borrow" the crowd before it broke up. Dark horse George Hawkins said people would teasingly ask him if he could name all the candidates. *Life* magazine did a six-page story "Anything Goes for Governor in Alabama," giving Wallace the best chance to win. Hawkins used a pine stump and a pitchfork as props; Jack Owen had a string band in Confederate uniforms serenade his audiences; Karl Harrison campaigned in a scaled-down wagon pulled by burros; and Shearen Elebash, the Yale graduate, banged out medleys of corny and sophisticated tunes on a piano in the back of a pickup truck. Winston Gullatte spent most of the campaign in a rocking chair on the veranda of his stately mansion: "The voters may get so nauseated over this hillbilly music they'll vote for me."[15]

But for sheer, absolute nonsense, Ralph "Shorty" Price from Barbour County emerged as the prize candidate. The garish, undersized Price was a typical political comic that Alabamians never really took seriously. But every four years they grinned at his antics, which always included some hard-hitting criticism of political personalities. He drove a battered jalopy with "State No. 1" painted on the side, as if he had a fleet of them. Price disliked Folsom and Wallace, who were one and the same to him. He referred to Wallace as a "gasbag" because he was always bragging on himself. Like Faulkner, Price claimed Wallace had double-crossed him. As the campaign grew more intense Patterson people took particular delight as Price associated Wallace with Folsom. Price told the voters that if Wallace were elected Big Jim would remain in the governor's mansion and Wallace would live in a chicken house out back.

Price went from town to town mocking Wallace with his "Wishy Washy Wallace" story until a rally in Geneva when Wallace decided it was time to stop ignoring him. Looking straight at Price, Wallace said he would continue "helping the mentally ill" if he were elected governor. The remark further infuriated Price. The Patterson camp capitalized on Price's anger by slipping him expense money to keep up the attack. For the rest of the primary, Price was furnished Wallace's itinerary and funds to get there. Patterson's campaign staff said they saw Wallace drive away time and again when he saw Price's painted car in town.[16]

Price's vendetta was but one of many unexpected windfalls that benefited Patterson. Alabama chiropractors, snubbed by the state medical association, gave him his first major political contribution—five thousand dollars—and helped build crowds for major rallies. The Creek Indians in Atmore endorsed Patterson as the only candidate that "Alabama Indians can trust." The Indians' concerns were segregation, states' rights, and individual liberties. What was later recognized as the best gimmick of the race was dropped into Patterson's lap when a Washington-area illustrator sought him out early in the campaign. Malcolm Ater had drawn a small comic book for Pres. Harry Truman in his 1948 campaign and thought Patterson had the kind of exciting events in his life for a similar book.[17]

Ater created a professional-looking comic book highlighting Patterson's life that cost about a penny a copy, making it affordable even in large numbers. Meriwether sent two hundred thousand copies to his coordinators with instructions to mail them the second weekend in April, just before the May balloting. The book had a completely unpredictable impact. Comic books were part of American pop culture in the fifties, and the Patterson book was so popular that voters kept it around the house. On a tour through the Sand Mountain region in northeast Alabama, when A. W. Todd's campaign workers tried to talk to the farmers about their candidate, hill people would pull a worn copy of Patterson's comic book from the bib of their overalls. After several such encounters, Todd told his workers that Patterson, not Faulkner or Wallace, was leading the race.[18]

The real coup of the campaign, however, was a simple editorial that developed into a slogan for Patterson. In early April, an obscure weekly, the *Greene County Democrat*, published an editorial entitled "Nobody's for John Patterson . . . but the People." The editorial, a few paragraphs about Patterson's platform, so commanded the attention of the public that it was reprinted across the state, with several newspapers claiming to have originated it. The editorial was the creation of Robert Nahrgang of Fairhope, who brought it to Patterson and Meriwether with a collection of short editorials he had written. Richard Martin of the *Democrat* agreed to run it. The slogan became a catchphrase that spread throughout the state in the final month of the campaign; it appeared on campaign literature, in newspaper advertisements, and on banners. The underlying suggestion of the slogan reinforced the perception that Patterson was positioned outside the state's political power structure, supported only by ordinary people.[19]

Newspaper endorsements followed this trend. Small town weeklies endorsed Patterson's candidacy, while big city dailies went for Wallace or Faulkner. The *Birmingham Post-Herald* was the largest state paper to endorse Patterson, because editor Jimmy Mills thought Patterson had earned the endorsement due to his "splendid work as attorney general." As balloting time neared, John Temple Graves, the *Post-Herald's* eminent columnist saw one candidate pulling ahead: "John Patterson, Alabama's famously fighting young attorney general who has gone into action for Alabama on so many fronts."[20]

Patterson's appeal to voters on several critical issues pointed to eventual victory. His humble background played well with Alabamians in the 1950s; his father's assassination garnered him sympathy; and his own role in defeating gangsters marked him as a genuine hero to an admiring public. Segregation, the issue that current events had tossed in his path, offered him yet another opportunity to appeal to the electorate. "Patterson verbalized what people were thinking and talking about among themselves about the school integration issue," recalled Robert Blackwelder, a young supporter who later taught political science. "They didn't want it to happen and when Patterson told them it wasn't going to happen in Alabama, they believed him." Another candidate, George Hawkins, believed that Patterson would have won even without the segregation issue: "He couldn't have lost the election considering all the important issues that he had going for him."[21]

On election day, John and Mary Joe Patterson drove to Phenix City and voted in the courthouse, then joined Meriwether and the staff at the Molton Hotel in Birmingham to await the election results. When the re-

turns started trickling in around 7:00 p.m., Patterson led the field. By
9:00 p.m. the primary results were in. Patterson led with 196,859 votes
to Wallace's 162,435. Faulkner finished third.

A cheering crowd estimated at ten thousand jammed the street in
front of the hotel hoping to catch a glimpse of Patterson. Ed Strickland,
reporting for the *Birmingham News*, witnessed the phenomenon: "Each
time a new vote total was announced a wild cheer would reverberate
through the hotel." He described hotel rooms and hallways packed with
supporters, encircling a beaming Patterson reaching out to shake hands
with them all. Meriwether, showing the strain of the campaign and little
sleep, did not join in the celebration, but was on the phone with campaign workers in other parts of the state, already preparing for the June 3
runoff with Wallace.

Later in the evening Meriwether persuaded Patterson—with some
difficulty—to go to the offices of the *Birmingham News* for a traditional
interview with the front-runner. A throng of cheering, celebrating supporters created an impassable mob in the hotel lobby, making it necessary
for Patterson's staff to smuggle him out through the service entrance into
the alley. Across town in the offices of the *Birmingham News*, which had
supported Wallace, he sat politely and answered questions, fifteen pounds
lighter, and pale with exhaustion. He didn't really mind; according to the
experts, he wasn't supposed to be the one sitting for the interview.[22]

1. Lt. Albert and Agnes Patterson as newlyweds, Brownsville, Texas, 1917. (Photo courtesy John Patterson.)

2. John Patterson with the bicycle he rode to deliver newspapers in Phenix City and Columbus. (Photo courtesy John Patterson.)

3. John Patterson in his army uniform. (Photo courtesy John Patterson.)

4. Thugs assaulting RBA members monitoring 1952 elections. This photo drew nationwide attention to crime in Phenix City. (Photo courtesy Jim Cannon.)

5. Albert Patterson during his campaign to clean up Phenix City. (Photo courtesy Jim Cannon.)

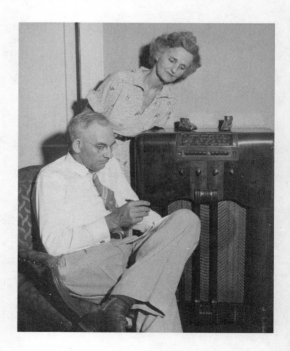

6. Albert and Agnes Patterson listen to election returns during the second primary on June 6, 1954. (*Columbus Ledger-Enquirer* photograph, courtesy John Patterson.)

7. John Patterson (*left*), June 18, 1954, the night his father was murdered. He is standing outside the Patterson law offices near the spot the crime was committed. (Photo courtesy Jim Cannon.)

8. *Left to right:* Hugh Britton, John Patterson, and Hugh Bentley at Albert Patterson's grave in New Site. (Photo courtesy Jim Cannon.)

9. John Patterson escorts his mother to court on the opening day of Albert Fuller's murder trial, 1955. (Photograph by Jim Robbins of the *Birmingham Post-Herald*, courtesy John Patterson.)

10. Arch Ferrell, who was acquitted in the Patterson murder trial. (Photo courtesy Jim Cannon.)

11. Underworld kingpins Jimmy Mathews (*left*) and Hoyt Shepherd. (Photo courtesy Jim Cannon.)

12. Governor Gordon Persons (*left*) appointing Lamar Murphy (*right*) as sheriff of Russell County. Former sheriff Ralph Matthews is at center. (Photo courtesy Jim Cannon.)

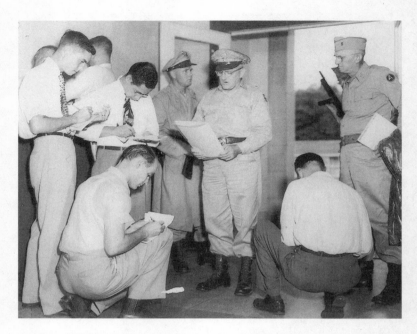

13. General Walter "Crack" Hanna reading the order establishing martial law in Phenix City. (Photo courtesy Jim Cannon.)

14. Alabama National Guard troops escorting "Ma" Beachie, most notorious of Phenix City madams. (Photo courtesy Jim Cannon.)

15. Alabama National Guard raiding a gambling hall. (Photo courtesy Jim Cannon.)

16. Alabama national guardsman watching seized gambling equipment burn. (Photo courtesy Jim Cannon.)

17. Attorney general John Patterson in a decrepit school-house in Marshall County, 1957. (Photo courtesy Jim Cannon.)

18. Judge Walter B. Jones, who administered the oath of office to John Patterson, Alabama's forty-ninth governor. (Photo courtesy Jim Cannon.)

19. Patterson (*right*) with longtime aide Joe Robertson. (*Birmingham News* photograph courtesy of Joseph G. Robertson.)

20. Patterson for Governor rally. (Photo courtesy Jim Cannon.)

21. Patterson rally in New Site High School, with Agnes Patterson in front row center. (Photo courtesy Jim Cannon.)

22. Governors Folsom (*left*) and Patterson at John's 1958 inaugural. (Photo courtesy Jim Cannon.)

23. John and Mary Joe Patterson at his gubernatorial inauguration, January 1958. (Photograph by Albert Kraus, courtesy John Patterson.)

24. John Patterson (*left*) and Bobby Kennedy, Birmingham, 1957. (Photo courtesy Jim Cannon.)

25. John Kennedy (*left*) and John Patterson during the 1960 presidential campaign. (Photo courtesy Jim Cannon.)

26. George Wallace (*left*) and John Patterson, 1961. (Photo courtesy Jim Cannon.)

27. John Patterson during the freedom rider crisis. (Photo courtesy Tommy Giles.)

28. Public Safety Director Floyd Mann in downtown Montgomery, May, 1961, as freedom riders approach. (Photo courtesy Tommy Giles.)

29. Trailways Bus terminal, downtown Montgomery, scene of 1961 mob attack on freedom riders. (Photo courtesy Tommy Giles.)

30. Sunday morning meeting on provisions for the safe passage of the freedom riders out of Montgomery. *Seated from left:* Floyd Mann, Byron White, Patterson, MacDonald Gallion. (Photo courtesy Tommy Giles.) Note portrait of Albert Patterson on wall behind John Patterson.

31. *Master Detective Magazine* official (*left*) presenting Police Officer of the Month citation to Floyd Mann (*right*), as Governor Patterson and Mrs. Mann look on. Mann received numerous awards and citations in recognition of his work keeping the peace in racially troubled Alabama. (Photo courtesy Tommy Giles.)

32. Tina and John Patterson. (Photo courtesy John Patterson.)

13
Alabama Elects a Boy Governor

John Patterson said he was as astonished as others were when he came in first in the May primary. During the final two weeks of the campaign, the crowds of hundreds had grown to thousands and money had flowed more freely. He said he was confident he was going to win, not sure of it, because something could always go wrong, but "I could feel it and the people could feel it too."

Not surprisingly, his strength came from the rural areas, but he also swept heavily populous Jefferson (Birmingham), Madison (Huntsville), and Mobile counties, and that surprised the experts. Wallace carried the Wiregrass region of southeast Alabama, his home region, and Montgomery County. The heaviest concentration of Patterson support was in northern and southwestern Alabama. The *Advertiser* called the Patterson victory the biggest upset in years. The *Birmingham News* headlined: "Patterson Surprises Wiseacres Who Said Campaign Couldn't Jell." He led in forty-three counties, took 31.8 percent of the vote (almost exactly what Baughm's straw poll predicted), and a new state record of more than 618,000 votes were cast.[1]

The morning after the election, Patterson's feelings of elation soured as he faced the most unpleasant part of the campaign. "Charlie Meriwether was on the phone early with losing candidates trying to outbid the Wallace people," Patterson remembered, "and left me to deal with the crowd wanting to make deals." For the next few days, he faced what he considered "the most disgusting part of Alabama politics," people converging on his Birmingham headquarters wanting to make campaign contributions in exchange for state business. A steady procession of hacks knocked on his door asking for jobs, favors, or contracts, forcing Patterson to post a guard; the more desperate threw envelopes of money through the transom and shouted out their offers. "It was the worst week I ever spent in my life. It seemed like everybody was trying to buy a ticket after the game was over." Repelled by the greed, Patterson gave orders that if they won the runoff, his early supporters, who had not asked for anything, would be given first consideration on state business.

In the meantime, Meriwether was busy talking to the Wallace camp about a deal that would have Wallace drop out of the race in exchange for Patterson's support in the next election. For days Meriwether contacted everyone he thought could influence Wallace, even offering a big share of state business if Wallace would withdraw from the runoff. Emmett Odom, a Wallace insider, went to Wallace with the proposal two times and each time Wallace answered with an emphatic no.[2]

Because, like Shorty Price, Faulkner still resented what he saw as Wallace's double cross in the 1954 race, he did not hesitate to support Patterson. Faulkner, a veteran campaigner, had an excellent statewide organization, which he turned over to Patterson, and several of his key supporters made sizable contributions for the runoff. Emory Folmar, a Faulkner adviser, gave Patterson five thousand dollars and began campaigning for him in Montgomery County. Patterson also collaborated with the Faulkner camp so he could raise enough to pay off a forty thousand dollar campaign debt. Assimilating Faulkner workers into his organization was a good decision for Patterson, although the sudden presence of staffers from a rival candidate created friction. Meriwether said, "I had a hell of a time keeping peace among our people and the new folks. Everybody was killing one another trying to get close to John." While dealmakers roamed the hotel and some of his own workers went on a weeklong drunk, Patterson started discussing runoff strategy with Meriwether and Hubert Baughm.[3]

A shaken and disappointed Wallace did not rest from campaigning but began blasting Patterson immediately after the vote, protesting that he did not have the "advantage of $10 million dollars worth of free publicity." Wallace had well-founded concerns about his chances in the runoff because of the dislike for the Folsom administration that had been clearly demonstrated at the polls. Candidates unable to shake the Folsom stigma—a long list of once-powerful men like Rankin Fite, Broughton Lambert, Fuller Kimbrell, Neil Metcalf, and others— lost control of state government. There was open rebellion against the Folsom crowd. These were the same people that Wallace had been allied with but was now trying to vainly to distance himself from.[4]

Grover Hall and Wallace developed a runoff plan to appeal to ordinary voters, conservatives, and businessmen, while steering clear of Folsom. Part of their strategy was to bring into the open Patterson's Klan following, a matter generally known early in the race but ignored by other candidates. By the end of the week, Wallace went on the attack in a televised speech from Montgomery. He not only placed the Klan in the foreground of the campaign but also attacked Patterson's record on segregation and the headline legal cases brought against the Folsom administration. Wallace claimed that the university had to retain out-of-state lawyers in the Autherine Lucy case because Patterson wouldn't intervene and that he had failed to get grand jury indictments against the Folsom crowd. "If Patterson will tell me who is getting the graft, I'll see that the grand jury gets the information," Wallace shouted at his rallies.[5]

But Patterson had changed campaign tactics. Wallace's hasty, hot attacks were met by silence as Patterson became a phantom candidate who drifted off into the Alabama countryside. On the Monday following the primary, Patterson assembled a small caravan of about a dozen cars and headed to rural Elmore County, outside Montgomery. "We put together a collection of supporters and began walking tours of the little towns and hamlets," Patterson explained. "We took our time and moved around the countryside at a slow, deliberate pace, taking time to visit and chat with folks." He spent an entire week in Elmore County while Wallace raged up and down the state, making charge after charge, challenging Patterson to a debate. The contrast of styles was striking: Wallace, a rumpled, frenetic bundle of energy, criticized Patterson while applauding his own record against crime, calling Patterson "weak" on the race issue and promising that he would go to jail for segregation. Patterson, calm and neatly attired, built on his strengths in the rural areas and refused to make any public comment about Wallace or the issues.

Patterson's "nonspeaking" runoff strategy was his own design. Realizing that Wallace, Hall, and the remnants of the Folsom crowd were on the attack, Patterson and his staff decided he would not make any public speeches or slug it out with Wallace in the media. It was a lesson he had learned from his father. Albert Patterson always told him never to react to anyone who attacked him because "the public doesn't like mudsling-

ing and they will like you for not responding to it." Patterson said his father was deliberately courteous to his mortal enemies, and every time he
went into the Russell County courthouse he made sure he shook hands
with the very men who eventually plotted his death. "I would ask people
about what I should do about Wallace and the big papers giving me hell,
and everybody told me to ignore them," Patterson explained. "They told
me that Wallace was hurting himself and not me." Another reason he
remained quiet during the runoff was that he didn't want to make any
more speeches. He had already given the only speech he had all over the
state. "I couldn't see going back to the same place and saying the same
things over again." Meriwether's media advertising, however, continued
at full tilt.[6]

When Patterson was finished in Elmore County, the caravan turned
north to Shelby County and Patterson did the same thing there. He
then went to Winston County, a Republican stronghold. The weather
was typical for a early summer in Alabama, hot and humid. Every day fifteen to twenty reporters trailed after the front-runner as he campaigned
through garages, sawmills, and country stores. Patterson said he enjoyed
the company of the reporters and found new ways to say "no comment"
when they asked about Wallace's accusations. The Birmingham and
Montgomery Patterson campaign headquarters further stonewalled the
press by not releasing his schedule.

The primary win changed the campaign's financial picture dramatically, allowing Meriwether to schedule previously unaffordable political
advertising. The sudden influx of money made it possible to buy bill-
boards and run a fifteen-minute commercial that Roy Marcato and Jim
Atkins had spliced together during the first primary, when Patterson came
down with laryngitis while campaigning in Huntsville. With their candidate unable to talk, Marcato collected all the film about integration he
could find, even getting news footage from Birmingham TV stations, and
put together a short film about the unrest and violence resulting from attempted integration. He took audio from several Patterson speeches and
dubbed it in to narrate the scenes. The film articulated the fears of voters that integration would disrupt education in southern schools; Meriwether ran it repeatedly in all state television markets.

Patterson had all the media coverage he needed to remain competitive with Wallace's harangues and mass media attacks. He continued his
walking tours and toyed with the corps of reporters who were always on

his heels. (One *Advertiser* reporter wrote a front-page story about driving four hundred miles without finding Patterson.) When Grover Hall referred to Patterson editorially as having "green eyes and a red neck," he approached *Advertiser* reporter Bob Ingram, pulled open both eyelids and told him to look into these green eyes and see if you can see no comment. Finally, tiring of the media game, he handed out mimeographed slips of paper that said: "I have nothing to say. Anything I say you will twist around and try to hurt me. You run your campaign and I'll run mine. John Patterson."[7]

Patterson's silence failed to insulate him from the Klan issue. About a week before the runoff election, he appeared on NBC's *This Is Your Life* to honor Hugh Bentley for his role in the Phenix City cleanup. Word of Patterson's appearance on the national television show leaked out, and Wallace attempted to buy the time slot on Alabama stations that normally scheduled the popular program. Wallace also demanded equal time from the network.

The show's host, Ralph Edwards, threw a postshow party for his guests at a Beverly Hills hotel. During the evening, Patterson was summoned to the phone. The caller, who identified himself as Bob Ingram of the *Montgomery Advertiser*, asked, "Do you know a man named Robert Shelton?" Patterson replied "No," and Ingram abruptly hung up. "I couldn't make any sense out of Ingram's phone call," he remembered, "and Ingram was acting unusually rude." On his return to Montgomery the next morning, he was greeted by a sensational front-page story headlined: "Klan Aids Patterson."

Positioned prominently at the top of the page was a photograph of a letter on Alabama attorney general office stationery signed by Patterson, containing the statement: "A mutual friend, Mr. R. M. 'Bob' Shelton, of ours in Tuscaloosa has suggested that I write you and ask for your support in the coming governor's race." Bobby Shelton was the grand dragon of the United States Klans, later reorganized as the United Klans of America. The form letter had originated in the Tuscaloosa Patterson campaign office when Shelton, a local resident, submitted a long list of names, many likely Klansmen, for the campaign secretary to contact. The secretary mailed them out over Patterson's signature. Since some of the Klan supported Wallace, a Klansman from Northport allowed Ingram to reproduce his copy of the letter. Hall was thrilled by the story and told Ingram he had won the election for Wallace.[8]

Patterson got the full treatment from the *Advertiser*. The front-page story carried Patterson's denial and the letter that contradicted him, as well as a reprint of a Patterson campaign cartoon showing soldiers with bayonets prodding black and white children into a schoolhouse. An accompanying photo showed a "Patterson for Governor" sign in Shelton's front yard. The paper reported that it had attempted to interview the editor of *Present Hour*, the Klan tabloid that endorsed Patterson. (The paper had denounced the "NAACP-loving George Wallace" as a Folsomite in sheep's clothing.) The story spread quickly with Wallace's heavy media backing, and the Patterson camp found itself embroiled in a controversy that they had intended to ignore. Meriwether publicly denied knowing Shelton.[9]

Out on the stump, Wallace and Hall fabricated a burlesque gimmick to exploit Patterson's nonspeaking campaign and his Klan ties. Wallace had campaigned with a four-poster bed covered by a patchwork quilt on the back of a pickup truck. At the end of a speech, Wallace would stop and ask, "Where is John Patterson?" He would look all through the crowd and repeat the question again. "You know what they say?" he asked the crowd. "They say politics makes strange bedfellows." Wallace would then lift the quilt and ask, "Is that you down there, John Patterson? Why don't you come out and face the people?" The audience would laugh and nod to one another. When the Ku Klux Klan article made headlines, he gave the scene a new twist. Wallace would raise the quilt and ask, "Who's down there between the sheets with you, John? Are you in bed with the Ku Klux Klan?" The crowds howled with delight.[10]

Patterson and Meriwether could no longer continue to deny that Patterson had connections with the Klan. Robert Shelton had joined the campaign early and worked with the headquarters staff in Tuscaloosa's Burchfield Hotel. Patterson admitted that he had also visited Shelton's home and made his campaign pitch to wall-to-wall Klansmen and their families. Shelton said he met Patterson before the governor's race at a motel near Garrett Coliseum, where the White Citizens Council rented a room for their headquarters. Sam Engelhardt and Walter Craig brought several campaign workers together to discuss campaign strategy, and Shelton was included because of his association with the council. Klan influence was a substantial factor in the governor's race, since it was estimated that there were about fifty thousand Klansmen in Alabama, roughly the same number as registered black voters. Shelton said it was the Klan's intent to build a force to oppose integration. "We liked Patterson because of his record against the NAACP and his law-and-order stand in Phenix City, but we also wanted to build a system beyond Patterson and the governor's office." Shelton did most of his work for Patterson out of the Birmingham office, dealing primarily with Meriwether. The Klan helped build crowds for Patterson rallies, put up or tore down campaign signs, and provided unsolicited protection for Patterson during major events. Shelton claimed that sometimes as many as forty to fifty armed Klansmen ringed Patterson audiences, even though Patterson denied any knowledge of it. The Klan never initiated any violence, but they did get involved in some prankish staple-gun battles with other candidates' campaign workers. Shelton said they once disabled A. W. Todd's entire caravan by pulling out distributor wires; they were mad because Todd's campaign manager called them a bunch of rednecks during a radio address.

Meriwether had received information that a contingent of the former Phenix City mob—Shepherd, Matthews, and the Davis brothers—were riding around the state on Wallace's behalf. Patterson, Robertson, and Meriwether were armed, and band members began carrying pistols after several threats were phoned in to the Montgomery and Birmingham headquarters. When Patterson and Robertson were driving to an engagement alone, one drove while the other sat in the back seat cradling a 12-gauge shotgun. During the runoff, when some of the old Phenix City gangsters began loitering around the lobby of the Molton Hotel, Shelton said he went down and told them that if they wanted trouble the Klan was with Patterson. Shelton said they then left. The underworld threat was real. The presence of the Klan, ironically, was a possible safeguard against violence.

The Klan publicity increased press scrutiny at the Birmingham offices, especially when *Birmingham News* reporter Fred Taylor and a photographer spotted Shelton talking to John Patterson's brother, Maurice. As they frantically tried to set up a compromising photo, Shelton was hustled into the ladies restroom where Mary Joe Patterson stayed with him until the reporters left. Meriwether acted as if he didn't know who they were looking for: "Who is Shelton? I don't know him. What does he do?"[11]

According to Shelton, the reason the media was at Patterson headquarters at the Molton Hotel was that the Phenix City crowd had set him up for a faked bombing at a local Jewish synagogue. He said the police—with the press—were tipped off about Shelton and were in the hotel trying to find him. Shelton was hurried out the service entrance and waited inside the Alabama Theater until Meriwether and staff worker Ralph Harden hurriedly got him out of town. Shelton said he had enough evidence to convince him that mob elements in Phenix City were trying to use the Klan to embarrass Patterson. In what sounds like a plot from a spy thriller, he said during the final days of the campaign, he was running from town to town eluding a Phenix City hit squad.[12]

Wallace pounded Patterson relentlessly on the Klan issue. Wallace claimed in a televised speech that Patterson's election would put "starch in all those dirty bedsheets" and result in the revival of the KKK as the "controlling political force in Alabama." Wallace even came up with a historical parallel: "The last time the Klan elected a politician in Alabama his name was Hugo L. Black." *Time* magazine helped Wallace when it published an article that suggested that the election of John Patterson would return the KKK to power in Alabama. Patterson finally made a weak clarification about knowing Shelton but not being aware he was a Klansman.[13]

As the Klan controversy raged, Patterson supporters urged him to break his silence and confront Wallace. A group of rabbis encouraged him to publicly disavow Klan support, but Patterson turned them down because he said he needed everyone's support to win. Maurice thought they had lost the election, and Meriwether believed the campaign had been seriously damaged. The *Advertiser* needled Meriwether about being a disbarred lawyer and a "Crump stooge." But Patterson held his ground and continued his low-key tour while the press threw charges at him.[14]

Surprisingly the Klan issue ran out of steam and in the last days of the campaign Wallace was once again on the defensive over his ties to Folsom. Recognizing the damage his Folsom connection was doing to his runoff effort, he claimed he would oust all Folsom appointees in state government. Wallace also said he had voted for the governor "but one time in my life" and that he was "irked" by the way he had been labeled a Folsomite. Folsom didn't make it any easier for Wallace when he admitted that he had voted for Wallace in the first primary. In the last days of the campaign, when it was apparent he was once again losing, Wallace desperately waved fistfuls of scandal sheets in front of his audiences claiming

Patterson was trying to smear him. In one speech, he held high a copy of *South* magazine with Patterson and his family on the cover and called it "the greatest enemy of the working man you can find."[15]

While segregation gripped the thoughts of run-of-the-mill Alabama voters, some people thought Patterson had distinguished himself when he talked about waste and corruption in government and made Folsom a campaign issue. Clarke Stallworth, the *Birmingham Post-Herald* reporter who traveled extensively with Patterson during the primary, thought good government was the key to Patterson's victory. The most important single point that put Patterson in the lead, according to Stallworth and observers that he interviewed, was "his frank stand against Folsom."[16]

On First Monday, Scottsboro's well-known market day, Patterson, the "invisible candidate," ended 128 days of campaigning with his hands swollen and fingers calloused; he was speaking from a flatbed truck less than thirty yards from a wildly ranting George Wallace. By 10:00 p.m. Tuesday night, Patterson had a 60,000 vote lead and a telegram from Wallace congratulating him. Patterson beat Wallace soundly—314,353 to 250,451—another record turnout. Albert Boutwell was elected lieutenant governor and MacDonald Gallion won the attorney general's post. Patterson carried 52 of 67 counties with a strong urban North Alabama vote to complement his strength in the eastern part of the state. On election night, NBC's David Brinkley predicted a "regime of bedsheets" for Patterson.[17]

Ed Strickland wrote for the *Birmingham News* that Patterson "did the thing that many politicians said could not be done. He took on almost all of the county and city political machines in the state and smothered them under a deluge of votes." Strickland noted that Patterson also defied tradition by moving around the state with his hand-shaking campaign in the runoff, instead of adhering to a carefully planned schedule of major speeches.[18]

Wallace was endorsed by an odd combination of the NAACP, the Folsom crowd, Jews, organized labor, suburbanites, Big Mules, and the education community. The big daily newspapers supported him eight to three over Patterson, but the rural weeklies backed Patterson fifteen to seven. A country grocer gave a *Montgomery Advertiser* reporter a memorable political lesson about Patterson's Klan support. The man pointed out that "they forget 80 percent of us, at least around here, are Ku Kluxers at heart." Patterson beat Folsom's 1954 landslide with a record vote, and did it without the help of the state's small contingent of blacks, the large labor vote, or the state's political elite. Common folk had spoken in great numbers and they taught Wallace a lesson he would never forget. Despite his protests, Wallace was the biggest Folsomite to be sent back home by the electorate.[19]

It was almost a month before Wallace drifted back into Montgomery; after the election, people said he looked like a hermit who had just come out of the woods. When he returned, he looked better and headed straight for the familiar haunts at the Jeff Davis Hotel and began talking about how "John Patterson out-niggered me." He made the same statement to Grover Hall and the staff of the *Advertiser* at a "victory" celebration the night of the election, and was seen and heard at restaurants and cafes all over Montgomery talking about how he was never going to be "out-niggered again."[20]

Ignoring Patterson's rising star and the emotional support of the people, Wallace blamed his defeat on race and made sure the politicians and power brokers in Montgomery heard him, thereby helping to create a negative impression of himself—more so than Patterson had—and an unshakeable place in American history as a racial bigot. Victory and defeat carried liabilities for Patterson and Wallace alike.

14
Trying to Build a "Better Alabama"

A dramatic twist of fate had thrust John Patterson into a profession he thought unpalatable, but he discovered it was to his liking. And he was a natural politician. Charlie Meriwether said he envisioned the opportunity in its entirety the day he drove to Phenix City to console the Patterson family, and he wondered why so many others had failed to see it. Patterson said some people suggested to him immediately following his father's death that he could take the nomination as attorney general all the way to the governor's office, but he had not seriously entertained the idea until well into his term. Even then he approached a run for governor with caution until he was sure that winning was indeed as likely as the people around him claimed. "I took my time evaluating the campaign for governor," he said. "I was concerned that the whole thing would fold on me once I got started, so I was careful about what people said to me about my chances to win."[1]

The morning after the runoff victory, Patterson and Meriwether quickly dismantled the campaign organization. They encouraged supporters and volunteers to go back to their homes and jobs, but many of the Patterson people were so inflamed by the victory that they hung around the Birmingham and Montgomery offices for days, partying and congratulating one other. "We had a hell of a time just trying to get everybody to go back home and go to work," Meriwether said. "I didn't think we were ever going to get them out of town."

During the campaign, Meriwether kept a set of financial records on a single steno pad and wouldn't allow anyone other than Patterson to examine its contents. Total campaign expenses came to $354,000, with only $85,000 of that spent in the first primary. On the day they closed the offices in the Molton Hotel, the two men sat down and carefully read the entries, one last time, committing the list of contributors and expenses to memory—then burned it. Meriwether didn't want it known that they had helped pay off Jimmy Faulkner's campaign debt.[2]

Patterson returned to the attorney general's office and began making plans for his administration. MacDonald Gallion had been on leave during the primary with his own race (Patterson made a sizable contribution to help compensate him for his loss of salary), and Jim Screws, an older assistant attorney general, ran the office while Patterson and Gallion campaigned. The *Montgomery Advertiser* absorbed its candidate's defeat with a fair amount of dignity and noted that Patterson was entering the next phase of his career with many assets: "His victory was overmastering, and hence on the scale of a mandate. He is young, strong and evidently quite decisive." Grover Hall also talked about Patterson as if he were something of an enigma. "We have looked keenly into his eyes and face and could get no sense at all of what lay behind. He was brisk and forceful and not without charm, but what was inside eluded us." Whatever it was about Patterson that Hall found so elusive was perfectly understood by a record number of Alabamians. During the runoff, voters not only purged another batch of politicians associated with the Folsom administration but also gave states' rights candidates control of the Alabama Democratic Executive Committee. Now that they controlled the party organization, Patterson and Meriwether installed Sam Engelhardt as chairman after a bitter fight with forces loyal to the National Democratic Party.[3]

Patterson's agenda as governor was just what he had promised during the campaign—an administration that would eliminate waste in state government, push for strict law enforcement, raise the old-age pension, continue the kind of road program that Folsom had started, and "just hold the line on segregation." Since he never had the support of the education community, no plans were made for a new school program. Patterson had to finance his programs without the aid of additional revenue as he had promised that no new taxes would be levied during his administration, claiming that everything proposed could be financed through the elimination of graft and corruption. "The problem was that we had no way of knowing if the Folsom administration wasted enough money to cover our programs," Patterson said. Patterson prepared for his governor's duties the same way he did the attorney general's office—he researched and read. "I read the messages and speeches to the legislature of some thirty governors, every history on every governor's administration in Alabama's history, including the Reconstruction era," he said. The most influential figure in his studies was Gov. Frank Dixon, who in 1939 organized Alabama's budget system and set up the state's merit system and the pardon and parole systems. Patterson wanted to know the mechanics of state government because he did not intend to give others the power to structure or define the limits of his administration. "I had seen in the Persons and Folsom administrations how important it was to take control of the office so that we would not be crippled by allowing other people to make critical decisions," Patterson explained. "I didn't intend to make the same mistakes." The only firm decision was that "those who went with us early would be favored in state matters." Patterson did not differ from Folsom on the philosophy that to the victor goes the spoils.[4]

The inner circle of the administration was made up primarily of people Patterson already trusted. Meriwether was named finance director, with Maurice Patterson as his assistant, while Joe Robertson continued as his executive assistant. Harry Cook, aide to defeated congressman George Huddleston, was asked to serve as press secretary. Ralph Smith, a law school classmate, was named legal adviser. Roy Marcato, the photojournalist who had worked without pay during the campaign, was rewarded with the position of director of the bureau of publicity and information.

Determined not to retain anyone even remotely associated with Folsom's personal staff in the governor's office, Patterson wanted to fire everyone who was not a merit system employee because they were all suspect. Mabel Amos, who worked for several governors including Folsom, remembered Patterson's first appearance in the office after the election: "When he came through the door, he thoroughly intended to fire me and everyone else in there." He would have if it had not been for Vaughn Hill Robison, senator from Montgomery, who persuaded Patterson to keep Amos and Kate Simmons so that he "didn't start off in the ditch." The two secretaries were extremely knowledgeable about the functions of the office, and Robison knew that Patterson was hell-bent on restructuring everything in the governor's office. Patterson agreed that Robison kept him from making a mistake.[5] "Selecting a cabinet wasn't difficult," Patterson explained. "I simply deferred to our friends, a few former classmates at the university, and supporters. I wanted to fill every slot with a career man."

Patterson was suspicious of the highway department leadership, having sued the department on numerous occasions while attorney general; he didn't feel they shared his views on waste and efficiency. In the end, he offered the position to Sam Engelhardt, who had lost his bid for lieutenant governor and who strongly supported Patterson in the runoff. Engelhardt's highway department knowledge was minimal, only some county road experience, but Patterson liked his "political acumen." Walter Craig of Selma, an Engelhardt ally in the White Citizens Council, was named his assistant.

The remainder of the cabinet selections followed the trend that Patterson wanted in his administration: Montgomery banker John Curry agreed to be the banking commissioner, with former army colonel Lehman Lewis named to the Small Loan Bureau in the department. Lewis applied for the job outright and was hired by Patterson to go to work immediately on the loan shark problem. A bit of intrigue surrounded the selection process for the state insurance department: Patterson wanted Robert L. Jones of Montgomery for the post, a friend from Phenix City days who had been important in recruiting people for the campaign. The problem was that Jones had a troubled past that insiders knew would raise credibility problems for the administration. Jones had been a professional gambler in Phenix City, became hooked on narcotics, and spent eight years in a Georgia prison. Patterson met Jones when he worked for his brother Leland Jones at the grocery store and liked him despite his past. Jones had rehabilitated himself and became an outstanding insurance executive in Montgomery. During the campaign they traveled together, often sharing the same bed. Patterson wanted Jones to have the appointment over the objections of his staff and was willing to take the heat for the nomination until Jones told him something that compromised the appointment. He told Patterson that when he filled out the registrar's form to vote in Montgomery, he falsely reported that he had never been convicted of a felony. Determined to pursue the appointment, Patterson sent an assistant attorney general over to the Montgomery County courthouse to find the document. "A thorough search failed to uncover the incriminating form," Patterson recalled, "but a few days later, word got back to us that Grover Hall had it and was going to publish it when Jones's appointment became official." Aware of the damage that would do to the administration, Patterson instead appointed Ted Rinehart, his army buddy, who had come south to work in the attorney general's office. Rinehart, who had an Andover–Princeton–Harvard Law School education, originally had been tapped as director of the State Department of Industrial Development. That post went to Leland Jones. "We reported that Robert L. Jones was ill and unable to accept the insurance commissioner's position," Patterson explained.[6]

The labor commissioner's post went to Olin Brooks, a lobbyist for L&N Railroad in Birmingham; Ed Azar, Patterson's Montgomery campaign manager, was named administrator of the State Alcohol Beverage Control Board. Patterson and Meriwether kept the liquor agents under close control "to keep the operation clean," Patterson said. They appointed supporters to lucrative positions and used the state's liquor trade to reward friends, particularly select people in Phenix City. RBA stalwart Hugh Britton became a liquor agent, and Cecil Padgett, star witness in the Fuller and Ferrell murder trials, was given a job with one of the liquor companies.

General Hanna, who had campaigned hard for Patterson, declined to be adjutant general; Henry B. Graham later accepted the post. Claude Kelley from Atmore, an outstanding conservationist, became director of conservation, and Ralph Williams, attorney and former law professor at the University of Alabama, headed up the State Industrial Relations Department. Floyd Mann, Opelika chief of police, was selected as director of public safety; Mann's appointment would prove to be crucial when the Freedom Riders came to Alabama. Alvin Prestwood, a twenty-eight-year-old assistant attorney general now at the Department of Pensions and Security, had the difficult task of helping Patterson deliver on his pledge to raise old-age pensions. Prestwood started to work immediately to find ways to fund the seventy-five dollar a month pensions. Patterson recalled that "Prestwood almost went into shock when I told him what we were going to do about the pensions. He couldn't believe we were going to have to get up all that money without raising taxes."

Two of Patterson's cabinet positions were held by men of eminent qualifications. Harry V. Haden, a recognized tax authority who had taught Patterson at the university, agreed to manage the all-important State Department of Revenue. Patterson especially wanted Haden's expertise to address equalization of the state's tax structure, which would increase revenue without raising taxes. Perhaps the most qualified member of Patterson's cabinet was Earl McGowin, an Oxford-educated Chapman lumberman with more than twenty years experience as a legislator. McGowin had also been conservation director in the Persons administration and Gov. Frank Dixon's floor leader in the House. It took some time for Patterson to persuade the highly successful McGowin (cousin to Mary Joe Patterson) to join his administration. "I wanted McGowin to take over the state docks at Mobile, where there was widespread corruption under the Folsom people," Patterson said. In the waning months of Folsom's term, Patterson obtained an injunction to keep the department from floating a bond issue that would have driven it even further into debt. He knew that McGowin would implement sound management principles at the state docks and that his presence in the cabinet would give the administration credibility in Alabama's political circles.[7]

During the time Patterson was putting together his cabinet and staff, he also met with legislators, informing them about his program and offering them a role in the administration. John Casey, a freshman House member from Heflin, was impressed with the team that Patterson assembled. "His ideas, which I shared, were very progressive for those days. He wanted the business community to assume its fair share of the tax burden, which certainly was a new approach since the big money interests always defeated those kinds of programs." Patterson's House leadership was made up of veteran lawmakers with considerable clout on Goat Hill, site of the state capitol. Conservative in their politics and eager to cooperate with the new administration, Charles Adams of Alexander City was chosen Speaker of the House, and Virgis Ashworth of Centreville, Joe Smith and Homer Cornett of Phenix City, Ira Pruitt of Livingston, Pat Boyd of Troy, and Kenneth Ingram of Ashland formed the core of the House leadership.

Even Patterson's political foes respected the way he organized the legislature. McDowell Lee, Wallace's state campaign manager and a second-term House member from Barbour County, met with Patterson and was told that he would not be given any key committee assignments because of commitments to his supporters. "But he wanted me to know," he explained, "that he would be dealing fairly with me for the next four years. Patterson started off knowing what the hell he was doing and consequently got everything he wanted in setting up his administration." Lee said Patterson organized the legislature like a veteran and convinced everyone that he was in control of state government.

In the Senate, Patterson threw his support behind Vaughn Hill Robison of Montgomery as president pro tem. Ryan DeGraffenried Sr. of Tuscaloosa, Donald Word of Scottsboro, Bob Kendall of Evergreen, and Dave Archer of Huntsville made up administration leadership in the thirty-five-member Senate. Robison said when Patterson called the senators to his campaign headquarters "he had his recommendations outlined and went into great detail about committee assignments. John told us he wanted people who would give his programs fair consideration." Like Lee in the House, Robison said the senators were impressed with Patterson's program; they left the meeting knowing who would be in control for the next four years.[8]

In contrast to his mainly urban and North Alabama support in the primary, Patterson's legislative leadership had a strong Black Belt representation. In the House, Black Belt legislators chaired some fifty-three committees, the highest number from that region in more than thirty years. In the Senate, administration leadership chairs were more equally divided between the Black Belt and North Alabama counties. Patterson insisted "that regional preferences were never a consideration, but the Black Belt legislators had the ability to get reelected and build seniority." The cities and the North Alabama region typically sent new legislators each term and they tended not to be team players, while the antique malapportioned representation system favored reelection of legislators from the more sparsely populated and predominately rural Black Belt counties. Patterson deliberately avoided the Jefferson County delegation, which was traditionally split and often difficult to work with. "We wanted people with legislative know-how who were mission minded. The Black Belt just happened to have the kind of legislators that our administration needed."

The Senate was a different story. Incoming Lt. Gov. Albert Boutwell showed signs of not wanting to go along with Patterson's committee assignments. (In Alabama the lieutenant governor's election is not linked to the governor's; the candidates run separately.) Robison said Boutwell expected key appointments for his supporters and pushed hard for Walter Givhan of Selma, darling of the Black Belters, as chair of the powerful Finance and Taxation Committee, the Senate's primary funding committee. Patterson nixed the idea, remembering that some Black Belt senators, including Givhan, aligned themselves with the Big Mules in North Alabama to stop Folsom's legislation. Givhan had also led the fight in 1931 to gerrymander the liberal Lafayette Patterson, John's uncle, out of his congressional seat. Patterson did not want that coalition to reunite, and he refused Boutwell's input on committee arrangements. "I wanted our administration to have an excellent road program, improve the state education system, and deal with reapportionment," he said. "I knew these were liberal ideas that would be killed by Black Belt senators, who were traditionally opposed to any kind of social program."

The cabinet and the legislative program were in place by the fall elections, and with the Alabama Democratic Party rallying around its nominees, Patterson had little concern over his Republican opponent, William L. Longshore of Birmingham. He made speeches at Democratic functions that were little more than glorified Patterson gatherings and was photographed riding a symbolic Democratic donkey. He brought a certain informality to his position as governor-elect but certainly more dignity than the unpredictable and bibulous Folsom. One small cloud appeared on the political horizon when the press discovered that Alabama's new football coach Paul "Bear" Bryant, trying to capitalize on the governor-elect's popularity, had asked Patterson to write letters to recruit high school prospects to his alma mater. But it did not cause any lasting harm to either man.

For Patterson and the reigning Democratic Party, the November general election looked more like a grand tour around the state than a political campaign. There were no schedules to keep, no flatbed trailers to haul from town to town, and no financial concerns. On November 4, 1958, John Malcolm Patterson, at age thirty-seven, became the youngest governor in Alabama's history, polling 239,633 votes to Longshore's 30,415.[9]

As Patterson prepared for his term of office, he faced problems that concerned most of the state's population. Segregation was certainly the most troubling because of increasing national pressure to integrate the South, and Patterson's victory placed him in a position of direct confrontation with the federal government. He also had the problem of instilling voter confidence in state government and delivering on his campaign promise to raise old-age pensions. While education had not been a campaign issue, as he traveled around the state Patterson had seen the deplorable conditions of the state's school system. There was also a need for legislative reapportionment to keep legislators from smaller counties from dictating policy for the rest of the state. Patterson also had to figure out how to keep his campaign promise to give the people honest, efficient government without raising taxes.[10]

But first came the inauguration and the biggest parade Montgomery had ever held for it: 140 floats, 150 cars, and 144 bands paraded for almost four hours on the cold, overcast morning of January 19, 1959. Unlike the Folsom parade, no blacks were invited to participate. Patterson planners insisted it was an oversight. Patterson said law enforcement officers persuaded him that it would be risky because of racial tensions. Folsom drove to the Patterson home the morning of the inauguration in a black limousine convertible, went inside and asked for a cup of coffee to help him sober up for the swearing-in ceremonies.

At noon, Judge Walter B. Jones administered the oath of office to Alabama's forty-ninth governor and Patterson delivered his inaugural address standing on the bronze star where Jefferson Davis had been sworn in as the first president of the Confederate States of America and placing his hand on the same Bible. The address was a more formal version of the Patterson campaign speeches. The most prominent issue was, of course, integration. "The Federal Courts have decreed that we must send our children to integrated schools contrary to our customs and traditions," he said. "I will oppose with every ounce of energy I possess, and will use every power at my command to prevent any mixing of the white and Negro races in the schools of this state." Fully one-third of the address focused on integration; the rest was devoted to the basics that customarily won the attention of the voters.[11]

Folsom escorted Patterson back into the capitol and asked for a personal favor from the new governor. "John, I want to use the state yacht every now and then." Patterson agreed and afterward, a thoroughly beaten Folsom walked outside and told the waiting press, "I've had enough."[12]

For the remainder of the day there were the usual inaugural festivities. Mary Joe Patterson greeted thousands of the Alabamians who streamed through the governor's residence, while her governor-husband celebrated over drinks with his staff and legislators in the capitol. That night at the inaugural ball at Garrett Coliseum, cameras caught Patterson nodding off to sleep in his chair and later dancing with Molly Patterson, his ninety-four-year-old grandmother. She died two weeks later, having seen her grandson make the long journey from the family's Goldville farm to the governor's mansion.[13]

15
Battling Black Belters
and Courting Kennedy

John Patterson spent little time adjusting to the governor's office. He saw to it that missing silverware was replaced (after the Folsoms left there wasn't enough silver left for a six-piece place setting, according to Patterson) and sent troopers to Cullman to retrieve a state car and two prison trustees that Folsom had taken back home with him. He reduced the serving staff from twelve to four, had most of the telephones removed, and ordered a security fence built around the mansion. The press referred to him as "Nervous John" after the fence went up. The Pattersons were financially secure with the twenty-five thousand dollar annual salary, by far the most comfortable income John had ever provided his family, and their needs were attended to by a staff, a pleasant change for a family that had spent much of its life in a cramped basement apartment.

Considering John Patterson's lack of experience, his first year in office has to be considered a success. He accomplished a number of things on his agenda, despite having what he saw as a pro-Wallace legislature. Exactly two weeks after taking office, he called the legislature into special session for a highway and road program. Intent on continuing Folsom's highway program, Patterson's plan called for obtaining federal matching dollars so Alabama could take part in the new Interstate highway system started by the Eisenhower administration. Before taking office, Sam Engelhardt and Patterson huddled with state highway department officials to study available matching federal funds. They found that Alabama could receive $326 million in federal highway funds for an investment of $60 million of state money. "I saw the program as a way to create jobs and keep money circulating in the state," Patterson explained. "It was a strong economic program for the state after we had gone through a period of recession during the fifties." He hoped to have the highway program fully funded at the beginning of his administration so he could use the money as leverage with the legislature. Highway department officials showed Patterson how he could fund a bond issue without raising taxes through gas tax money that had not yet been pledged to other programs. The plan sailed through both houses by mid-February without a dissenting vote, and Patterson scored his first legislative victory. Engelhardt thought it was simply a matter of presenting something the legislators couldn't turn down. Legislative support grew out of the administration's commitment to pave county roads and city streets. When Engelhardt pointed out that this was essentially illegal, Patterson retorted that they would give the law a liberal interpretation, as Folsom had always done. With new highway funds available, one of Patterson's first road projects was building a traffic exchange covering some forty acres on the south end of Phenix City. He was on hand the day bulldozers begin demolishing ramshackle saloons, corrugated tin buildings, and cheap dives in old Girard. The section that had been a blight on the town and caused its citizens so much grief and embarrassment was gone.[1]

The regular legislative session opened in early May with lawmakers facing the paradox of calls for more money to keep public schools open and legal machinery to close them in case they were integrated. Patterson said he didn't want a lot out of the regular session, but he introduced legislation to increase education expenditures by $42 million and asked for the power to abolish the public school system if desegregation suits threatened Alabama. The possibility of integration made some lawmakers reluctant to fund education, and Patterson realized that racial conflict would be used as an excuse to keep from addressing the state's deplorable education system.[2]

Opposition to administration bills came from a small core of Black Belt legislators who aggressively opposed Patterson's property tax equalization plan. The proposal brought instant and heated opposition from the less populated counties with large timber, strip mining, and cattle interests. The Black Belters claimed that their constituency of large landowners was already overtaxed. The opposition stymied Harry Haden's plan to achieve tax justice by equalizing property assessments. When the scholarly Haden began correcting and reorganizing the faulty tax procedures, a storm of protest erupted from the Central and South Alabama counties and the industrial delegation from Jefferson County.[3]

In a public statement, Patterson informed legislators that Haden's program would mean equalization of taxes within counties, as well as among counties, and would provide "the long-range solution to many of our school financing problems." He predicted that tax equalization would generate another $43 million in annual taxes. The idea was far too progressive for Black Belters and their Birmingham confederates. Patterson admitted, "When I saw considerable opposition mounting, I backed off and let the matter quiet down before it inflicted further damage to my other legislative plans."[4]

Patterson abandoned the tax equalization issue to maintain good relations with the legislature because he wanted to introduce his agenda for major improvements in education. Realizing that the education issue would have to be separated from other legislative items, he called a special session of the legislature to be held during the regular session—the first time that the state legislature had ever met for the sole purpose of addressing public education issues. The gallery was jammed with school officials who had come to hear the governor's remarks. The special session for education was the culmination of many people's concerns, according to Patterson.

Following his win in the Democratic primary there was a great rush by education leaders to apprise him of the desperate needs of education in Alabama. State education expenditures were well below the national average, slightly more than a hundred dollars annually for each white student; less than seventy dollars per black in the "separate but equal" school systems. Blacks made up about one-third of the total school enrollment. What Patterson heard from the education community persuaded him to make education a major issue once he took office. The administration identified education as a priority and sought an opportunity to make significant gains for public schools. Speaking to the special session, Patterson said that Alabama's public school system needed attention or "we might see it collapse." Citing an acute shortage of teachers, he spoke of children—black and white—attending school in condemned buildings, some heated by pot-bellied stoves and with outhouses as toilet facilities.[5]

In addition to the $42 million increase in general appropriation to education, Patterson asked for a series of tax reforms, most of them to be achieved by removing tax exemptions, to raise money for a $100 million revenue bond issue for capital improvements, with the majority of the money going to higher education. He claimed the bond issue did not contain "one penny" to support an integrated school, which legislators were dead set against funding. At the same time, he asked for the authority to close any school where federal force was used to threaten segregation and to cut off state funding for any integrated school.[6]

The House passed the series of bills without serious opposition, but once the education package reached the Senate, the enemies of education from the Black Belt and big business tried to dismantle the bond issue. Frank Rose, president of the University of Alabama, one of many educators who personally lobbied for the bills, was shocked to find that state senators would lie to him and curse him to his face. Alabama Power Company, the region's chief utility company, and other power providers allied themselves with the Black Belt representatives to try to kill the school funding program because the bills removed tax exemptions on equipment and power poles. Disappointed House members wept openly when the chamber of commerce, Associated Industries of Alabama (AIA), and the Alabama Mining Institute collaborated to oppose funding for public education. Lt. Governor Albert Boutwell supported the utilities lobby.

To counter big business's opposition to the school bond issue, Patterson threatened to remove federal income tax payments as deductions on corporate state income tax returns. Only then did Boutwell, the chamber of commerce, and the powerful AIA lobbying force agree to allow the bills to come to a vote. In the meantime, Patterson himself was getting votes through arm-twisting and vote-buying with state patronage. On the day of the vote, Sen. Vaughn Hill Robison discovered they were one vote short because of the conspicuous absence of a South Alabama senator who had pledged his support. Patterson explained that he had tried unsuccessfully to reach the senator by phone at his equipment sales business and even sent a state trooper to locate him. Patterson finally got through to ask why the man wasn't in Montgomery. The South Alabama senator explained that his business was struggling badly and he had thirty-five dump trucks on his lot that he was unable to sell. Patterson understood the price of the vote for the education bill and called Sam Engelhardt at the highway department. "Sam," Patterson asked, "do you need thirty-five dump trucks?" Quickly grasping the political importance of the question, Engelhardt answered that he needed the trucks if the governor said he did. Patterson got the final vote that carried the bond issue for education.

Patterson gave education its first bond issue of $100 million plus $42 million in appropriations for teachers' salaries, a 15 percent raise. The Alabama Education Association hailed him as one of the great friends of education, calling the bond issue "the greatest single increase in funds available to education since the founding of our public school system, more than 100 years ago." Patterson felt that he had been seriously damaged by the bitterest fight of his administration. The education battle had been surprisingly costly, and Patterson said he had bargained away "all of [his] marbles" acquired in the road program. When the "Eisenhower recession" hit an already struggling state economy and a hundred-day steel strike affected the state's steel industry, Alabama's economic climate changed. The education budget had to be prorated (reduced by the same percentage as a revenue shortfall) because of a sharp decrease in revenue. Education leaders demanded that Patterson call another special session to raise taxes. Patterson refused because of the state's weak economy and a belief that working people could not afford additional taxes. Educators, who previously lauded him as one of Alabama's great governors for his unqualified support of education, turned on him in anger. "After all the months of hard work, I wound up with the hostility of education instead of their support," Patterson explained. He said educators never understood the battle legislators went through to generate funds for schools.[7]

As the special session on education got under way, Patterson forces were jockeying another historic piece of legislation into place. Rep. Bob Gilchrist of Morgan County sponsored a regulatory bill for the small-loan industry aimed at the loan sharks that Patterson had fought to a stalemate as attorney general. Gilchrist wasn't an administration team player and Patterson didn't care for him personally. "Gilchrist had real political ambitions and just horned his way into the bill and made it his own, because he saw it would get a lot of press," Patterson said. The governor allowed him to spearhead the small-loan bill in the House to get the legislation passed. The administration had a model of the bill from a national organization that worked with loan shark abuses.[8]

This would be Patterson's final assault on loan sharks and would result in a major contribution to Alabama's working class. The issue had become personal for Patterson, who had investigated numerous cases of usury. "What we found by interviewing poor blacks and whites around the state really got to John," Joe Robertson recalled. "No one, including state authorities, realized the extent of the problem."[9]

The powerful loan shark lobby, a decades-old force in the legislature, struck back at administration bills. Les Allenstein of Gadsden—owner of several small-loan companies and leader of the industry's lobbying arm, the Alabama Finance Institute—prowled the capitol hall with teams of lobbyists, all of them with cash and favors at the ready. Robertson said the lobbyists "were everywhere, talking to the legislators. You knew they were there and that they were up to something behind the scenes." Ralph Mead from Cherokee County said he was offered five one hundred dollar suits for his vote, but turned it down to support the bill. At the same time Attorney General MacDonald Gallion brought a court suit against some three hundred loan companies, members of the Alabama Finance Institute, because of violations of usury laws, a move that put still more pressure on the legislature.[10]

The controversial bills didn't encounter serious problems in the House, passing 86 to 9. To head off possible sabotage by loan company lobbyists, Patterson threatened the Senate with a special session even before the bills arrived. Nevertheless, Black Belt senators employed every delaying tactic they could muster against the bill. Administration supporter Vaughn Hill Robison stubbornly kept the Senate in session around the clock, refusing to recess even to eat or sleep. A small group calling itself the "Filthy Five" filibustered after failing to weaken the bill. Senators slept at their desks and others slipped away to their hotel rooms in relays (with offers of prostitutes from the lobbyists) in order to keep enough members on the floor for a quorum. They ate picnic style around the Senate chambers. Patterson had folding cots placed in capitol corridors for naps. Again, Patterson pledged to build roads and schools to get key votes, and even sent select brands of liquor to legislators' rooms. The filibuster was finally broken after forty-two hours with what newspapers reported as "an adroit parliamentary move." Lt. Governor Boutwell suddenly recognized Robison who brought up the bill for a vote. It passed 25 to 2 with one day remaining in the session. Only two of the Filthy Five voted against it.[11]

The loan legislation was considered a Patterson triumph. The strongest feature was a penalty clause that specified jail terms for those found in violation of the new law, a victory for Patterson's law-and-order agenda. "The best testimonial to the strength of the act is the fight the loan sharks waged to quash it," the *Advertiser* wrote. The law fixed rates at a level profitable enough so that national companies would do business in Alabama, but small-loan companies said the law would put 90 percent of them out of business—exactly what the administration wanted. The results of Patterson's campaign against the small-loan industry, set in motion while he was attorney general, were far-reaching. Abuses had been so widespread and entrenched in Alabama's business climate that the new law was nothing short of an economic revolution for the average Alabama family. It eliminated a system rooted in plantation practices, a system that held poor people in economic bondage. Patterson's press statements pointed out that because of the small-loan legislation, working-class families in Alabama—black and white—could finance appliance and furniture purchases at affordable rates. It could well be Patterson's most important contribution to the people of Alabama.[12]

Patterson's first-year achievements also included Earl McGowin's unraveling the mess at the state docks in Mobile and restoring them to a profitable basis, although the state owed some $1.5 million in debts from the Folsom administration. The *Montgomery Advertiser* called it "one of the finest performances in the way of political and economic reform of [McGowin's] long public service career." Patterson began a weekly radio program, an effective communications medium in the 1950s, to tell the people about state problems. The tax equalization plan created such a storm of controversy that it hampered his legislative programs with members of the South Alabama delegation. Despite that setback, he got more legislation passed in that first year than most governors did in a much longer period. United Press International rated the 1959 legislature as "the most successful in state history."

Two issues, however, caused a sharp decline in Patterson's popularity during his first year in office. Patterson had promised the electorate that he would "stop up the holes in the bucket" so new taxes would not be necessary. But in order to fund his programs, the administration passed $37 million in new taxes. Many Alabamians felt betrayed by the tax increase from an administration that had only months earlier loudly condemned the practice of raising taxes. The editor of the *Leeds News* wrote an article entitled, "Dear John: We Can't Hear You Anymore." Patterson was reminded that during the campaign he had been the "Man on the White Horse . . . hollering that if you were elected there would be no new taxes and no extension of any present tax." Although it was impossible to suppose he could have pushed through programs costing more than half a billion dollars without raising taxes, taxes had been a basic Patterson campaign issue, and the inability to fund his programs without additional revenue damaged his credibility.[13]

Accessibility also became an issue. Harry Cook, Patterson's press secretary, said the most difficult matter Patterson faced was the number of people who wanted to see him. "Great conflicts arose within the administration because of the overwhelming demands on his time—everyone wanted to see the governor," Cook explained. "There just wasn't enough time to see everyone. It became a real problem for the staff to conduct state business." Cook said it was months before procedures could be set up to make efficient use of the governor's time. Patterson was hurt by what the press and the public perceived as a "closed door" policy in the governor's office.

Reporters, supporters, and others who wanted to see Patterson were frequently turned away by Joe Robertson in the governor's anteroom. The practice, however necessary, was irritating to people who had previously had access to Patterson, and it contradicted Patterson's campaign pledge to be available. Many supporters who waited to see Patterson only to be turned away vowed never to support him again. Others went to Charlie Meriwether who always had access to the governor's office. "That was about the only way you could get in to see John, because everybody found out pretty quickly that his secretary wasn't going to let you in," said Gordon Wooddy of Piedmont.

Joe Robertson made no excuses for protecting the governor's time. "There was just no way John could see all those people and get anything accomplished," he explained. Patterson said that, in the beginning, he and Robertson tried to see as many people as possible but it became unworkable because "the people who wanted five minutes ending up staying an hour." While the tightly managed schedule maximized Patterson's time, he still put in twelve to fourteen hours a day in his capitol offices. Mabel Amos said that Patterson was a governor who studied everything closely and stayed at his desk until he had his day's work finished. Maintaining a strict schedule did create more work time, but it proved costly to Patterson's popularity.[14]

The biggest political uproar Patterson caused during his first year in office didn't come from Alabama, but from Washington, D.C. In mid-

June, he and a group of state officials went to the capital for a confidential meeting with Massachusetts senator John F. Kennedy. Patterson and Kennedy had met in 1957 in Birmingham when Kennedy addressed the Alabama League of Municipalities, headed by Ed E. Reid, executive secretary. In that speech Kennedy addressed the "unsavory" labor racketeering that he and his brother Robert were investigating in Senate hearings; he did not mention the raging civil rights debate. He also said he would not be a candidate for the 1960 presidential campaign and that Lyndon Johnson of Texas had the best chance at the Democratic nomination. At that gathering Kennedy asked to meet Patterson, whom he knew by reputation from the Phenix City cleanup. The introduction that night began a promising friendship for the two young regional politicians, and Patterson began making calls on Kennedy whenever he had business in Washington. They met in Georgetown the morning Patterson testified against pending civil rights legislation.[15]

Ed Reid and Grover Hall (who had temporarily suppressed his hostility to Patterson) advised Patterson to support Kennedy when it became apparent the senator would run for the presidency. While Patterson admired Kennedy and considered him sympathetic to the South, he did not want to get involved in the campaign. Reid and Hall persisted, saying it would be good for Alabama if the governor came out early for Kennedy, and Patterson began mentioning the senator in speeches without actually endorsing him. Like others in the South, Patterson liked Kennedy's moderate position on race, even though it was not a topic they addressed in their meetings. "I also felt that if Kennedy were president, he would give the South time to accept the dramatic social changes that the civil rights activists were demanding through the court system," Patterson said. Patterson, Ed Reid, Charlie Meriwether, Ralph Smith, Joe Robertson, and Hubert Baughm breakfasted with John Kennedy at his Georgetown townhouse on N Street the morning of June 15, 1959. Kennedy was accompanied by his brother-in-law Stephen Smith. The Alabamians were predictably impressed by the well-appointed house and the elegant ambience of the Kennedy lifestyle. Jackie, attired in her riding habit, looked in on the meeting and spoke politely when her husband introduced "my friends from Alabama." Joe Robertson was amazed at Kennedy's steady stream of profanity.[16]

John Patterson has not revealed the content of any of his conversations with Kennedy. He did say that "we reached an understanding about his position on several issues that day, the Democratic Convention being the most important." Patterson further declined to comment on Kennedy's opinions on integration, Martin Luther King, or the South's position in the emerging civil rights fray. Meriwether said, "When [Patterson] left that meeting he was convinced that Kennedy would be less aggressive about the civil rights issue and that he would have an entrée in expressing the viewpoints of Alabama and the South in regard to the conflict between the southern states and the federal government." He also said Patterson believed that through Kennedy he would have input to help the South buy time for people to accept the great changes that were inevitable following the 1954 Supreme Court decision.[17]

Ralph Smith, Patterson's legal adviser, said Kennedy had courted the South following the 1956 Democratic Convention, when southern delegates supported him for the vice presidential nomination instead of Estes Kefauver of Tennessee. Ironically, many southerners didn't trust Kefauver on the integration issue. The Alabama delegation eventually voted heavily for Kennedy at the 1960 convention. "Kennedy was pleased to have our support," Smith said, "and a tacit understanding for the future was reached at the Georgetown meeting." Kennedy's southern strategy, according to Smith, involved little more than an unantagonistic response to their conservative viewpoints. Ted Sorensen said the Kennedy camp was surprised by the strong southern interest but no plan evolved to solidify such support, other than trusting to opportunity and instinct in dealing with the South.[18]

Patterson said his group left the meeting feeling good about Kennedy, believing they had gained ground on a matter of national importance. Negative repercussions from the meeting began when Reid decided to telephone Grover Hall with the news. Patterson says Hall persuaded him to give the *Advertiser* an interview to discuss his opinion of Kennedy. Unaware that his comments would create serious political fallout, Patterson spoke enthusiastically about Kennedy. "The senator is a man who is sympathetic to our problems in the South and particularly in Alabama," he said. "That's the kind of man we need in the White House." Patterson went on to say that he intended to do everything he could to help Kennedy win the nomination.[19]

Speculation arose about Patterson's motives for supporting Kennedy so early. Meriwether said he noticed considerable jealousy among East Coast factions because of the Kennedy-Patterson friendship. Republicans, who were quick to criticize the relationship, convinced Jackie Robinson to criticize Kennedy for meeting with an avowed segregationist. Patterson's public endorsement and its consequences, so many months in advance of the convention, embarrassed both men and reduced the effectiveness of their relationship. The issue was kept alive when Engelhardt said he wanted to raise a slate of delegates pledged to Kennedy, and Hugh Sparrow suggested that Patterson could be considered a strong vice presidential candidate if Kennedy won the nomination.[20]

It took almost two days for the state press to reach Kennedy for a comment, and then a Kennedy spokesman only remarked that the senator was "always appreciative of the governor's interest." A week later Kennedy put distance between himself and Patterson, at least publicly. The *Birmingham News* sent a reporter to interview him about the endorsement, and the paper reported that Kennedy was "startled and bewildered by Patterson's open avowal of support." Kennedy said they didn't discuss civil rights and that his future votes on civil rights might embarrass Patterson. Patterson's endorsement of Kennedy had been criticized, notably by Adam Clayton Powell, who Kennedy feared would influence black politicians. Kennedy strategists would only tell the *News* that their objective was to build a reserve of strength among Dixie delegates for the second ballot of the convention. Kennedy said he would have preferred for Patterson to wait and come out with an endorsement in the preconvention months of 1960.[21]

Back in Alabama, Patterson was taken to task in religious circles for supporting a Roman Catholic. The Methodist *Christian Advocate* ran a front-page editorial by T. P. Chalker entitled "Patterson and Roman Hierarchy." The article condemned the endorsement, saying it was a "grave mistake to support a Roman Catholic" and suggesting that American democratic liberties were endangered by the Catholic church. "On a given Sunday, all of the Methodist ministers in the state, and many Baptists, preached a sermon on my endorsement of a Catholic for president," Patterson said, "including my own pastor at Saint James Methodist Church in Montgomery." Patterson said he called his minister to his office and demanded to know where in Methodist principles religious intolerance was specified as church doctrine. Disgusted by the narrow vision of Alabama Methodists, he did not return to the church for almost twenty years, and then it was to attend a wedding.[22]

The Kennedy matter drew ire from more than the churches. A group of "white Christians" later identified as Klansmen crowded into the governor's office to question him about being used by "Communist-Jewish integrators." Patterson, with the press in attendance, became angry at the hectoring and reverted to his stock response whenever his segregationist principles were questioned, by snapping that if any school in Alabama is integrated "it will be over my dead body."[23] Patterson's unbending segregation stance was constricting his personal and political room to maneuver. Whatever the problem or issue, he found the safest ground was to denounce integration. During his first year as governor, that was his response to success, to failure, to controversy. While his administration had an unmistakably progressive character, the reactionary nature of state politics and the racial tone of the 1958 gubernatorial campaign painted John Patterson into a very small corner. He was now on a fast track for a historic encounter with the people whose support he believed he needed.

16
MLK, Castro, and a New Romance

Battles in the state legislature with Alabama special interests were valuable experiences for the young governor, and it showed. One anonymous legislator told the *Birmingham Post Herald* that the governor learned fast: "He has a quick mind and he's anxious to learn. And he works hard." The same could be said about Finance Director Charlie Meriwether, who initiated stringent business procedures for state financial functions that had been loosely managed during Folsom's last term. Meriwether also had the benefit of a new competitive bid law designed to control state contracts and reduce costs on state purchases. He set up a system that required all state contracts to come through his office, rather than allowing individual departments to award them. He also negotiated contracts that reduced operating costs or enabled the administration to expand state services within the existing budget. For example, he negotiated a tire contract with the B. F. Goodrich Tire Company in Tuscaloosa at 5 percent less than the lowest bid; within a year it had saved enough money to purchase every car the state needed. (The press fussed over the contract and attempted to tie it to the governor's relationship with Klansman Robert Shelton, an ordinary company employee who had nothing to do with the letting of contracts.) According to newspaper reports, during the first year of the Patterson administration, contracts were 11.5 percent under projected operating costs.[1]

Alvin Prestwood, director of the Department of Pensions and Securities, faced the Herculean task of doubling old-age pensions without additional revenue. Prestwood nevertheless had the lion's share of the work completed in a few months and was paying Alabama pensioners sixty-five dollars a month, a 70 percent increase. The administration increased pensions at a rate five times the national average according to Prestwood: "Patterson's theory was if you're going to do it, then do it where it's significant help to the pensioners." But the administration's efforts to raise pensions came under continual attack by Black Belt legislators who didn't want poor blacks receiving state benefits. Prestwood said that white families were receiving the bulk of the pensions, although statistically they weren't. Patterson, aware of the deception, told Prestwood not to worry about the politics and to keep raising the pension payments.[2]

Alabama was beginning to experience some of the economic benefits the rest of the nation had been enjoying. Business research by the University of Alabama for that period showed increases in virtually every category of the state's business life, with cotton production expanding more than 50 percent and the value of building contracts rising over 14 percent. Industrial growth for new capital investments for Alabama industry rose $100 million during Patterson's first year in office, then an all-time record, and more than 1,643 miles of county roads were under construction in all 67 counties, another record for the state. Patterson and Meriwether were able to save the state some $5 million dollars on the school building program through bond negotiations. "Governor Patterson will have some justification to punch in the nose the next guy who asks when he is going to start stopping up the holes in the bucket," wrote Bob Ingram of the *Alabama Journal*. The state launched an extensive airport construction program and continued developing Folsom's inland docks program at six major Alabama cities. Patterson and Earl McGowin also began "Good-Will Trade Missions" to the Caribbean and South and Central America to promote the Alabama State Docks at Mobile, which were earning a profit under McGowin's management.[3]

Just as the state was taking a turn toward prosperity, Patterson received his baptism into the modern civil rights movement. In early 1960 lunch counter sit-ins were staged by Alabama State University students in Montgomery. In late February a group of students sat in at the lunch counter of the Montgomery County courthouse, and Patterson threatened to have them expelled from school. Within a week, eager for a confrontation with state authorities, a crowd estimated at more than one thousand black university students demonstrated on the capitol steps. The previous night, Martin Luther King had encouraged the student body to protest until it turned "the Cradle of the Confederacy upside down."[4] Patterson, who was in Washington opposing Senate legislation to create federal voter registrars, was content to allow the State Board of Education to handle student dissent. He asked Alabama State University (ASU) president H. C. Trenholm to make the students "behave themselves and obey the law." But he had no intention of involving himself in the matter until a milkman from a local dairy appeared at the governor's office and asked to talk with him. Patterson agreed to see him after being told the man had important information about ASU.

The milkman told Patterson about a scam going on at the university's central cafeteria. He explained how the dairy truck unloaded part of the milk order at the cafeteria and then drove over to the cafeteria manager's house and unloaded the rest. Furthermore, the milkman told the governor, other suppliers were delivering their products under the same arrangement. Patterson asked State Investigator Willie Painter to look into the accusation; Painter, dressed as a milkman, rode the route to confirm what the governor had been told. Painter reported that indeed it was all true. (The dairy fired the milkman when the university identified the whistle-blower.) Patterson ordered an investigation of university operations and discovered that the cafeteria was running huge monthly deficits. Patterson said he also learned that the cafeteria was feeding hundreds of civil rights demonstrators. The investigation revealed other irregularities. Patterson claimed that the ASU registrar was holding more than fifty thousand dollars of student activity fees, in cash, in his desk drawer. He also said he felt the school had serious academic shortcomings. Patterson asked officials at the University of Alabama and Auburn University to put together a team to help ASU with its academic problems, "so they could get back to studying like a university." President Trenholm instituted disciplinary measures (some 150 students were not readmitted for the next quarter) and made extensive changes in the staff that resulted in numerous resignations.[5]

The investigation also revealed that Lawrence D. Reddick of Georgia, a professor of history, and a group of out-of-state students were the leaders of the demonstrations. The State Board of Education expelled nine students and put on probation twenty others who had sat in at the courthouse lunch counter. Nonetheless students and faculty generally ignored Trenholm's orders to stop participating in demonstrations. "They were using the university like some foreign countries use their universities, to organize turmoil and overthrow the government. I didn't think the state should be supporting that kind of activity," Patterson claimed. He asked Trenholm to fire Reddick but the ASU president refused.

Patterson then called a meeting of the State Board of Education, presided over it himself, and presented the results of the investigation. The board, which included three Patterson appointees, was reluctant to fire Reddick, but did so, in part because Patterson had invited the press to hold the board accountable. Later Trenholm, who was popular with the local white power structure, was relieved as president by the board because Patterson felt he had lost control of the university. Patterson was severely criticized for his role in the controversy, especially for Trenholm's dismissal. To many, Patterson's response was regarded as nothing more than an overtly racist overreaction, which considering Patterson's aggressive posture on segregation, was a credible interpretation.

Patterson made regular statements to the state media charging corruption at ASU and expressed misgivings about its academic integrity. In the end, there were two positive results from the controversy: Patterson's intervention did shake up the school's questionable academic practices, and the case of the nine expelled students went all the way to the U.S. Supreme Court, resulting in a landmark decision that required due process for students of higher education. Patterson later expressed regret over his involvement and surmised that, as with the Tuskegee boycott, he had been the biggest loser.[6]

Alabama State became the source of further legal difficulties after Martin Luther King's indictment on charges of falsifying his 1956 and 1958 state income tax returns. Chafing at King's ability to create unrest, Patterson suspected that King might be hiding income and personally reviewed his state income tax returns. When he discovered that King's income didn't match his lifestyle, Patterson said he saw an opportunity to "unhorse King" by getting a conviction that would send him to prison.

Patterson instructed an investigator from the State Revenue Department to go to the black-owned bank in Atlanta where King maintained his account and "bluff his way into getting King's financial records." Bank officials, who became flustered when the investigator flashed his credentials and demanded King's records, allowed him to examine them. The investigator found that King had accumulated more than sixty thousand dollars in unreported honorarium income. The bank called King to warn him about what was afoot and he quickly filed an amended state tax return and made the proper payment. Patterson wanted to prosecute anyway, contending that King was guilty of fraud. Alabama officials arrested King and brought him back to Montgomery for trial.

Fred Gray represented King in what he believed was the civil rights leader's most serious legal trouble. "If Dr. King were convicted," Gray wrote in his book *Bus Ride to Justice*, "this would . . . show that while leading thousands of African Americans in Alabama, and delivering his message of nonviolence around the world, Dr. King had been a dishonest man who had failed to properly report his income." The matter was further complicated when, in an effort to raise funds for King's legal defense, a group of civil rights activists placed a full-page advertisement in the *New York Times* that contained two false statements. The ad alleged that Montgomery police had herded four hundred ASU students into a wire stockade and hosed them down and that Governor Patterson had ordered the school cafeteria padlocked "to starve the students into submission." The ad was signed by such prominent people as Eleanor Roosevelt, Marlon Brando, and Harry Belafonte. Patterson responded angrily that the ad was "very inflammatory, malicious in its entirety and grossly misleading," and that King's case would be treated like any other citizen's: "He's got to pay his income taxes like anyone else." An *Advertiser* editorial called the ad, "Lies, Lies, Lies."

Montgomery police chief L. B. Sullivan filed a libel suit against the *Times* in Montgomery Circuit Court and won a five hundred thousand dollar judgment, which the newspaper appealed to the U.S. Supreme Court. Reacting to Sullivan's success, Patterson filed a million dollar libel suit, saying he would build a home for the elderly with the money. However when Sullivan lost his appeal, Patterson saw he had little chance with his suit and decided to settle out of court. The paper agreed to pay Patterson's legal fees of some seventeen thousand dollars and issue an apology for the erroneous advertisement. As for King's case, his attorneys argued that this was the first time anyone had been tried in Alabama on charges of perjury relating to state income tax evasion. King's legal team was shocked when an all-white jury in Montgomery, the Cradle of the Confederacy, found him not guilty.[7]

Spring 1960 held other interesting political diversions for Patterson. He and Sam Engelhardt attempted to put together a slate of Democratic Convention delegates pledged to Kennedy and began raising money for the campaign. By April, Kennedy had beaten Hubert Humphrey in Wisconsin and was headed into the West Virginia primary to confront the religion issue. By this time, Patterson, Meriwether, Engelhardt, and John Overton were delivering cash contributions in twenty-five thousand dollar chunks, according to Patterson.

When Kennedy won the West Virginia primary and it looked as if he could be the Democratic nominee for president, Patterson's attempts to form a slate of delegates to the convention found opposition immediately on the basis of Kennedy's religion and liberalism. Once again Patterson was in hot water with the state's electorate. A newspaper survey in the first week of April showed that of 107 convention candidates, only 3 favored Kennedy. The effort to raise a slate of Kennedy delegates was further hindered by opposition from the states' rights faction in the Alabama Democratic Party, customary Patterson allies.

Patterson said Kennedy was "so unpopular that we had to hide the fact that the delegates were committed to him." With Engelhardt's help, Patterson recruited people to run whose names began with A or B for ballot position and even found a truck driver from the Gadsden area named Frank M. Dixon, the same as the popular former governor. They also recruited "professional delegates," businessmen who were willing to trade votes in return for state business, and a few delegates agreed to vote for Kennedy in exchange for convention expenses. Patterson further accommodated delegates by using the state plane to ferry them to the convention in Los Angeles.

All the wheeling and dealing got Kennedy exactly fourteen of Alabama's thirty-six votes, but the state would cast the first vote in the roll call and start the nomination trend rolling—at least the Patterson team thought they would. When the convention opened, Patterson employed a buddy system to keep his slate of delegates in the fold. Some candidates used Hollywood starlets to sway delegates, but Lyndon Johnson's organization applied the most pressure, according to Patterson. It was a test of perseverance for him to keep his delegates, especially with the state press reporting how they were voting. Kennedy delegates received letters and phone calls from home criticizing them for supporting a Catholic.[8]

John Kennedy was as intrigued by his southern supporters as the southerners were by the beguiling New Englander. He had made speeches in Alabama, South Carolina, Arkansas, and Georgia to large and enthusiastic audiences. When key votes on civil rights came up in 1957, Kennedy twice joined the minority and made efforts to avoid committing himself fully on the issue. *Birmingham Post Herald* columnist John Temple Graves hailed him as "a novel personality capable of becoming the living antithesis of Earl Warren." Kennedy responded to Graves by saying he hoped that "a moderate philosophy on behalf of the national interest" would enable him to "feel a common bond with many southerners." When Kennedy announced his intention to run for president, he did not list civil rights as a major issues.

As convention time neared, Kennedy was asked by a newsman how he hoped to retain the support of ardent segregationists like Patterson and also win black support. He replied in perfect vacillation: "Well, Governor Patterson has announced his support of me, and as far as I know that support still stands. It seems to me the real question here is that if—I think I have made my views quite precise on civil rights. I hope I have." Patterson's endorsement endangered Kennedy's liberal, black support, and he once referred to it "as a millstone around my neck." However, he never repudiated his southern supporters, especially Patterson's. Sam Engelhardt said the Kennedy organization courted Patterson for well over a year, often accommodating his segregationist viewpoint. "They would make little remarks to try and convince us that they were not strong on civil rights," Engelhardt said. Kennedy's racial ambivalence was noted elsewhere in America. Those who watched Kennedy work his way through the system believed that he regarded civil rights as a strictly political issue and rarely did he display any determined principle on the subject. Victor Lasky wrote in *J.F.K.: The Man and The Myth* that Kennedy conceded that in civil rights matters he had the disadvantage of his environment, that "he had never known enough Negroes to know how they think." One black editor wrote that Kennedy was weak on civil rights for so long, that he wouldn't know a forthright statement on racial equality if it were dragged across his breakfast table.[9]

Kennedy went to Los Angeles knowing that he had not only significant southern support but also enough votes to win on the first ballot. Kennedy didn't need all of the Alabama votes. Bobby Kennedy instructed Patterson to cast only six of Alabama's votes on the first ballot instead of the entire fourteen; they were instructed to cast the remaining votes on a second ballot. Patterson said the delegates pledged to Kennedy turned surly and threatened to bolt to other candidates, but before the rebellion could develop Kennedy cinched the nomination on the first ballot with Wyoming's votes.[10]

According to Patterson, John Kennedy and other members of his family thanked him on several occasions for his support, and that fall Patterson joined Kennedy on campaign stops in the South. About two weeks before the election, Patterson became concerned that Richard Nixon was about to take credit for a secret mission that the Eisenhower administration had organized against Castro; he phoned Kennedy for a private meeting in New York. They met in Patterson's suite at the Barkley Hotel and Kennedy listened attentively to a firsthand account of a CIA plot to equip and train a force to invade Cuba. "If the invasion was a success," explained Patterson, "and Nixon used it in the campaign, I wanted Kennedy to be prepared to handle it." Patterson said Kennedy acknowledged the information, thanked him for bringing it to his attention, and accepted another large cash contribution for the campaign. During the final days of the campaign, Kennedy spoke of strengthening the "non-Batista democratic anti-Castro forces in exile." Nixon reacted angrily to the statement, thinking the CIA had revealed details of the invasion. Although Kennedy was given two general briefings on international issues by the CIA's John Foster Dulles, his organization insisted that they had learned about the invasion plan from their own sources. Obviously, Patterson was one of those sources.[11]

Patterson and the state of Alabama had become involved in the planned invasion when CIA officials approached Maj. Gen. George R. (Reid) Doster, commander of the Alabama Air National Guard, about assisting a U.S. government mission. The CIA was interested in Alabama Air National Guard pilots who flew old B-26 medium bombers, as state guard personnel had been cleared for security during earlier CIA projects. General Doster and a CIA official met with Patterson to obtain his approval for state participation in the project.

The CIA representative explained the plan to the governor and said Alabama personnel were wanted because they were more patriotic and would help maintain the required secrecy about the mission. "I asked him if Eisenhower knew about it, and when he told me he did, I agreed to allow the Alabama National Guard to help support the mission," Patterson explained. "After having been in World War II and the Korean War, I wasn't about to turn down an opportunity to fight communists in Cuba."

Patterson restricted the role of the guardsmen to training purposes and stipulated that no Alabama personnel would take part in the actual invasion. The CIA official agreed. Doster, who kept Patterson apprised of the operation's progress on his trips back and forth to the Guatemalan training site, told him in mid-October that "it could go down any time now." Patterson then went to New York and talked with Kennedy.[12]

The invasion did not take place that fall, but in April 1961, after Kennedy was president. The effort, doomed from the start, was further compromised by Kennedy's reluctance to allow more American force to aid the mission. Poor intelligence, an ill-planned beachhead, and a lack of support by the Cuban people made the disaster an embarrassment for the American government. Behind the scenes the Soviet Union threatened to aid Castro unless Kennedy halted the invasion; that could account for Kennedy's reluctance to provide air support. Doster was incensed by the CIA's bungling of the entire affair, which took the lives of four Alabamians. Kennedy went on television the day after the invasion and denied that Americans were involved.[13]

"It taught me a real lesson," Patterson said. "You can't let patriotism blind you in politics. I would never again be as eager to do something of that nature without thoroughly investigating it." He said everybody was running for cover when the mission failed and "nobody wanted to claim the men who had died down there." At a White House luncheon with Kennedy a few weeks afterward, the president told Patterson that some day he hoped to be able to do something for the Alabamians who died in the invasion, a hope that was never fulfilled.

Two years later, Sen. Everett Dirksen (R.-Ill.) conducted a one-man inquiry and for the first time announced publicly that four American pilots had been killed. The pilots were lost when the Alabama Air Guard flew the last mission over the beach in an attempt to support the landing after anti-Castro Cuban pilots refused to fly. Only then did Kennedy acknowledge that four Alabamians had been killed in a "volunteer flight." Widows of the pilots were cowed into silence when the CIA threatened to cut off monthly support checks sent by the agency as death benefits.[14]

In the spring of 1960, Patterson began a not-so-discreet affair with Tina Sawyers. Florentina (Tina) Brachert Sawyers was the buxom, stunning hostess at the Riviera Restaurant where Patterson and Joe Robertson often stopped for lunch. Patterson was friendly with owners Gus and Nick Polizos, who had supported his campaign for governor. "John became fond of Tina and we began eating there more often," Robertson said. "Tina would make a fuss over John when we would come in and he liked that." A relationship developed and Robertson said he began driving them to out-of-town liaisons.

Tina Sawyers, her husband, an air force sergeant, and their two daughters had arrived in town in 1959 when Sergeant Sawyers was transferred to Maxwell Air Force Base to manage the NCO Club. Sawyers had married Florentina Brachert in 1950 in Haunstetten, Augsburg, Germany, where he was then stationed. Tina was one of five children of Leonhardt and Florentina Brachert. Leonhardt, a design engineer who manufactured sports equipment, had been drafted and assigned to a Messerschmitt airplane factory during World War II. He had worked as an engineer on the German jet fighter in an underground factory near Fussen until the war ended. Leonhardt Brachert had resumed the operation of his sports equipment company when his twenty-year-old daughter married the American.

It is difficult to gauge the effect the relationship had on Patterson's political career. Mabel Amos said there was not a hint of the romance in the governor's daily routine; what she knew about their relationship came from talk around Montgomery. Charles Meriwether, staunchly loyal to Patterson, offered no opinion on the matter. On the other hand, Joe Robertson believed it hurt Patterson politically. Robertson said as the talk got around Montgomery, "the old biddies would come to the Riviera to eat and stare at Tina, and often she and her sister accompanied John on state trips." Robertson said he cautioned Patterson about the liabilities of the affair and did what he could to contain public exposure. "John just let his heart overcome his political judgment," Robertson said.

Gossip about the governor's affair eventually reached Mary Joe, but she chose not to confront her husband. At this point in their marriage she was accustomed to her husband's infidelities; in the past, there had been situations that threatened their relationship. The most serious was a period of several weeks in early 1954, when John returned to Germany to continue an affair begun during his second tour of duty with the army. Mary Joe said at the time she didn't believe he would ever return to Alabama. As she did in the past, she simply looked the other way when stories about the governor's girlfriend at the Riviera began sifting throughout Montgomery. The affair hurt and embittered Mary Joe Patterson; she remained in the marriage because of her love for John.[15]

The relationship with Tina Sawyers, which continued throughout Patterson's term in office, did some damage to his public image. But a far worse storm was approaching.

17
Freedom Riders Tarnish
Patterson Administration

Patterson's third year as governor began in grand style, with a whirlwind schedule of events celebrating the incoming Kennedy administration. The contrast between the staid, conservative Eisenhowers and the young and zestful Kennedys was remarkable, and the delegation from Alabama came like others to applaud a new era for the Democratic Party.

Patterson took some thirty people to Washington for the inauguration as he felt they had had a part in Kennedy's election. John and Mary Joe Patterson stayed at the Shoreham Hotel, attending parties and receptions as a snowstorm paralyzed the capital. At a reception Kennedy hosted for Medal of Honor winners and state governors, the president-elect had bittersweet news for Patterson: "I'm going to take Charlie away from you." Turning to Meriwether, Kennedy shook his hand and said, "I'm happy to know that you're coming up here and will be on board with us."[1]

Months earlier, Steve Smith had called and said the Kennedy administration would have a place for Meriwether, suggesting either an undersecretary position or a directorship at the Export-Import Bank. Kennedy was forthright in paying his political debts. After the campaign he asked Patterson what federal appointments he wanted. Patterson discussed possible appointments with Meriwether and Sam Engelhardt and proposed three positions that he would like to name: the customs agent for the Port of Mobile; the farmers home administrator for the state; and the Treasury Department's bond sales agent for Alabama. The three posts were significant positions that Patterson wanted to fill with supporters to help him organize the state for Kennedy's reelection in 1964.

Kennedy instructed Patterson to prepare dossiers on the three appointments and send them to the White House, a request Patterson interpreted as a gesture of at least partial agreement. Months later when the appointments were announced, much to Patterson's dismay not one of his nominees was chosen. Angered at being ignored, he flew to Washington and met with Kennedy only to learn that Alabama's congressional delegation had made the appointments. The president left it to his campaign director, Larry O'Brien, and to Alabama senator John Sparkman to explain why it was necessary for the administration to use federal patronage to help his programs in Congress. "Not one member of the Alabama delegation campaigned for Kennedy, and we had taken all kinds of heat for him on this religion thing for over a year," Patterson said. "It made me mad as hell."

The disappointment was offset somewhat by Kennedy's earlier promise to lend his support to the proposed Tennessee-Tombigbee Waterway. During the campaign, Kennedy sent Patterson a telegram confirming his pledge to include funds for the project if elected; the message was copied and sent to political operatives across the state and included in Democratic newspaper advertisements. Kennedy was assassinated before he could deliver on his promise to start funding the project. Pres. Richard Nixon signed the Tenn-Tom measure into law in October 1970.[2]

Whatever anger and frustration Patterson experienced over Kennedy's appointments was soothed to a great extent by Meriwether's nomination as one of five directors of the Export-Import Bank in Washington. The move was instantly labeled as a political payoff by the press—which it was. The *Montgomery Advertiser* wrote that "Kennedy owed Patterson and Meriwether much—they volunteered and fought all the way for Kennedy. And Kennedy paid off his pals in unflinching Truman style." John Temple Graves said Kennedy had been ashamed to acknowledge Patterson's support, but "now lets the governor name a friend for a job." Probably the most distorted allegation was made by national columnist Drew Pearson, who wrote that Patterson "demanded Charlie Meriwether's selection to the Export-Import Bank, where he would be in charge of loans to African Negro republics." Meriwether, contrary to Pearson's claim, was given oversight of Far Eastern loans.[3]

Meriwether's nomination caused the most bitter debate of all Kennedy appointees and was the subject of two full days of hearings before the Senate Banking Committee. Senators Wayne Morse (D-Oreg.) and Jacob Javits (R-N.Y.), the most vocal opponents, sifted through FBI reports seeking incriminating information to sabotage the nomination. Jewish support in Alabama and business contacts in New York eventually convinced Javits to back off from his opposition. Meriwether was not at all ruffled by the opposition, which he interpreted as an attack on southern racial attitudes. He told the committee that he favored segregation in Alabama, but he didn't "care a hoot in Washington." Back home, the *Advertiser* said the attacks didn't bother Meriwether because he had the hide of a rhinoceros.[4]

The Senate Banking Committee approved Meriwether's nomination by a slim 5–4 margin and sent it to the full Senate for confirmation. Charges of anti-Semitism and racism were brought against Meriwether, and Senator Morse made undocumented charges of alcoholism and a police record. Alabama senator John Sparkman accused Morse of McCarthyism, setting off a shouting duel in Senate chambers between the two men.

Kennedy remained firm in support of Meriwether in the face of fierce antisouthern opposition. The Senate voted for confirmation 67 to 18. At a news conference shortly after the vote, the president expressed confidence in Meriwether: "I informed the Senate that I looked over Mr. Meriwether's FBI record before I sent it to the Senate. Mr. Meriwether is now a member of the Export-Import Bank, confirmed by the Senate by a rather large figure, and I am confident he will do a good job."[5]

Meriwether's move to Washington was a severe loss to Patterson; his extensive political experience had been an asset since Albert's death. Patterson, who trusted Meriwether without reservation, had seen his fortunes skyrocket under Meriwether's guidance. Some in the state saw Meriwether as a kingmaker manipulating Patterson behind the scenes, but both men are quick to dispel that notion. "John was his own man, despite what some of the politicos have said," Meriwether asserted. "Sometimes he took my advice and sometimes he didn't, but the decisions he made were his own and not mine." Meriwether remained in Washington for five years, well into the Johnson administration before he resigned and returned to Alabama. Maurice Patterson served the remaining two years as finance director for Alabama.[6]

Meriwether's move to the nation's capital occurred at a critical time for Patterson, although neither of them could have foreseen it. The courts were striking down Jim Crow laws in state after state: Virginia failed in its massive resistance effort; Arkansas was overwhelmed by federal forces in Little Rock; and in January 1961, the University of Georgia went through court-ordered integration and a series of campus riots. Patterson, his legal adviser Ralph Smith Jr., and Attorney General MacDonald Gallion knew that Alabama would be confronted with the same crisis even though the NAACP, which was spearheading integration suits elsewhere, had no official status in Alabama.[7]

Patterson and Smith, preparing for Alabama's expected legal fight, had begun seeking scientific data to substantiate their defense of segregated education. They set out to develop an argument based on the premise that there were differences between the races in learning patterns and social behavior that made separate schools better for both races. In Reed Surratt's *Ordeal of Desegregation,* Smith explained the position: "It was my feeling, and one shared by Governor Patterson, that he should explore every avenue in our efforts to preserve racial segregation. I think that many people in the South sincerely believe that the mental capacity of the Negro is inferior to that of a white, yet these same people think that science has proven to the contrary. Actually, scientific data supports the contention that the white race, intellectually, is superior to the Negro, and that is the point we seek to make with this study."[8]

Patterson had a slightly different rationale for the search for justification of the state's segregated school system. "I was looking for evidence that because of learning and social differences, a segregated school environment would be more conducive at that time to each race getting an education." Later he stressed that the study had nothing to do with racial inferiority.

Smith contacted Frank Rose, president of the University of Alabama, and asked if the university faculty could conduct a study of the mental, sociological, and psychological capabilities of blacks and whites. No contracts were signed, but the sociology department agreed to do the study and the governor's office offered to pay the university ten thousand dollars. Smith was referred to Charles D. McGlamery, chairman of the sociology department, and informed the professor that the purpose of the study was to show the superiority of the white race. McGlamery, a young, idealistic PhD, was "shocked by the request because the conclusion was predetermined and not demonstrable by a scientific study." He told Smith the sociology department would do a study for the governor's office but not on those conditions. At odds about how the study should be structured, McGlamery refused to cooperate with the project and Smith was forced to look elsewhere.⁹

Smith's search landed him at Columbia University in New York City, where he learned that a retired professor in North Carolina had a manuscript that made some general genetic and social behavioral comparisons of blacks and whites, but was unable to get it published. Smith journeyed to Chapel Hill and made arrangements with Wesley Critz George, retired professor of embryology and former head of the Department of Anatomy at the University of North Carolina Medical School, to publish his work as a scientific document. Compiling studies of some forty-one scholars worldwide in the field of genetics and anthropology, and others in related disciplines, George claimed that blacks were intellectually inferior, that criminality among blacks was higher than among whites, and that the Negro brain was smaller than the brain of white people. George contended that the Supreme Court had deprived Americans of "their right to a firm foundation of truth" in the Brown decision. The study provided the kind of scientific support that Patterson and Smith were looking for. They had a thousand copies published at a cost of five thousand dollars. George was given most of the copies for distribution to university libraries around the country and Patterson passed out the remainder in Alabama. "I approached Dr. Rose about giving George a job at the university, but he turned me down," Patterson said. "He said the whole sociology department would quit if he did that."

Patterson and Smith thought they had what they needed to confront the federal government in an integration case: "We had the scientific data to carry to the U.S. Supreme Court. Ralph Smith and I looked forward to putting the Supreme Court in a position of saying that the study wasn't true, after they had based much of the Brown decision on Gunnar Myrdal's theory. We had no illusions of winning; we just wanted some substantial information to argue the case." Myrdal, a Swedish scholar, had published an influential study, *An American Dilemma*, contending that intelligence develops through experience and socialization and not genetics. But the anticipated confrontation never took place, although Patterson continued to "sock the tar baby" as Ray Jenkins, then reporting for the *Advertiser*, dubbed the governor's segregationist efforts. "John Patterson couldn't resist the old Southern temptation to sock the tar baby.

He . . . kept up the racial game." Jenkins felt that Patterson got caught up in an absolutely hopeless situation.[10]

But the "racial game" didn't seem hopeless to Patterson as he turned to legislative duties in May 1961, the same week that astronaut Alan Shepard rode a rocket 302 miles into space. His report to the second session of the biennial legislature contained references to their previous accomplishments, including a balanced budget and a surplus in the state treasury. Patterson then approached the Alabama legislature with the most sensitive subject that they would face during his term—redrawing legislative districts—reminding legislators that there had been no reapportionment since the adoption of the 1901 Alabama Constitution. Patterson said, "The continuous failure of the Legislature to reapportion itself now makes it possible for about 28 percent of the people of Alabama to elect a majority of the members of both houses."[11]

The move was a bold one according to Patterson: "The drive for reapportionment was a very liberal view for the time." Patterson, after gaining virtually everything he asked for during the first legislative session, felt he had nothing to lose by forcing the issue. "I just believed in it. The people in Birmingham and North Alabama just didn't have any voice in state government. We had to fight the Black Belters—who were strictly conservative—for everything we got." Some sixteen counties in the sparsely populated Black Belt controlled a majority of the votes in the legislature.[12] Patterson's initial proposal for the Alabama legislative dilemma was to expand the districts to 120 House seats and 40 seats in the Senate. The strategy behind the proposal was to force a greater distribution of power, breaking up the Black Belt system that controlled the legislature. Neither the public nor the legislature showed much enthusiasm for the plan and it died of neglect.

Continuing to push for legislation, Patterson pointed out "a flagrant abuse of the legislative process," where population imbalances had some state representatives with as few as seven thousand constituents in their districts, while others represented as many as a hundred thousand. With legislators reluctant to correct the unbalanced districts, the issue went to the federal courts, which ruled in *Sims v. Frink* that primary elections could not be held with large population imbalances. Forced into a corner, the legislature drew up two plans for the 1962 elections to be submitted to the federal courts for review.[13]

The problem of equitable legislative representation in the state legislature was accompanied by another similar issue. The 1960 national census revealed that while the state had gained population, it was not enough to keep nine congressmen in Washington; Alabama had to reduce its congressional delegation to eight. Patterson said he didn't have a structured approach about how to eliminate a sitting congressman and the congressional delegation couldn't agree on a plan. Patterson said the solution was provided by former governor Frank Dixon. "Governor Dixon paid a call to my office with the suggestion about the '9–8 Plan,'" where all the congressmen would run at large with the low vote-getter being eliminated. Dixon also proposed that the next legislative session would redraw the lines for eight congressional districts. The idea was accepted by all parties concerned as a fair approach to the problem.

Dixon's 9–8 plan meant congressional candidates had to campaign statewide. In the elections Frank Boykin of Mobile was eliminated, partly as the result of his much publicized involvement in a Maryland savings and loan scandal. The issue of district lines had not been resolved by the time the Wallace administration came to power, and Alabama's congressional delegation had to run statewide a second time in 1964. Carl Elliott of Jasper was forced out by the state's conservatives and segregationists. Sample ballots marked with Wallace's slogan "Stand Up For Alabama" were distributed throughout the state; Elliot's name was omitted from the sample ballot.[14]

In May 1961, while the Alabama legislature filibustered over reapportioning legislative districts, a true crisis was in the making: freedom riders were on their way to Alabama. The Congress of Racial Equality (CORE) had recruited thirteen people to take an integrated journey south to demonstrate that southern bus terminals were violating the nondiscrimination provisions of the National Motor Carrier Act of 1935. Their trip began in Washington, D.C., on May 4, the same day the legislature met for its second session, and encountered only minor resistance as the riders attempted to use terminal restrooms and lunch counters in Virginia and the Carolinas. On Mother's Day, May 14, the thirteen freedom riders divided into two groups to travel from Atlanta to Birmingham, one riding Greyhound and the other Trailways. The only scheduled stop was late morning in Anniston, Alabama.[15]

Patterson and Public Safety Director Floyd Mann, aware that the freedom riders would eventually come through Alabama, anxiously tracked their progress through newspaper stories. By the time the riders got to Atlanta the story was a headline event. Mann sent Eli L. Cowling to Atlanta to ride the bus and monitor the riders' conversation with sophisticated listening devices. "We wanted to know what their plans were so we would be prepared for trouble," Mann explained. Cowling stationed himself on the Greyhound bus with the riders and headed toward Alabama.

The Kennedy administration didn't want the rides to continue any more than the southerners did. President Kennedy was preparing for a summit meeting with Soviet Premier Nikita Khrushchev in Vienna when the rides began. He called Harris Wofford, the administration's point man on civil rights, and angrily ordered him to "Stop them! Get your friends off those buses!" Kennedy didn't want to be embarrassed in front of the Russians. Attorney General Bobby Kennedy wasn't even aware the rides were under way.[16]

A crowd made up primarily of Klansmen lay in wait at Anniston's downtown terminal. Some two hundred men exploded into mob violence when the bus arrived. Cowling stood motionless and silent in the door of the bus as the enraged rabble beat the vehicle with clubs and slashed the tires, taunting the riders with shouts of "communists" and "Heil Hitler." No law enforcement officer was on the scene to control the violence, and the driver sped away unaware that the tires were seriously damaged. The crowd gave chase in a caravan of forty cars until the bus limped off the highway with flat tires about four miles west of Anniston. Once again the mob went to work, smashing windows with chains and clubs and tossing in a fire bomb to flush the riders out.

The freedom riders owed their lives to Cowling's protection, according to Floyd Mann. The Alabama state investigator opened the door with his pistol drawn and blocked the entrance into the bus. "If Cowling had not been on that bus everybody would have been burned to death," Mann said. Alerted by passing motorists, the highway patrol arrived and scattered the angry crowd by firing several shots into the air, but not before the riders had been severely beaten by the mob. A picture of the burning bus flashed across the nation and around the world.[17]

The following week racial violence in Alabama was the subject of an avalanche of news stories as world attention turned to the plight of the freedom riders trying to make their way across the South. Birmingham police commissioner Eugene "Bull" Connor arrested the entire group after local Klansmen had beaten them a second time. The *Birmingham News,* in an attempt to help identify the assailants, published front-page pictures of rioters attacking the riders. When federal authorities became involved, Governor Patterson and President Kennedy reverted to their regional positions. Robert Kennedy huddled with Justice Department officials Burke Marshall and John Seigenthaler about how to get the freedom riders safely out of Alabama. Seigenthaler met the "sad befuddled group" at the Birmingham airport and helped get them on a plane to New Orleans. In the meantime another group had formed in Nashville to take up the journey at Birmingham. Seigenthaler tried without success to head them off; instead he found himself assigned to trying to ensure their safe conduct through Alabama.[18]

As the freedom riders headed toward Montgomery, what neither federal nor state authorities knew was that the FBI and the Birmingham Police Department had been involved in the Birmingham attack. The truth would not be made public until years later. In 1980 the *New York Times* published two articles written by native Alabamian Howell Raines detailing the contents of a Justice Department report that said the FBI "knew about and apparently covered up involvement in violent attacks on blacks, civil rights activists, and journalists by its chief paid informant inside the Ku Klux Klan." The 302-page report said that of the hundreds of militant segregationists waiting for the CORE bus to arrive, Gary Thomas Rowe Jr. was "one of the handful [who were] most responsible for the violence at the bus station." Investigators detailed Rowe's role in beating blacks, photographers, and reporters during the Birmingham mob scene.

Rowe, who was recruited to infiltrate the local Klan, did "missionary work" (his term for perpetrating violence against blacks) for six years with the Klan while reporting to the FBI. Rowe said he had "complete access" to the files of Lt. Tom Cook of the Birmingham Police Department, the intelligence officer for the force. He also said Police Commissioner "Bull" Connor promised the Klan fifteen minutes with the freedom riders at the bus station before moving in, and police deliberately avoided arresting Klansmen. Rowe said he notified the FBI about the plan three weeks prior to the attack.

Klan leader Robert Shelton said he heard rumors of the planned attack on the riders but denied that his organization was involved. He said that Rowe, who for a time served as his bodyguard, "fantasized" about his role in the Klan and was a "lying dog all the way through." Justice Department investigators uncovered messages in bureau files in Birmingham corroborating Rowe's testimony that FBI director J. Edgar Hoover was informed of the attack well in advance. One message quoted Bull Connor as saying that he wanted the riders beaten until "it looked like a bulldog got a hold of them." Hoover chose not to inform federal or state authorities about the threat and took no action within his organization to prevent it, saying that the FBI was an investigating body not a police body. Patterson said violence and embarrassment to the state could have been avoided if Hoover had notified the proper authorities.[19]

Protecting the freedom riders was further complicated as neither Alabama authorities nor the Justice Department believed they were responsible for protecting the activists. Both believed their presence would intrude on the role of local law enforcement and only if local authorities obviously could not or would not provide adequate protection could they intervene. "At that point in time," Public Safety Director Floyd Mann explained, "the Highway Patrol didn't go into areas where we were not invited. We let the city and county authorities handle their own matters." Patterson said intervention on his part would have been disastrous. "Had I intervened directly and forcefully in the police affairs of Birmingham and Montgomery, they would have dumped the whole thing on me, disappeared from the scene, worked against me, and given me all the blame. We were trying to make them do their duty."[20]

Nevertheless Patterson and Mann began making preparations to maintain order should the state be forced to protect the freedom riders. Both contend that after the Anniston violence, they monitored the riders on a minute-by-minute basis and started riot control training with selected Alabama National Guard units; state troopers were given similar training at Gunter Air Force Base. By the time the second bus departed Birmingham for Montgomery, preparations were complete and included an emergency communications system. "There was never any fear on my part that we couldn't handle the situation," Patterson explained. "I would have filled every jail in Alabama before I would have let that thing get out of control." The plan did not come too soon. The federal authorities, especially the U.S. attorney general Robert Kennedy, were taking a new interest in the freedom riders.[21]

Robert Kennedy had an angry confrontation with company officials over dispatching another bus to continue the rides: "Somebody better get

in the damn bus and get it going and get those people on their way. . . .
We have gone to a lot of trouble to see that they get to take this trip and I
am most concerned to see that it is accomplished." Media accounts of the
conversation convinced southerners that the administration was sponsor-
ing the riders, when actually the Kennedys had tried to stop them. In his
study of the conflict, historian J. Mills Thornton said that throughout
the freedom rider crisis the Kennedy administration was reluctant to intervene: "Both John and Robert Kennedy felt a strong political obligation
to Governor Patterson, and they were loath to do anything that would
put him in a bad light." He suggested that the Kennedys felt beholden
because Patterson had been one of the first public figures to endorse Kennedy's campaign for president.[22]

But communications between Patterson and Robert Kennedy were quickly
falling apart. "I was getting calls from him about every other day," Patterson said, "and we weren't exactly friendly with one another to begin with.
He had a hard time getting Greyhound to put another bus into service for
the riders, and he kept calling me, sometimes in the middle of the night at
the mansion, to talk about it." During the calling and negotiations with
Robert Kennedy, Patterson kept up his public defense of segregation with
statements about how agitators were finding out that Alabama was not
the Congo. He claimed that the freedom riders were communist inspired
and their ride "timed to embarrass us abroad."

The fate of the freedom riders continued in limbo until the late afternoon of May 19, when President Kennedy attempted to reach Patterson
by telephone. The first time the president called, Patterson had his secretary tell Kennedy that he was out; a few minutes later Kennedy called
back and Patterson instructed her to tell the president that he was out
on the Gulf fishing. Kennedy then placed a call to Lt. Gov. Albert Boutwell, who was upstairs in the capitol presiding over the Senate. Boutwell
hurried downstairs in a state of excitement over Kennedy's call. "Boutwell was absolutely flabbergasted that I wouldn't talk to the president.
He didn't know that I had been talking to Robert Kennedy about the
situation for an entire week." Patterson explained to Boutwell that he
had been expecting the phone call for days and knew what the president wanted. "He called to ask me if I could guarantee the protection of
these people," said Patterson. "If I said no, then he would send in federal
forces. If I said yes, and something happened to them then he would use

it as an excuse to send in federal people also. It was a no-win situation for me." Ralph Smith said, "Patterson was incensed because he felt the Kennedys were putting him in the ridiculous position of having to protect Alabama's troublemakers. The president was trying to make him responsible for the actions of outside agitators." Patterson said he was also angry because the Kennedys were treating him as if he were a "vassal" of the federal government.

Patterson said he could have guaranteed the safety of the freedom riders if they had agreed to the state's terms of protection. "These people didn't come down here for the purpose of testing interstate travel accommodations. They came here to go out into the community and cause trouble for publicity. It's difficult to guarantee that they wouldn't be molested rambling all over town." The riders had made a number of appearances in Birmingham while they waited for the journey to continue.[23]

The Kennedys pressed Charlie Meriwether into service to try to influence Patterson. Meriwether was traveling through the Atlanta airport on a return trip from Florida to Washington when the plane was called back as it prepared to taxi onto the runway. He was asked to go to the nearest phone where Robert Kennedy was waiting: "If you can get into Montgomery and get anything done, we'd appreciate it," Kennedy asked him. Meriwether flew directly to Montgomery and went to see Patterson. "I told John that regardless of how bad he thought the situation was in Alabama, we were getting a bad image across the nation. I didn't try to tell him what to do, just how it was hurting the state." Patterson listened and asked Meriwether to sit in on some of the meetings.

Behind the scenes, Patterson negotiated with federal authorities to ease the crisis. "John was extremely worried about the situation," Meriwether said. "I think he did everything he thought was right, considering the fact that the public expected him to resist this thing. After all, he told them he would." Mann said the governor stayed on the phone or in meetings during his waking hours trying to deal with the freedom rider conflict, while at the same time keeping tabs on the Alabama legislature in session upstairs in the capitol. Mary Joe Patterson said her husband was entirely consumed by what was happening to the state; he slept fitfully at nights and was more than a little irritable with the family and staff. While he maintained the familiar segregationist rhetoric that played so well publicly, he also fussed and fought with federal officials in an attempt to resolve the problem.

When the freedom riders finally left for Montgomery, Floyd Mann placed sixteen Alabama State Highway Patrol cars in front of the bus and sixteen behind it. A state surveillance plane flew up and down the ninety-mile route, and guards monitored the trip from overpasses. Before the bus left, Patterson met with John Seigenthaler to discuss protection for the freedom riders. Patterson assured Seigenthaler that he had the means and the desire to protect citizens and visitors on state highways, but "I'm not going to say that I'm going to protect a bunch of goddamn foreign trouble-makers who come in here to stir up trouble." Seigenthaler called Robert Kennedy in Patterson's presence and conveyed the message that the state would provide safe passage of the bus to Montgomery, and he believed the governor was sincere about his commitment. When the bus left, Patterson issued a double-edged statement to the press promising "to protect visitors and others on the highways" while making heated comments about trouble-making outsiders.[24]

Montgomery police chief L. B. Sullivan assured Patterson and Mann that local law enforcement would handle the situation once the bus arrived, so the state dropped its massive escort at the city limits. Reliance on Montgomery police protection was a mistake, especially in light of incidents in Anniston and Birmingham. "We heard later that Sullivan gave the Klan fifteen minutes before he came in," Patterson said. An angry mob of about one thousand whites was waiting at the bus station. Soon clothes and suitcases were flying through the air as the crowd assaulted the new group of riders while, for the third time, the local police looked the other way. The manager of the bus terminal locked the door to his office and refused to answer the telephone.

The riders were attacked with fists, clubs, sticks, and pipes as they attempted to get off the bus. Seigenthaler recalled that "the bus terminal looked like an anthill; people crawling, shouting, just a constant movement; people running, pushing, shoving, fighting to get in on these freedom riders who had just gotten off the bus." Floyd Mann had seventy-five state troopers stationed nearby, "in anticipation that the Montgomery police weren't going to do their job." Mann and his assistant Bill Jones waded into the mob with drawn pistols, straddling downed riders and ordering the mob to release newsmen they were beating. Seigenthaler, who was savagely clubbed when he tried to help one of the female riders escape, was hospitalized with a serious head injury. When the Montgomery police did arrive, they began directing traffic. As order was being restored,

Mann, Jones, and Tommy Giles, Patterson's photographer, helped get the wounded to the hospital using a state car. Federal officials near the terminal merely acted as observers. FBI agents were seen around the perimeter of the riot taking notes. John Doar, from the Justice Department, was on the phone in the U.S. attorney's office nearby; watching from a window, he reported on the melee at the bus station to Robert Kennedy in Washington. Kennedy immediately ordered Deputy Attorney General Byron "Whizzer" White to mobilize U.S. marshals and get them to Alabama as quickly as possible. By nightfall, some six hundred federal marshals had assembled at Gunter Air Force Base in Montgomery.[25]

Patterson was predictably outraged by what he believed was an "unwanted and unneeded" invasion of federal forces. He also saw the federal position as encouraging strife. "Now the federal government comes in here and illegally interferes in a domestic situation they themselves helped to create." Two hundred federal agents patrolled the hospital where the freedom riders were taken by state police (ambulances were not available for the beaten riders), and a group of marshals escorted Martin Luther King into the city. Patterson and Robert Kennedy argued over the phone about who would take responsibility for King's safety.

Another crisis developed at the First Baptist Church when King addressed a mass rally in support of the riders. Federal marshals ringed the church as a mob of several thousand whites surrounded it, their threats and cursing audible inside the hot, crowded building. At the Justice Department, Burke Marshall listened to a round of telephone calls to Byron White, to King inside the church, and to Patterson in the governor's office. "Dr. King was very upset," Marshall said, "panicky you might say, about this mob outside." King thought they were going to burn down the church. Local radio and television stations pleaded with people not to go to the church, but the pleas only increased the size of the mob with latecomers and curious bystanders.

King had reason to fear the throng of angry whites. They had already burned a car belonging to Virginia Durr, who years before had accompanied E. D. Nixon to get Rosa Parks out of jail, and were prepared to do the same to the black church. Tom Posey, Patterson's personal aide, was reporting on the scene from a pay telephone booth (Patterson said the mob sounded like a swarm of bees from his office); Floyd Mann had positioned himself with about one hundred state troopers in a nearby school yard. Again, the Montgomery police merely watched from a distance as the mob turned violent and started throwing stones and bottles at the federal marshals. The marshals, many of whom had been pressed into service from ordinary desk jobs, shrank back from the violence, and the mob charged. No match for the crazed whites, the marshals scattered as some of the mob battled their way up to the front door of the church before Mann's troopers stopped them. As Posey described the scene to Patterson, the governor called out the specially trained units of the Alabama National Guard and quickly regained control. Patterson declared "limited" martial law and within minutes soldiers with bayoneted weapons patrolled Alabama's capital. The legal documents had been prepared in advance. Patterson insisted he never lost control of the situation: "My order to them from the beginning was to do everything possible to maintain law and order and protect people and property."[26]

Robert Kennedy called the governor's mansion soon after the National Guard secured the city and was met by a furious outburst from Patterson: "I told him: Now you got what you wanted; you got yourself a fight; and you've got the National Guard called out and martial law, and that's what you wanted. We'll take charge of it now with the troops, and you can get on out and leave it alone." In Washington, the administration saw the riot as a breakdown in law enforcement and President Kennedy issued a statement: "I call upon the governor and other responsible state authorities in Alabama . . . to exercise their lawful authority to prevent any further outbreaks of violence." The U.S. Justice Department got Judge Frank M. Johnson to issue injunctions against the KKK, the States' Rights Party, and others who had tried to stop the bus rides. On Sunday morning, Patterson, Floyd Mann, McDonald Gallion, and other state officials, met with Byron White and explained their frustration at dealing with "trained teams of agitators." A seething Patterson asked for whatever information the federal authorities had on the freedom riders to determine if any of them were communist or "of the persuasion." White could not assure the governor that the information would be available to the state, which further convinced Patterson that the federal government was involved in the matter.

During Byron White's three-day visit, the telephone operator at the federal installation transmitted to the governor summaries of all White's telephone conversations with Robert Kennedy and the president. Patterson readily acknowledged the covert reports. The first one he received from the telephone operator concerned White's initial phone call to the president, during which White reported that everything was under control in Alabama. He told President Kennedy that the federal troops sent to quell trouble over the freedom riders could be recalled. The troops remained in Montgomery.

When the freedom riders left the capital, a large contingent of heavily armed Alabama State Troopers escorted them to the Mississippi state line. The conflict did serious damage to the state's public image and to Patterson's political career. Patterson's anger was fueled by the recognition that he had been caught in an uncompromising contest between the state and federal government. His posture as a defiant, anti-integration stalwart made his involvement in the crisis a disaster. The *Montgomery Advertiser,* which called the freedom riders "slobbering trash," felt that the governor had been too virulent and ran an editorial entitled "The Governor of Alabama a Mob Leader?" While he had the public support of Alabama's congressional delegation and other southern governors rallied behind him as did the majority of Alabamians, in the end, local law enforcement was allowed far too much leeway in dealing with events. On the other hand, administration sources said it would have been an extremely unpopular political move for the state to seize control of local affairs prematurely. Press Secretary Harry Cook said Patterson didn't want to intervene unless local law enforcement broke down. Patterson's position as an intransigent segregationist limited both his political will and moral authority to use state power to maintain order. Some of his anger likely sprang from his realization that he had cornered himself.[27]

Robert Kennedy said the president was "fed up" with Patterson and with the freedom riders, both of whom did enormous political damage to the administration, in a region where they had been moderately popular just two years earlier. It is difficult to assess exactly what the Kennedys expected of Patterson. While they viewed him as someone with whom they were friendly, the Kennedys did not see Patterson as a political ally, according to Ted Sorensen. But it can be surmised that they believed Patterson could be persuaded to accommodate federal responsibility and lend his leadership in controlling Alabama's racist element. The historian and Kennedy authority Arthur Schlesinger Jr. remembered "that both John and Robert Kennedy were disappointed by Governor Patterson's performance during the Freedom Riders crisis."[28]

The error, in Patterson's later analysis of events, was to ignore President Kennedy's call: "When they said the president was calling me, I didn't take the call because I knew what the call was about." Patterson later considered that it was a final appeal by the president to take decisive action to quell the racial controversy before federal marshals were sent into Montgomery. Whether the president's personal appeal to Patterson would have made a difference can only be left to speculation, but Patterson believed that his refusal to take the call "was one of the biggest mistakes I ever made."

Floyd Mann's leadership under trying circumstances was noted by state and federal authorities and the press. Patterson relied on Mann's considerable law enforcement expertise, and federal authorities, particularly Justice Department officials, regarded him as competent and cooperative in controlling mob violence. Schlesinger described him as "a man of courage," and numerous historians took care to detail his instincts for managing the crisis. Major newspapers in Alabama were prompt in reporting that Mann's personal valor probably kept numerous beatings by Klansmen, including of national newsmen, from becoming murders,. At one point, Robert Kennedy attempted to use Mann and Gen. Henry Graham to circumvent Patterson's authority. Patterson said when he discovered what the attorney general was attempting to do, he threatened to fire both men if they "violated my instructions." Kennedy checked to see if the governor indeed had such authority; he did.[29]

The Kennedy administration was shaken by black demands for immediate redress of the inequities of the century-old segregation problem and called for a "cooling off" period following the freedom rides. Black leaders were openly suspicious when the Kennedys advised them to concentrate their energy on voter registration, a less confrontational method of advancing their cause. Alabama remained in a state of racial agitation for months, its public image badly tarnished by a week of violence in May.

For Patterson, the remainder of his third year as governor mirrored his determination to continue developing administration programs, despite the explosive drama of the freedom rides. In September, he called the legislature back into special session to enact general appropriations bills and saw the final passage of congressional redistricting in time for the fall elections. In the process he defended troublesome Jefferson County when the Alabama legislature attempted to divide the county and place it in four different congressional districts.

On a lighter side, Patterson's old friend Hugh Sparrow of the *Birmingham News* began reporting monthly mansion expenses, just as he did during Folsom's spendthrift administration. And when there was not any hard news, Sparrow would sit in Patterson's anteroom with pad and pencil and simply write down the names of his visitors. Then, in his Sunday column, he would comment on all the people who saw the governor that week. "It would make some people mad as hell to have their name connected with a visit to the governor's office," Patterson said. "Many of them would leave if Sparrow was sitting in the waiting room."[30]

John Patterson said he received a lot of correspondence supporting his clash with the freedom riders, most of it lauding his firmness in dealing with federal authorities. He knew things would never be the same after what happened in the spring.

Scandal Spoils Patterson's Big Finish

Alabama's constitution at the time did not permit a governor to succeed himself in office, so Patterson was looking ahead to a return to office in 1966. With his mind fixed on reelection in four years, John Patterson said he set about to protect the administration as much as possible during his final year. "I believed that my chances for a second term were good, if I didn't accept the lame duck role passively or allow the upcoming governor's race to upstage the accomplishments of the administration." In early January, Patterson launched an eight-point program to keep his political program visible and viable during the campaign season, which included an avalanche of Wallace demagoguery.

"As naive as it was," Patterson said, "I planned to run again from the very beginning. I wanted to get through the last session of the legislature with as little controversy as possible, and have an efficient administration." His plans were in place by late 1961, when Ralph Smith resigned to set up law offices in Montgomery where Patterson would join him at the end of his term. John and Mary Joe shopped for a new home, purchasing an elegant, five-bedroom mansion in preparation for their return to private life. The acquisition of the new house, the formation of the law practice, and the celebration of eight years of public service made the prospects of continued success seem entirely realistic for the Patterson family. All that remained was for him to finish his term without serious damage, remain politically active for the next four years amid the Wallace furor, and position himself as the top contender for 1966 when Wallace in turn would be ineligible.[1]

There were good reasons for his belief that another term as governor was possible. The administration had overcome staggering economic problems and made significant improvements in the state's stagnant business climate and financial strength. Industrial, construction, employment, trade, finance, and agricultural sectors of the state were showing impressive annual increases. Alabama's business environment improved substantially and Patterson reported industrial growth of almost fifty thousand new jobs, representing business investments of $663 million. No preceding governor had seen that kind of economic growth in one administration. On the negative side, Patterson's involvement with the Kennedys hurt him, while the freedom rider episode reinforced his reputation as a die-hard segregationist.[2]

To the surprise of many, Big Jim Folsom opened the 1962 gubernatorial race by qualifying for a third term. In the waning months of his second disastrous administration, Folsom had told an audience at the University of Alabama Governors Day celebration that he would not run again, "if the Lord will let me stay out of office." He was soon joined in the gubernatorial race by George Wallace, recognized as the front-runner because of the 1958 runoff with Patterson. Ryan DeGraffenried, a progressive state senator from Tuscaloosa County favored by urban, business, and education interests, qualified as another top contender. With Patterson on the sidelines, some in his campaign organization lined up with Attorney General MacDonald Gallion, who supported most of the Patterson program. Gallion also continued the same aggressive style as attorney general, generating considerable public attention particularly on segregation matters. Yet in spite of what many assumed was a close relationship, Patterson refused to endorse him for governor.

Behind the scenes, according to Seymore Trammell's unpublished account of the Wallace campaign, a few Patterson insiders attempted to strike a deal with the Wallace camp. Trammell, who later became Wallace's finance director, said that some Patterson people wanted to throw their support to Wallace in return for Wallace's help in 1966. No such deal was arranged, Patterson said. "There was some talk about it, but I felt that if I wanted to have any chance to come back in politics, I needed to stay out of other people's campaigns." Patterson remained neutral, and members of his administration were advised to stay out of the governor's race and start preparing for '66.[3]

With the state preparing for the next governor's race, Patterson launched the most extensive trade mission of his administration, a fifteen-day trip to Central and South America. The governor's press releases stated that the lengthy journey covered more than twelve thousand miles of port to port travel, occasionally disembarking in the middle of an afternoon coup. He entertained Latin American shippers aboard the state yacht and attended official receptions resembling those given heads of state. "Earl McGowin had the state docks in excellent condition so we felt like the state had something to offer shipping interests in those countries," Patterson explained. With increased trade volume and more effective management, by the end of 1962, the state docks, which had once operated in the red, earned more than $2.2 million.[4]

In spite of Patterson's efforts to keep a high political profile, he was completely overwhelmed by the 1962 race. Wallace, having learned his lesson on the race issue, campaigned on a promise to defy any federal court school integration orders, predicting that federal authorities would "back down from the firm resistance of a governor." Folsom ran another populist campaign, and DeGraffenried, a racial moderate, called Wallace's defy-the-court scheme "loud mouth talk" and "empty threats." Wallace's race-baiting was effective. With Alabama voters still excited over the Kennedys and freedom riders, he took a solid lead in the primary, with DeGraffenried barely edging out Folsom for the runoff spot. Gallion ran fourth. Wallace went on to beat DeGraffenried handily with a promise to "stand in the schoolhouse door" to stop forced integration. With that promise, Wallace secured his future just as Patterson fixed his in 1958. And fulfilling it would portray Wallace and the state in the worst possible way as the nation wrestled with the emerging modern civil rights movement.[5]

As the Democratic primary settled in for another season of racial demagoguery, Patterson called for a final special session of the legislature to settle the unresolved reapportionment issue. Without realizing it, when organizing his administration, Patterson had contributed to the traditional system of power by giving Black Belt legislators more committee appointments than any governor in almost thirty years. Patterson had simply been searching for legislative experience, but the high visibility of Black Belt legislators in the administration made it more difficult to make substantive changes in district realignment. A bigger concern was the fear that a correct balance between population and the legislature would result in the election of blacks to public office. Some of the Black Belt counties were as much as 80 percent black; reapportionment would make the election of African American members to the state legislature inevitable.

In late March, the U.S. Supreme Court had assumed jurisdiction in the apportionment of the state legislature, with a three-judge federal court acting on the pending case. The court set a deadline of July 16 for the legislature to reapportion itself or subject the state to federal intervention. Patterson deplored the role of the federal courts even though he had pushed hard for change in the two previous regular sessions. The case had made its way to the Supreme Court after plaintiffs from Birmingham and Mobile alleged a denial of equal protection under the law because of malapportioned districts and the failure of the legislature to comply with the Alabama constitution. Some three months prior to the petition, the U.S. Supreme Court made a landmark decision in *Baker v. Carr,* which, for the first time, found district apportionment in the state of Tennessee to be in violation of the Fourteenth Amendment. In *Sims v. Frink,* the Alabama complainants pointed out that the 1901 Alabama constitution required the legislature to reapportion itself after each decennial census on a population basis, which in effect was the one-man, one-vote principle. The court told the legislature to create single-member districts as near equal in population as possible. An every-county survey on voting strength by the University of Virginia found that Alabama's rural counties elected 83 percent of the House members and 86 percent of the senators. Yet the same counties contained only 59 percent of the population.[6]

Patterson's first solution was to propose, for a second time, the expansion of the legislature to 40 senators and 120 representatives, an idea that had died of neglect the previous year. It was one of many bills introduced to correct the district imbalance and satisfy the federal courts. The dominant rural bloc launched a lengthy filibuster to stall the bills and came close to turning the special session into a shambles. Within ten days, however, administration forces prevailed, gaining passage of two laws for the federal court's review. Highly populated Mobile, Madison, Jefferson, Tuscaloosa, Calhoun, and Etowah Counties increased their representation at the expense of five Black Belt Counties, which lost their powerful single-seat districts. Jefferson County (Birmingham) almost tripled its representation.[7]

The federal panel considered the merits of the laws and within a week ordered immediate reapportionment by taking parts of the two acts and writing them into an order. The court more or less accepted the acts as a compromise—calling the action "moderate"—stating that it hoped a better apportioned legislature would in turn complete the task. The order said the action would suffice for the 1962 elections but that the judges would return and finish the job if the legislature did not do it themselves. The press was quick to praise Patterson. The *Birmingham News* called the reapportionment laws "Patterson bills," because "no other legislature in half a century has been able to pass a single act of reapportioning its seats." Patterson was magnanimous in the face of the historic achievement, giving the legislature credit for the work while playing down his leadership role. "I was relieved to get the bills through the legislature," he said. "It was my last chance to help correct a very serious state problem, and I didn't really care who got the credit as long as we reapportioned the legislature." Even more remarkable was the fact that district lines were redrawn at the peak of racial unrest, when some legislators were exploiting the explosive integration issue to frustrate change.[8]

Having escaped the special session with only minimal political damage, mainly from defeated Black Belters, Patterson said he was optimistic about his chances for another term in the governor's office. During the session, his strategy was to do as little as possible to antagonize the electorate, staying in the background and intervening only when it seemed to work in his favor. In the waning days of the session, he was blindsided when headlines in the *Montgomery Advertiser* charged the administration with a major scandal in the highway department. Patterson was stunned when Joe Robertson tossed the June 6 morning edition on his desk with headlines that read: "Gallion Requests Court Halt State Road Stripe Deal." Reading the story, he realized it sounded like something from the Folsom era.

For some several weeks, Gallion's staff had been turning rumors about a contract for painting center lines on state highways into facts. *Advertiser* reporter Charles McWilliams came to Gallion with evidence that in recent months a number of ordinary people around Montgomery were cashing sizable payroll checks from a local contractor. The IRS, which picked up on the matter when it found numerous discrepancies while auditing tax returns of bogus partners of the contractor, turned the information over to the attorney general. The material was developed into hard evidence for an injunction to halt highway striping by the local contractor Joe T. Barton. Gallion claimed the state lost some $842,242 in the scandal.[9]

Patterson's first suspicion was that Grover Hall was trying to "fly-speck our administration." He denied the charges without full knowledge of what had happened in the highway department, saying they were "exaggerated, misrepresented, and overcolored." He told the media that Gallion was being used by people bent on political revenge against him, claiming that Hall hired McWilliams for the sole purpose of smearing him. Calls to the highway department, particularly to Walter Craig, did little to clarify the charges. Patterson decided to accept Craig's explanation, and, rather than investigating any wrongdoing, he zealously defended his administration without full knowledge of the facts.[10]

Ray Jenkins didn't believe the stories were political attacks on Patterson: "Grover Hall used to get kind of personal with John, sometimes calling him squint-eyed in editorials. But I think McWilliams simply stumbled on the story." Gallion and others in state government maintained that the scandal was not generated by vengeful opponents but by misguided and careless elements inside the administration. Further, the scandal had been going on for almost two years, with a lot of gossip about it circulating around Montgomery. If anything, the paper was tardy in exposing the story.[11]

The background of the paint stripe contract was uncomplicated and completely within the legal guidelines defined by state law. In March 1960, when Maurice Patterson offered the business to the public, he said the notice was posted on a bulletin board outside the purchasing department in the capitol, asking for "per mile" bids. The job also specified outside white lines, which were being added for the first time as a safety feature. There were some 8,771 miles of highway involved. "When the bids came back, there were four of them with the lowest being $39.50 per mile from Alabama Sign and Marking Company," Maurice Patterson said. "We sent it over to the Highway Department and they let the contract." Highway Department officials considered the bid reasonable.[12]

The scandal developed during the second year of the contract, when Walter Craig manipulated its renewal. The owner of the company that won the contract, Joe T. Barton, told the state that he would renew the contract for another year without raising the price, a savings for the state. The legal department found no problems with extending the contract for the same price and authorized its continuance. Gallion said the scheme basically involved Craig, Barton, and Hubert Baughm, "the background man who was behind the scheme." Baughm, editor and publisher of *South* magazine, had assured Patterson after the story broke that it was not a kickback scheme and he was only doing public relations work for Barton's company. Gallion claimed Barton "[doesn't have] a single employee, doesn't have a single piece of equipment, and maintained no office outside his home," but acted as a kind of broker for the scheme by subcontracting the striping to W. Howard Williams of Montgomery for $20.00 a mile, half the contracted price. Williams was able to stripe the highways at a greatly reduced savings, because he had developed technology that painted at higher speeds under pressure, making it possible to do the work quickly and cheaply. The profits were split among the principals, who in turn laundered the money at the Montgomery Country Club, and spread exorbitant sums to lesser players in the form of fake payroll checks. Barton received $843,242 for 21,000 miles of striping in twenty months. Officials in the Highway department estimated that Barton made some $600,000. When the money was broken down Barton was getting $7.50 per mile, while Baughm was given $7.00 and Craig $5.00 of the $19.50 per mile profit.

Gallion said neither Sam Engelhardt nor John and Maurice Patterson were aware of the lucrative arrangement until the *Advertiser* published the story. Maurice said his office began to "get some feedback on the project by the end of the second year. But I really didn't know what was happening until I was served with a subpoena from the sheriff's office." John was convinced that Grover Hall was trying to torpedo his reelection chances. Calling in Fred Bodeker, the reputable Birmingham detective who had uncovered the big vote steal in the 1954 election, Patterson asked him to investigate the reporter. Bodeker planted an operative in the apartment next to McWilliams and his wife at the Hilltop Arms; he gained the confidence of the couple to the extent that the three of them made the rounds at local bars together.[13]

Patterson's concerns about the motives of the investigation were confirmed when he started receiving confidential reports from Bodeker. The operative said that McWilliams was "prone to brag about his ability and forcefulness" and talked of Grover Hall wanting to "scare the Patterson crowd." In the following weeks, Patterson read reports that McWilliams had Tina Sawyers and her sister under surveillance, and the reporter said he had talked to people in Phenix City who told him that Patterson had murdered his father. McWilliams said he was going to write a book and title it "Story of a Man Who Killed his Father, Put a Saddle on the Casket, and Rode it into the Governor's Office."

The case mushroomed into even greater notoriety when McWilliams and Assistant Attorney General Joe Malone were discovered on Patterson's Tallapoosa County farm taking pictures and peering in the windows at his family during breakfast. When McWilliams refused to leave the property, Tom Posey, the governor's aide, forcibly removed him, and Mary Joe Patterson had them arrested. The governor stated publicly that the incident was conclusive proof that the *Advertiser* and the attorney general were "in concert" to smear him.

At the same time, Fred Bodeker also investigated Gallion to see if he could find something to "dampen his spirits," according to Patterson. Bodeker's operative discovered that Gallion was negotiating with the Wallace camp for a deal to support Wallace in the runoff against DeGraffenried in exchange for money to pay off his campaign debts. The deal was well documented, including a long list of telephone calls linking Gallion to Wallace's campaign leaders who had encouraged the attorney general to extend the paint stripe controversy.[14]

The investigation went on for months, with the *Advertiser* keeping up a steady stream of stories about the scandal, most of them by McWilliams. Gallion eventually filed suit against Maurice Patterson, Joe Barton, and Sam Engelhardt in an attempt to recover the $950,000 the state had spent on the contract. Walter Craig was the only one of the leading conspirators indicted for his part in the scandal. Hubert Baughm and Joe Barton, who were not indicted, agreed to testify against Craig. Surprisingly, the U.S. Justice Department granted immunity from prosecution to anyone testifying against Craig, while the IRS extended tax exemptions for money siphoned off in the deal. Such an arrangement, Patterson surmised, would have obviously required the approval of Attorney General Robert Kennedy and the state's attorney general.

Craig's trial made headlines and the *Advertiser* published a detailed account of the proceedings, as the assistant highway director defended himself against bribery charges. It was like shooting fish in a barrel, with Baughm and Barton giving the court a detailed description of the check-cashing scheme from which both witnesses had made huge profits. The trial was cut short when two jurors claimed they had received death threats if they voted to convict Craig; the judge declared a mistrial. Craig's defense counsel claimed that the news coverage was so badly slanted that they were forced to take out paid newspaper advertisements to explain his client's position on the death threats. A second trial failed to produce a conviction and Craig went free—the jury deliberated only half an hour before finding Craig not guilty.

The suit against Maurice Patterson, Sam Engelhardt, and Charlie Meriwether (included because he had been finance director) continued into the next administration, when Patterson took the cases as attorney and filed a motion demanding a trial. He told District Attorney David Crosland that he intended to find out why the U.S. Justice Department made deals with people who had masterminded the kickback scheme in an attempt to convict Craig. The day after Patterson made his intentions known Attorney General Richmond Flowers dropped all the cases. Flowers had testified at the trials that no deals were made. After eight months of heavy-handed journalism by the Montgomery press, two trials, and a myriad of backroom deals by state and federal authorities, not one member of the administration was convicted. Nonetheless Patterson's political career suffered a major setback. *Newsweek* termed the scandal "a personal jolt and a costly political liability" for Patterson. In those pressure-filled months, Patterson realized that greed had wrecked an otherwise efficient administration and his trust had been betrayed by longtime friends. "I was deeply hurt by what people like Hubert Baughm did to promote the scheme," Patterson said. "It was an extremely painful experience that provided my political enemies a field day in the papers. It was also the worst possible thing that could happen right before we left office."[15]

During the height of the scandal, Patterson was faced with a personal dilemma. An application from the Alabama Electric Cooperative (AEC) in Covington County to build a steam-generating plant with federal Rural Electrification Administration (REA) funds on the Tombigbee River was submitted to Maurice Patterson. State law at the time required the approval of the finance director and the agreement of the governor. Alabama Power Company strongly opposed the co-op's plan to build a $20 million plant that would generate and distribute electricity. The administration began to get tremendous pressure from utilities around the state. Power company executives and allied legislators suggested that the governor should turn down the cooperative's request or simply do nothing about the application, which would kill for the project. Patterson leaned toward approving the loan because the steam-generating plant would provide cheap power to the southwest portion of the state.

The big utilities went to considerable lengths to forestall the project. Patterson was contacted at his farm one July weekend by two legislators close to the administration who wanted to discuss the generating plant project with him. Patterson knew the lawmakers were running interference for Alabama Power Company but invited then down anyway. Their offer was extremely attractive. "They stated that the power company expected to lose the case with the REA now pending before the finance director, and that they were in a desperate situation and that if the REA prevailed, it would just about put them out of business" wrote Patterson in a memo following the meeting. If he denied the co-op grant, which essentially meant doing nothing, all the charges would be dropped against his brother Maurice Patterson and investigations of his administration would cease. When Patterson reminded the two legislators that the investigation was in the hands of state authorities, he was told, "that has been arranged." The men asked the governor to meet with an Alabama Power Company official at his office on Monday to further discuss the matter. Patterson agreed to hear their entire proposal before making a final decision.

On Monday morning, a high ranking official for Alabama Power Company walked into the governor's office with the same two legislators. He gave Patterson the impression that he was confident they were going to be able to work out a compromise on the steam-generating plant. The official not only restated the offer to get the charges dropped against Maurice but also told Patterson the company was prepared to put him on an annual retainer of $100,000 for the next five years.

After mulling the offer over for a few moments, Patterson told the utility executive that such an agreement would damage his political career. "I told him that they had put me in a position where I couldn't help them if I wanted to. I also told the gentlemen that I had never dishonored myself so far in life and I wasn't about to start now. The answer is no." He told them he was going to approve the application. The power company official was taken aback by the answer and the two legislators were noticeably shaken, said Patterson. He should have turned them down at the farm over the weekend, he said, but he wanted to see who would call on him. Alabama Power Company would return to oppose him later in his career.

Patterson said the pressure to accept the offer was enormous: his brother faced indictment in a major scandal; his administration was suspected of highly placed wrongdoing; and he was being offered long-term financial prosperity for him and his family. But the incident allowed him to emerge from his tenure in public service with his self-respect intact—regardless of how the media portrayed him.[16]

As a lame duck governor, Patterson found plenty to do politically during the remaining months of 1962. He helped carry the Democratic banner across the state that fall against nominal Republican opposition and kept himself visible with the electorate. He led the drive to bring the USS *Alabama* back home, mainly with donations from Alabama schoolchildren, and started construction on the Alabama Industrial Relations Building. (When Wallace took office, the Patterson cornerstone disappeared and one with Wallace's name replaced it.) An eight-story highway building was constructed that was later converted to the legislative state house. In North Alabama, the state broke ground for a new $3 million center for space research to support the nation's space program, which later expanded into the University of Alabama in Huntsville. President Kennedy visited Redstone Arsenal in September to watch a test-firing of Saturn rocket boosters, but Patterson did not join him for the visit as he had joined Eisenhower in 1960. Alabama and South Carolina were the lone remaining southern states without some form of integration. Riots at the University of Mississippi created a very un-Faulknerian scene at Oxford, and Patterson predicted "there will be chaos, violence and destruction" if Alabama was threatened by the same federal forces.[17]

By the time John Patterson turned control of the state government over to Wallace, he had gone through a personal and political transformation. He had come to Montgomery with the sound of gunshots still ringing in his ears; he was leaving amid the mixed chorus of curses from civil rights activists and hosannas from their opposition. His political star had risen the same year the Supreme Court ruled in *Brown v. Board of Education,* a decision that reshaped the nation's social, educational, and political life. He did not set out to make a defense of segregation the centerpiece of his public life. But events transpired to make him ease the fears of his white constituency by publicly defending the norms of traditional white southern culture. John Patterson knew that southerners would someday have to accept an integrated society, but he thought the inevitable could be delayed for a little while.

However history may judge Patterson with regard to the civil rights movement, he achieved some notable successes during his two terms in state government. His crusades as attorney general were sensational enough to turn an underrated gubernatorial candidacy into a record victory. Sympathy accounted for part of the unstoppable energy that fueled his candidacy, but hard work on tough, contentious issues earned him the respect and confidence of most Alabamians. The state needed positive leadership to carry it through the emerging shift from agricultural to urban culture and into the mainstream of economic and governmental progress. Patterson gave Alabama something resembling instant reformation.

His support of education, small-loan laws, and reapportionment were large progressive strokes that by themselves would have made his tenure successful. Add in special attention to aged pensioners, a record highway program, industrial growth, and sound fiscal management in state departments, and Patterson's administration shines as one of the most productive in state history. McDowell Lee, who viewed state government from the vantage point of secretary of the Alabama Senate for several administrations, believed that Patterson eclipsed all other Alabama governors in recent times because of his administrative abilities: "John Patterson had one of the better administrations in the last thirty years."

Others agreed. "It will be hard for even the severest critics to paint the Patterson administration—try as they may—as anything much less than good," the *Birmingham News* observed in an overview of Patterson's service. "For the record clearly is one of substantial accomplishment, of tangible achievement, of service to the state." The *Alabama Journal* likewise viewed the Patterson administration as "one of the great periods in Alabama history." The state's weekly and small-town newspapers, Patterson's strongest media support, chimed in with similar acclaim for his administration.[18]

That recognition was an asset to Patterson's plan to run again in 1966. Administration sources put together a long list of accomplishments in booklet form, and Press Secretary Harry Cook compiled a collection of Patterson speeches into a slick 486-page book, *Messages and Addresses of John Patterson*. The books were printed at state expense and circulated to

Alabama colleges, universities, and public libraries. John Patterson didn't know what it would take to be governor of Alabama a second time, and he certainly didn't know what the dominant issues would be in four years, but he knew he had been careful in his preparation. "It's really hard to describe the feeling of being governor. It surpasses everything I have ever been a part of in life—except the Battle of El Guettar. I believed then that we could do it one more time."[19]

19
Twice Embarrassed at the Polls

John Patterson spent his last day as governor of Alabama preparing for George Wallace's inauguration. In early December John had moved Mary Joe, Albert, and Babel to their new home on Felder Avenue to give the Wallaces time to prepare the governor's mansion for the transition. On that final day, he called for Wallace in a limousine, rode with him at the head of the inaugural parade to the capitol, and escorted him to the platform. When Wallace began his fiery "segregation forever" speech, Patterson slipped quietly off the platform and went to his office to say good-bye to his staff. Afterward, Tom Posey drove him home, where his family and a small group of friends were waiting for him. For the first time in years, the phone no longer rang incessantly.

When Patterson returned to his law practice with Ralph Smith, he found few clients clamoring for the legal services of a former governor. He was hard pressed to maintain his comfortable Montgomery lifestyle and the family farm in Tallapoosa County, which, through steady land acquisitions while he was governor, had grown to more than twelve hundred acres. Patterson struggled to remain solvent, in a sense marking time until the campaign season opened once again. Politics, not law, was still his main interest.

Preparations for the 1966 race were much the same as for the first campaign. "About a year after leaving office," he explained, "I went back to my files and began communicating with my supporters and started making speeches around the state." Contributions came in steady but not large amounts, and Patterson began spending more and more time away from his already struggling law practice—much as his father had. Meriwether resigned from the Export-Import Bank to help with the campaign, although he decided early on that he wouldn't be the official manager: "There was too much attention focused on me by that time. People in Alabama really hated the Kennedys, plus I had been implicated in the paint striping scandal while I was in Washington. I decided it would be best for John and the campaign for me to remain in the background." Vaughn Hill Robison was tapped as official campaign manager, with Ralph Smith in a prominent role as coordinator.[1]

Once the campaign started, Patterson was unable to determine his position in the race. "We couldn't tell much about it at that point," he explained, "because we always got a good reception wherever we went. We couldn't get a good reading on where we stood." Meriwether thought Patterson's chances for reelection were excellent: "We knew we had a couple of issues that would hurt us in the campaign, but John had a good administration that we felt would make him a leader in the race."[2]

Within two years after becoming governor, Wallace had completely seized the race issue and become the very image of southern resistance with his defiance of federal authority. The 1964 presidential race gave Wallace's stance on civil rights even greater national dimensions, making him reluctant to step away from the governor's office and the considerable resources that supported his political jaunts around the nation. By state law, Wallace couldn't succeed himself and he began devising ways around the problem.

Confident that his personal popularity combined with Alabama's anger with the Kennedys and the civil rights movement would give him broad public support, Wallace ordered a special session to force through the legislature a succession bill that would call for a statewide vote on a constitutional amendment. Citing "widespread public demand" for the governor to succeed himself, Wallace called the session for September 1965. Legislators did not fall into step with Wallace's political plans, however. One House resolution pointedly said that the session was called "for the sole and selfish purpose" of satisfying Wallace's personal ambitions. A small group of House members fought the bill for more than a week before losing by a 74 to 23 vote. [3]

Across the rotunda in the Senate opponents were ready to kill the succession amendment. Forming what was described as a "community of interests," Wallace opponents allied to keep Wallace from assembling the necessary three-fifths vote to pass the constitutional amendment. Vaughn Hill Robison worked closely with Ryan DeGraffenried and a few other senators to stop Wallace's power play. George Hawkins of Etowah County said the succession bill created the most constituent pressure that he experienced in the legislature. Hawkins fought the succession proposal because he thought Alabama needed to move beyond Wallace: "I thought it was very inappropriate for Wallace to want to change the rules to benefit himself. I believed that we had had enough of him." Kenneth Hammonds of DeKalb County stood against the administration and said openly on the Senate floor that Wallace was following the "same cycle as Adolf Hitler." Word spread in Montgomery that Wallace was intimidating senators with threats to cut off state funds for their counties; he went to the home counties of opposing senators, walking the streets and telling people to contact their legislators on his behalf. Patterson supporters also reported that a lot of money changed hands to line up votes for the amendment.[4]

Vaughn Hill Robison's parliamentary skills held the bill at bay for more than a week. A group of North Alabama senators filibustered the measure for another two weeks while Wallace forces applied greater and greater pressure. The Senate chambers echoed with some of the harshest debate that body had heard in decades, with senators on both sides demanding public apologies. A. C. Shelton of Calhoun County told of public pressure "inspired by agents of the administration." Wallace attempted to garner Shelton's support with an offer of $25,000—the governor's salary at the time—and by naming one of his sons insurance commissioner. Julian Lowe of Randolph County said the administration cut off funds to a college in his district after he voted with opponents of the bill. In the end Wallace could muster only 18 votes, 3 short of the 21 needed to pass the bill. With Wallace's political future presumably settled, campaign money almost immediately started flowing to Patterson, over $250,000 in a matter of a few days. A seething Wallace publicly acknowledged that Patterson had played a role in defeating the amendment.[5] But in the end, all the efforts to stop Wallace proved futile.

Tragedy struck one of the leading candidates in the spring of 1965 and thrust Wallace firmly back into Alabama's gubernatorial picture. Flying from a campaign stop in Fort Payne to Gadsden where his family waited, Ryan DeGraffenried and his pilot's plane crashed on a wooded hillside during foul weather. They were both killed. Two days later Lurleen

Wallace qualified to run for governor, an obvious stand-in for her husband. "She ain't all that sharp," Wallace said at the time, "but she can take care of herself."[6]

Mrs. Wallace's presence changed the campaign dramatically. Patterson insiders attended her first campaign appearance, which was held in Phenix City. By the end of the rally, his political advisers had reached a consensus: voters would give her a phenomenal reception. They also believed that the site had been chosen to demonstrate Wallace's drawing power in Patterson's hometown and to retaliate for his role in denying George Wallace another term. When Wallace decided to run his wife for governor, Meriwether saw Patterson's reelection chances disappear: "With Wallace preempting everyone on race, our well-publicized association with the Kennedys, and Mrs. Wallace's popularity, which was stronger than George's, we were finished before we started."[7]

Patterson knew his chances against the Wallaces were slim, but he felt compelled to see the matter through."We all knew what was happening," he said, "but we worked hard at being optimistic for the sake of the campaign. We had collected all of that money, so I felt I owed it to our people to hoe the row out." Campaign workers defected until there were "damn few of them left at the end," Joe Robertson said. "The money dried up when Lurleen got in the race; the whole thing just fell apart." Even some of Patterson's staunch Phenix City supporters went over to Wallace.[8]

The 1966 race also marked the first real test of the black vote. The Twenty-Fourth Amendment (ratified in 1964) abolished the repressive poll tax that had long kept southern blacks from voting, and the passage of the 1965 Voting Rights Act saw Alabama's black vote grow to some 125,000, a dramatic surge but not impressive enough to attract the interest of the ten-candidate field. Only Richmond Flowers openly sought black support. Patterson, like the other candidates, relied on conventional campaign strategy, denouncing Wallace's "intemperate ranting and raving," and charging that he was violating the state constitution by running his wife: "A man who won't honor the Alabama Constitution is not a defender of our rights, and this is true no matter how loud he talks, or how much he cusses liberals." Patterson brought back the Sunny Valley Boys to entertain his modest audiences and passed out revised versions of the Patterson comic book. This time the tactics didn't work.[9]

When the vote tally from the May 3 Democratic primary came in, Patterson had failed to carry a single county. Polling a meager 32,335 votes, he placed sixth, just ahead of the aging Folsom but far behind Mrs. Wallace's 400,000-plus votes. Flowers came in a weak second with 142,716, more than 80 percent of which were estimated to be black votes. Hugh Sparrow called it a "blank check" victory because the Wallaces didn't have to make a single specific pledge to the voters. It was an embarrassing disappointment for Patterson. He thanked his campaign workers at the Molton Hotel in Birmingham and slipped out during the "crying and depression," drove down to the Goldville farm, built a fire, had a couple of drinks of whiskey and went to bed. Getting on with life, he said the next day he went to the Montgomery courthouse, made the rounds of all the offices and shook hands with officials and employees, and told everyone he was back in the law business.[10]

After the sound trouncing, John Patterson believed his political career was over. He didn't foresee getting involved in another statewide race and could salvage no comfort in the wake of defeat. He said he considered returning to Phenix City but decided he had a better chance of succeeding professionally in Montgomery. He formed a new law partnership with his old army pal Ted Rinehart; Ralph Smith returned to his hometown. Patterson liked Rinehart because he was bright, articulate, and a proven ally. Rinehart said the partnership made a "prosperous but not extravagant living. We didn't have any large retainers from the big corporations; just a good general practice that included some people we knew through politics." With politics out of the picture, Patterson settled into a routine that resembled the life of an average middle-class attorney in America. The routine included regular trips to Atlanta to see the now-divorced Tina Sawyers who left the state in 1963 after the *Advertiser*'s investigation of the paint-stripping scandal.[11]

The lull of private life did not linger, however. By 1970 politics drew Patterson into yet another state race. This time it was the chief justice position on the Alabama supreme court, which was being vacated by seventy-eight-year-old chief justice Ed Livingston, who had been on the court since 1939. "Serving on the supreme court was one of my major ambitions," Patterson said. "So I qualified early hoping that it would scare potential candidates away from the race." State supreme court races were traditionally dull affairs. For years, the court had been controlled by older men who tended to be segregationists on race issues and conservatives on economics. Often cases would linger for years before decisions were reached. Even in the fire of southern politics, candidates for the office didn't hire hill-billy bands or have fish fries and barbecues to draw crowds, relying instead on name recognition and relationships within the law profession for campaign support. There had not been a contested race for the chief judgeship in sixty-four years, still more incentive for Patterson to position himself early.[12]

This time his candidacy would be short-circuited by unforeseen professional rather than political problems. The central problem was his relationship, or more precisely his lack of a relationship, with the Alabama Bar Association: Patterson had risen to the state's top law position and then the governorship without an apprenticeship in the state bar association. "I had failed to cultivate necessary friendships among my peers and had made only token appearances at bar association meetings prior to the race," he said. When it became apparent that he might be elected without serious challenge, several influential lawyers looked around the state for candidates to keep Patterson from becoming chief justice by default. Some state attorneys openly opposed Patterson because they did not want a controversial politician to head Alabama's top court.

In an article entitled "Attorneys Seek Candidate to Run for Chief Justice," the *Montgomery Advertiser* reported on a bar association meeting in Birmingham where two state attorneys, Howell Heflin of Tuscumbia and C. C. "Bo" Torbert, a Lee County state senator, were considered as possible candidates against Patterson. Heflin appeared to be the best bet because of his strong name recognition. The Heflin name was synonymous with old-line Alabama politics. "Cotton Tom" Heflin, Howell's uncle, had served in the U.S. House of Representatives and Senate for some thirty years. The group settled on Heflin primarily because of that connection, consoling Torbert with the promise of future endorsement. A sizable campaign contribution, reported at some $100,000, went with the endorsement. The bulk of the money came from trial lawyers.[13]

Patterson found himself frozen out of the customary round of personal appearances and speeches. "There just weren't any invitations," he said. "I believe that the word was passed around to leave me out, and they did." To his dismay, even when he made an inquiry, Patterson couldn't get a major speaking invitation. Further problems arose when letters to the editor appeared in newspapers throughout the state, reminding readers of the paint stripe scandal and Patterson's endorsement of Kennedy. "I did some checking and discovered that many of the letters were submitted by fictitious people with vacant lots as addresses," Patterson said. He tried without success to call attention to the bar association's role in the campaign; his appeals went unnoticed by the press and the voters.

The large newspapers endorsed Heflin, further weakening Patterson's efforts. He had neither the finances nor the organization to counter his opponent's strength. A full-page advertisement in the *Birmingham News*, paid for by a group of Jefferson County lawyers, incensed Patterson with the claim that "radicals are trying to tear down the very existence of our judicial system." The majority of state lawyers were of the opinion that Patterson wasn't qualified for the position. Patterson understood what was happening: "They thought I was going to do violence to their system." His campaign organization was extremely meager, consisting of a small room near his own law offices, where Ralph Harden of Tuscaloosa worked as campaign manager. They spent less than nine thousand dollars, with Patterson trying to "make up the difference in shoe leather, phone banks, and people from our other campaigns."[14]

The critical support of the Alabama Bar Association swept Howell Heflin into office as chief justice of the Alabama supreme court, the second lopsided defeat for John Patterson in four years. "It was a terrible political mistake," Patterson said. "At the time I didn't know a lot about how the legal profession operated in regard to supreme court vacancies. It was a regrettable error on my part."[15]

Patterson admitted that life was "pretty gloomy" following the 1970 loss. "A lot of people thought it was all over for John Patterson," he recalled, "including most of my close friends." Charlie Meriwether said Patterson's political career "didn't seem to have a lot of promise during that period, and frankly, as much as I believed in John, I didn't see a lot of hope for him following the supreme court race." He was only forty-nine and a capable attorney, hardly the description of an elder statesman.

Campaign wounds and hurt feelings healed over the next fourteen years, before political opportunities came again. During the interim, however, two significant changes occurred in his personal life. The most dramatic was his relationship with Mary Joe, which, by accounts from friends who knew the couple well, was moving toward inevitable separation. The Rineharts and the Robertsons noted more and more conflict between John and Mary Joe, and their social companions sensed that the twenty-eight-year relationship was ending.

John continued seeing Tina Sawyers during this period. Robertson described the relationship as an "on-again, off-again romance." Patterson would only say that he had asked his wife to stop her heavy smoking and drinking because it was damaging her health, and for a short time she did. Mary Joe Patterson saw no fault in their marriage other than her husband's marital infidelity, specifically his relationship with Tina. Whatever the cause, John divorced Mary Joe on June 10, 1975. She kept the Montgomery house and John the family farm in Tallapoosa County. Mary Joe Patterson expressed bitterness toward John and Tina, and interviews with her prior to her death revealed an abiding distress over the lost marriage. John and Tina were married September 30, 1975, in Fulton County, Georgia.[16]

The same month he divorced Mary Joe, Patterson was offered an opportunity to teach at a state university. Responding to an invitation from Ralph Adams, president of Troy State University, Patterson began teaching college students about politics in Alabama and the South. He held the job for more than sixteen years. "Teaching the course kept me current with American and southern politics," Patterson explained. "I made friends with an entire generation of young men and women. There were times when I felt I was getting more from the students than they were from the teacher. I appreciate Dr. Adams's giving me the opportunity to be associated with Troy State."

The intervening years helped soothe old political wounds. Patterson and Wallace mended their fences, a great part of the understanding coming during the period while both men were out of office. "To our mutual amazement," Patterson said, "we discovered we had the same set of friends and the same group of enemies." The relationship went further when Patterson supported Wallace for a historic fifth term, often representing Wallace at speaking engagements when the governor was campaigning elsewhere. During Wallace's final political campaigns, Wallace repented of his racist behavior and portrayed himself as a "progressive reformer." Before the assassination attempt that crippled Wallace, Patterson volunteered for Wallace's two presidential crusades, traveling with the Wallace team and introducing the governor at campaign stops in Texas and Florida. Patterson's efforts for his former foe proved worthwhile. In April 1984, with a vacancy to fill on the Alabama court of criminal appeals, Wallace repaid his former antagonist with the appointment, setting off an uproar among black legislators who remembered Patterson's strident opposition to racial integration. Lost in the outcry was Patterson's reapportionment plan—the plan that had enabled blacks in Alabama to win elections and thus oppose his appointment as judge. Patterson closed his law office and moved into the same offices in the supreme court building that he had occupied as attorney general. That fall and again in 1990 he ran unopposed for additional six-year terms.[17] At the conclusion of his term in 1996 Patterson continued working criminal appeal cases in semi-retirement until 2003, when reductions in the court system mandated by budget constraints ended his judicial career.

He did have one final part to play in the Alabama court system. In 2004 Gov. Bob Riley asked Patterson to serve as chief justice for a special Alabama supreme court to hear former chief justice Roy Moore's appeal to retain his position on the court. The Moore case attracted national attention when federal district judge Myron H. Thompson ordered the removal from the Alabama Judicial Building of a two-and-a-half ton granite monument engraved with the Ten Commandments. Judge Thompson ruled that Moore's moving the monument into place late at night, its considerable size, and its location in the judicial building violated the establishment clause of the First Amendment of the U.S. Constitution. Thompson said the presence of the monument endorsed the Judeo-Christian faith.

The case had gone through the customary sequence of federal court appeals and court of judiciary rulings by the time Patterson and supreme court members heard Moore's oral arguments on April 30, 2004. Justice Janie Shores, Judges Kenneth Ingram, Braxton Kittrell, Edward Dwight Fay Jr., J. Richmond Pearson, and Harry Wilter Jr., all mature and seasoned jurists, made up the court. The seven judges had been selected by a random drawing from a pool of twenty retired justices and judges. According to Patterson, the facts in Moore's case were never in dispute. "When we gathered around the table after hearing oral arguments," Patterson explained, "there was a general consensus that there was a correctness of the federal court that left us with no other choice under the circumstances of the case than to affirm the court of judiciary's ruling." Moore's refusal to obey a lawful and binding order of the U.S. District Court, under the facts of the case, warranted his removal from office, the special court concluded.

The court further ruled that the federal court neither applied an improper "religious test" in analyzing the issues nor did it violate Moore's constitutional rights to his religious beliefs when he was removed from office. Patterson said the federal courts and the court of the judiciary had made rulings that were fully supported by the evidence. The fact that Judge Moore testified under oath that he would do it again became important to their decision. Reaching back to 1963 and the George Wallace era of federal defiance, the court cited *United States v. Wallace* that "the rule of law does require that every person obey judicial orders when all available means of appealing them has been exhausted. . . . The rule of law will prevail." The U.S. Supreme Court ended the matter when it declined to hear Moore's appeal. The special court submitted its report to Governor Riley on November 5, 2005. Later Riley appointed Finance Director Drayton Nabors, attorney and insurance executive, to replace Roy Moore as chief justice.[18]

Patterson's colleagues on the special court honored him with a resolution of appreciation for answering the call to serve Alabama once again under "extraordinary circumstances." There was personal significance for Patterson's service: while he presided over the Moore case, he occupied the chief justice's office for more than eight months. Sitting on the bench during Moore's appeal realized his career ambition to serve as chief justice. Ironically, in John Patterson's final case as judge, he was defending the controversial decision of a black federal judge.

Today, in his "reclining years" he talks of the past in candid terms, readily admitting errors in judgment when he was part of the emerging civil rights movement. But the constant, persistent element in his daily thought is the dramatic event that shaped his future when he was a restless young attorney, eager to do other things with his life. Phenix City and his father are in his mind, and scenes of the past play over and over again, as Patterson relishes the good he was able to accomplish as attorney general and governor and reflects on the things that caused him regret. "I think about Phenix City every day," he said. "I relive it all, everything that took my father's life—everything that changed mine. I will for the rest of my life."[19]

Conclusion

Although unaware of it at the time, Patterson served during a historic period: between 1954 and the mid-1960s, Alabama—indeed the South, the entire nation—underwent cataclysmic social change. Alabama was pushed, willing or not, from the obsolete Old South into the emerging New South. The politicians might talk among themselves about the inevitability of change, but to the voting public they had to present the staunch and constant face of the unreconstructed segregationist. It was into this maelstrom of radical change and fierce resistance that John Patterson stepped as a reluctant and untried politician.

Assessing John Patterson's place in Alabama politics is not a simple matter. Thrust into a career he had once shunned, he tried his best to live up to his father's standards—and his own. As attorney general and even more so as governor, he provided critical leadership and tried to instill in the people and their elected officials an awareness of the benefits that can accrue from growth and change. While Alabama clung to its affection for Dixiecrat politics and its agrarian past, John Patterson preached the gospel of progressiveness. Positioned in history between the flamboyant Folsom years and the unforgettable Wallace dynasty, Patterson's tenure can be easily overlooked. It should not be.

Patterson initiated changes as attorney general that turned the office into the crime-fighting unit his father, and then he, had promised to make it. The success of this approach gained Patterson considerable attention and smoothed his path to the governor's mansion. Though his crowd-pleasing efforts with the NAACP, the Tuskegee boycott, and Alabama State University do not redound to his credit, they ought to be assessed in the context of the times.

On the other hand, Patterson's legal assault on loan sharks has a timeless merit, and its far-reaching effects on the state's economic system were unequivocally positive. The attorney general's office set in motion the government mechanisms that destroyed a usury system that had held a multitude of Alabamians, many of them black, in bondage. It may well be the most significant long-term contribution that Patterson made to "the people."

During the 1958 gubernatorial campaign, Patterson made the best of his position as a political outsider. His campaign themes of establishing law and order, putting an end to waste, and restoring good government appealed to the electorate. His outsider image also allowed the voters to see in him their own hopes for a more efficient state government. The sober, well-groomed Patterson must have been a welcome change from the often inebriated and disheveled sitting governor, and his composure played well against a wild-eyed and strident Wallace.

Public outrage over his father's assassination and Patterson's persona would, under normal circumstances, have been enough for a solid base in the 1958 governor's race. But the 1954 Supreme Court school desegregation decision inflamed southern tempers. Patterson and other candidates believed, with good reason, that to survive politically they had to take a strong position against integration—the stronger the better.

While Patterson was attorney general, his attacks on the NAACP gained him name recognition and the reputation of someone who was willing to face off against enemies of the southern way of life. But the integration issue lured Patterson into ever-increasing conflict and an unyielding position. By the time the freedom riders arrived in Alabama, Governor Patterson found himself unable to manage the crisis with any degree of restraint or objectivity. According to administration insiders, his fury during the 1961 race crisis seemed directed more toward the federal government than the racist hooligans in the streets. Patterson believed he had been betrayed by the Kennedys, who had given him inconsistent signals on their attitude toward integration. Patterson neither managed the crisis competently nor used the issue to forge lasting political strength, as his successor so famously did.

The tone for the freedom rider clash was set in 1958 when Patterson's campaign rhetoric foreshadowed his response to civil rights conflict. Expectations of Alabama's electorate also accounted for his intense reaction to federal intervention. He promised the people a fight and he gave them one. Patterson's volatile public defense of Alabama's traditional segregation practices, branded him as a wild-eyed racist who might lead a revolt among the keyed-up population. His determination to fulfill his promise to oppose integration at all costs has prompted some historians to paint him as a misguided man, but nonetheless a man of ability and force. Patterson bears the political scars from once having been in a fierce struggle over the modern South's greatest moral issue—and lost. He accepts whatever historical blame is due him in the matter.

The Patterson family drama is an important component of Alabama's history. His father's assassination made John Patterson heir to the bitterly fought battle in Phenix City that was later seen as a struggle between good and evil. The tragedy created for him an unparalleled fund of sympathy among Alabama's electorate, and Albert Patterson's crusading image gave him a running start for the governor's office. Patterson translated those advantages into a successful political career. Commentators of the period surmised that people saw John Patterson as a political reincarnation of his father. In realizing his own agenda, he also achieved Albert Patterson's goal of defeating crime, particularly in Phenix City.

Of all that has occurred in John Patterson's life, Phenix City remains the most persistent memory. John and his family still grieve over the tragic loss of Albert L. Patterson.

Appendix: The Patterson Cabinet

ABC (Alcoholic Beverage Control) administrator: Ed Azar, Montgomery; assistant, Billy Vickers, Newsite

ABC Board: chairman, Morgan Reynolds, Clanton; members, Charles Eslen, Birmingham; J. C. McDowell, Piedmont

Adjutant general: Henry V. Graham, Birmingham

Aide to governor: Tom Posey, Montgomery

Banking director: John Curry, Montgomery

Civil defense director: Joe Foster, Huntsville

Conservation director: Claude Kelley; William Younger, Montgomery, was later named director; assistant, Joe Kilgore, Jasper

Executive secretary: Joe Robertson, Birmingham

Finance director: Charles M. Meriwether, Birmingham; Maurice Patterson, Phenix City

Highway director: Sam Engelhardt, Shorter; assistant, Walter Craig, Selma

Industrial development director: Leland Jones, Phenix City; assistant, Porter Howell, Marion

Industrial relations director: Ralph Williams, Tuscaloosa; assistant, Charles Voltz, Gadsden

Insurance commissioner: Ted Rinehart, Montgomery; assistants Bill Page, Huntsville; Earnest C. "Sonny" Hornsby, Tallassee

Labor commissioner: Olin Brooks, Birmingham; assistant, E. J. Barnett, Birmingham

Legal adviser: Ralph Smith, Guntersville; assistant and, later, chief adviser, Robert Bradley, Montgomery

Pensions and security director: Alvin Prestwood, Enterprise; assistant, John Tyson, Greenville

Press secretary: Harry Cook, Birmingham; assistants, Bob Harper and Tommy Giles, Montgomery

Prison director: E. M. McCullough, Montgomery; assistant, Frank Lee

Publicity and information director: Roy Marcato, Birmingham

Public safety director: Floyd Mann, Opelika; assistant, Bill Jones, Scottsboro

Revenue commissioner: Harry Haden, Tuscaloosa; assistant, Guy Sparks, Anniston; Ralph Harden and Chester Walker of Tuscaloosa later served as assistant commissioners

Selective service director: Walter Thompson, Gadsden; assistants, Bobby Blalock, Pell City: Kenneth Ingram, Clay County

State docks director: Earl McGowin, Chapman

Notes

In the text, an endnote number appears at the end of a passage on a particular topic, which may extend over several paragraphs. Citations for the passage are grouped together in the endnote.

Chapter 1

1. Interviews with Grace Patterson Harry, Goldville, Ala., 16 February 1985, and John Patterson, Goldville, 29 December 1984. *New York Times,* 30 November 1931. Judge Jack Coley of Alexander City was a member of the group. Nancy B. Smith, Enterprise, Ala., granddaughter of Congressman Lafayette L. Patterson (Albert's older brother), has compiled a family history; Isabel C. Patterson, "Builders of Freedom and Their Descendents" (Montgomery, Ala.: State Department of Archives and History, 1927), relates the family migration to Alabama and includes much family history.

John Love Patterson, eldest son of John Graham, inherited Leander, his father's seven-hundred-acre farm, and its slaves. John Love developed a gristmill on Town Creek and was a tradesman as well as a prosperous farmer, occupations vital to the South during the Civil War. John Love was exempt from service at the beginning of the war, which was just as well, since he opposed secession and was said to have debated the issue with William Lowndes Yancey. John Love Patterson was drafted during the third year of the war, serving at Camp Watts near Notasulga, the largest conscript camp in the Confederacy. Patterson saw action when Union general James Wilson's raiders skirmished near the camp, and again when the camp was emptied to defend Girard, across the Chattahoochee River from the Confederate manufacturing complex at Columbus, Georgia. Patterson returned home with nothing more than a sack of salt slung over his shoulder.

At forty-three John Love Patterson married Mary Elizabeth Bryant of Hackneyville, age seventeen; they had five daughters. John Love also had a son at the time of this marriage. Several years before the war, Patterson had an affair with Ellen Fields, the teenage daughter of a local sharecropper. The girl became pregnant and the Fields family secluded her until a boy was born in March 1858. A few days after the birth, Ellen's father and brothers walked over to Leander and left the child on the doorstep. The Fields family then left the area; talk was they went to Texas. The boy, Delona, later married Mollie Green Sorrel; Albert L. Patterson was their second son.

2. Russell County Historical Commission, *The History of Russell County, Alabama* (Dallas, Tex.: National ShareGraphics, 1982), 68; Anne Kendrick Walker, *Russell County in Retrospect* (Richmond, Va.: Deitz Press, 1950), 107–11; F. L. Cherry, "The History of Opelika, " *Alabama Historical Quarterly* 15 (1953): 183.

3. John Patterson interview, 29 December 1984; Alabama National Guard, "Brief for General Hanna," provides details on club locations and gambling.

4. "I'll Get the Gangs That Killed My Father!" *Saturday Evening Post*, 27 November 1954; John Patterson interview, 29 December 1984.

5. Interviews with John Patterson, 29 December 1984, and Grace Patterson Harry, 19 February 1985.

6. Interviews with John Patterson, 29 December 1984, and Ruth Benson Cole, Mount Olive, Ala., 17 January 1985.

7. John Patterson interview, 29 December 1984; Robert B. Roberts, *Historic Forts: The Military, Pioneer, and Trading Posts of the United States* (New York: Macmillan, 1988), 21–22.

Chapter 2

1. John Patterson interview, Goldville, 29 December 1984; Paul D. Harkins, *When the Third Cracked Europe: The Story of Patton's Incredible Army* (New York: Army Times, 1969), 49, 64.

2. John Patterson interview, 29 December 1984; John Patterson to A. L. Patterson, Fort Sill, Oklahoma, 23 August 1942, John Patterson's Personal Files.

3. John Patterson interview, 29 December 1984.

4. John Patterson to A. L. Patterson, Tunisia, 2 March 1943, Patterson Personal Files; John Patterson interview, 29 December 1984.

5. John Patterson interview, 29 December 1984.

6. John Patterson interview, 29 December 1984; Colonel V. R. Rawie to author, Las Cruces, New Mexico, 29 June 1985; *The Barracks Bag Express* (regimental newspaper), 19 May 1943; diary of Franklin McElhenny, 1941–1944 (McElhenny was the regimental surgeon; Patterson obtained a copy of his diary after the war); "A Combat History of the 17th Battalion WWII" (author unknown; n.d.), 29; John Patterson to A. L. Patterson, Italy, 30 November 1943.

7. John Patterson interview, 29 December 1984.

8. Ibid.

9. Circuit Court records, Tuscaloosa County, Ala. (Case No. 5568), 17 January 1946.

10. University of Alabama records, Tuscaloosa; Harry Haden interview, Huntsville, Ala., 17 December 1984.

11. John Patterson interview, 29 December 1984.

12. Interviews with Joe Robertson, Montgomery, Ala., 18 December 1984; John Patterson, 29 December 1984; and Joe Kellett, Fort Payne, Ala., 21 December 1988.

13. Interviews with Irby Keener, Centre, Ala., 6 August 1985; Joe Robertson, 18 December 1984; and Mary Joe Patterson, Montgomery, 9 January 1985; Judge of Probate records, Chilton County, book no. 19, 333 (marriage license).

14. Interviews with Joe Robertson, 18 December 1984, and John Patterson, 29 December 1984.

15. Interviews with Mary Joe Patterson, Montgomery, 9 January 1985, and John Patterson, 29 December 1984.

16. Interviews with Mary Joe Patterson, Montgomery, 9 January 1985; John Patterson, 29 December 1984; and Jim Cannon, 17 October 2006; information provided by the Mary Mother Catholic School, Phenix City, Ala., 18 October 2006; Alabama National Guard, "Brief for General Hanna."

17. John Patterson interview, 29 December 1984.

Chapter 3

1. Hilda Coulter interview, Phenix City, 12 August 1985, and John Patterson interview, Goldville, 23 June 1985.

2. *Columbus (Ga.) Ledger,* 7 May 1946; John Patterson interview, 23 June 1985; Edwin Strickland and Gene Wortsman, *Phenix City* (Birmingham: Vulcan Press, 1955), 21; *Saturday Evening Post,* 15 June 1965. See also Alan Grady, *When Good Men Do Nothing: The Assassination of Albert Patterson* (Tuscaloosa: University of Alabama Press, 2003); Grady's primary research was based on newspaper accounts of Phenix City and the Albert Patterson murder.

3. William D. Barnard, "Southern Liberalism in Triumph and Frustration: Alabama Politics, 1946–1950" (PhD diss., University of Virginia, 1971), 25, 46; William D. Barnard, *Dixiecrats and Democrats* (University: University of Alabama Press, 1974), 19.

4. Barnard, "Southern Liberalism," 294; Roy L. Smith Jr. interview, Phenix City, 2 October 1985; Carl Grafton, "James E. Folsom and Civil Liberties in Alabama," *Alabama Review* 32 (January 1979): 12.

5. George E. Sims, "The Little Man's Big Friend: James E. Folsom in Alabama Politics, 1946–1958" (PhD diss., Emory University, 1981), 251–52; John Patterson interview, 23 June 1985; *General Laws: Legislature of Alabama, 1947,* act no. 378, 269–70 (this act created the Twenty-Sixth Judicial Circuit for Russell County); *Alabama Laws: Legislature of Alabama, 1949,* act no. 304, 438; George E. Sims to author, Plainview, Tex., 1 July 1985; "Report of the Special Legislative Committee Investigating Pardons and Paroles," legislative document no. 4, 1961, 284–98.

6. John Patterson interview, 23 June 1985; Sims, "The Little Man's Big Friend," 252; *Journal of the House, 1947*, 2560.

7. John Patterson interview, 23 June 1985; *Gadsden Times*, 4 May 1950; *Official and Statistical Register*, Secretary of State Files, Montgomery, 1950, 530; Albert Patterson Files, John Patterson Papers, Alabama Department of Archives and History, Montgomery.

8. *Life*, October 1954, 47; Hilda Coulter interview, Phenix City, 12 August 1985, and John Patterson interview, 23 June 1985.

9. Roland Joseph Page, "The *Columbus [Ga.] Ledger* and the Phenix City Story: On Winning a Pulitzer Prize" (master's thesis, Florida State University, 1966), 8–13 (quotation); *Attorney General vs. Daniel*, 6 July 1916, Alabama Records, 196:704; *Columbus (Ga.) Advocate*, 30 April 1938 (quotation); *Columbus (Ga.) Inquirer*, 20 July 1954; Emmett Perry, "The Story behind Phenix City: The Struggle for Law in a Modern Sodom," *American Bar Association Journal* 42 (December 1956): 1147.

10. *Phenix Citizen*, 18 June 1970, 7 November 1968.

11. Page, "The *Columbus [Ga.] Ledger*," 16–17; interview with John Luttrell Sr., Saint George Island, Fla., 10 December 1985; Albert Patterson Files, John Patterson Papers.

12. Albert Patterson Files. John Patterson reports that while he practiced law in Phenix City, jury and grand jury selection could be predicted months in advance. The jury box would be brought into the courtroom and placed on the judge's bench. The clerk would unlock the box and take out a packet of juror cards secured with a rubber band. The clerk would deal off the top until the required number of names was selected for the regular jury panel and the grand jury for the term.

Chapter 4

1. Francis H. Keller, *The Korean War: A Twenty-five-Year Perspective* (Lawrence, Kans.: Regents Press, 1977), 112–13; Joe Robertson interview, Montgomery, 18 December 1984.

2. Interviews with John Patterson, Montgomery, 29 December 1984, and Mary Joe Patterson, Montgomery, 9 January 1985; John Patterson to Mrs. A. L. Patterson, Frankfurt, Germany 12 March 1953.

3. *Sunday (Columbus, Ga.) Ledger-Inquirer,* 28 October 1951; *United States vs. Poorthunder*, U.S. Military Records; interview with John Luttrell, 10 December 1985 (quotation); John Patterson to A. L. Patterson, Gelhausen, Germany, 10 May 1953; Mrs. Hugh Bentley interview, Phenix City, 8 December 1985; Margaret Anne Barnes, *The Tragedy and the Triumph of Phenix City, Alabama* (Macon, Ga.: Mercer University Press, 2003).

4. Strickland and Wortsman, *Phenix City*, 188; *Birmingham News*, 6 August 1954; Hilda Coulter interview, Phenix City, 12 August 1985 (quotation); *Phenix City Herald*, 12 July 1950.

5. Strickland and Wortsman, *Phenix City*, 191; John Luttrell interview, 10 De-

cember 1985 (quotation); *Columbus (Ga.) Ledger*, 9, 10, 11 January 1952; Hilda Coulter interview, Phenix City, 12 August 1985.

6. *Columbus (Ga.) Ledger*, 16, 17, 18 January 1952.

7. Ray Jenkins interview, Baltimore, Md., 11 November 1985.

8. *Columbus (Ga.) Ledger*, 23 January 1952; Ray Jenkins interview, 11 November 1985.

9. Hilda Coulter interview, Phenix City, 8 December 1985; *Columbus (Ga.) Ledger*, 8 August 1952; *McCall's*, "The Angry Women of Phenix City," September 1955, 58 (quotation).

10. United States District Court for the Middle District of Alabama, Alabama Supreme Court Records, 27 February 1952 (quotation); Hilda Coulter interview, Phenix City, 8 December 1985. Mrs. Coulter kept many of the radio scripts.

11. *Columbus (Ga.) Ledger*, 10 March 1953 (Ferrell said it was a "friendly fight"); *Phenix City Herald*, 22 February 1952; *Columbus (Ga.) Inquirer*, 14 February 1952; Hilda Coulter interview, Phenix City, 8 December 1985.

12. *Columbus (Ga.) Inquirer*, 25 February; 21 March 1952; Alabama State Supreme Court Records, Montgomery, 5 November 1952; interview with Grace Patterson Harry, Goldville, 16 February 1985.

13. *Columbus (Ga.) Ledger*, 16 July 1952 (quotation); *Columbus (Ga.) Ledger*, 6, 20, 21 May 1952; *Montgomery Advertiser*, 26–28 July 1952; Albert Patterson Files, John Patterson Papers; *Records of the Wickersham Commission*; *A History of American Criminal Justice* (New York: Oxford University Press, 1997), 154–57.

14. *Columbus (Ga.) Ledger*, 27 July 1952 (quotation); John Patterson interview, 10 October 2005; *Columbus (Ga.) Ledger*, 22, 25–26 July 1952.

15. *Columbus (Ga.) Inquirer*, 22 July, 6 March 1952.

Chapter 5

1. Page, "The *Columbus (Ga.) Ledger*," 58–59; *Columbus (Ga.) Ledger-Inquirer*, 6 May 1952 (quotation); Grady, *When Good Men Do Nothing*.

2. Alabama Supreme Court Records; *Columbus (Ga.) Ledger-Inquirer*, 19, 27 June 1954; *Montgomery Advertiser*, 9–12, 14 June 1953; *Columbus (Ga.) Inquirer*, 2 July 1952 (quotation).

3. Hilda Coulter interview, Phenix City, 8 December 1985.

4. John Patterson interview, Goldville, 29 December 1984.

5. Charles M. Meriwether interview, Birmingham, 13 December 1984; *Montgomery Advertiser*, 12 March 1961.

6. In October 1918, 1st Lt. Albert Patterson was wounded in the right hip and leg at Saint Etienne, France, as he led a charge on a German machine gun position, for which the French government honored him with a Croix de Guerre. It took him two years to recuperate at Fort McPherson, Georgia. Albert Patterson recounted his war experiences to John during their law partnership. "History of the 36th Division," Patterson family records; John Patterson interview, 29 December 1984; Albert Patterson Files, John Patterson Papers.

7. Barnard, *Dixiecrats and Democrats*, 144; George E. Sims, *The Little Man's Big Friend: James E. Folsom in Alabama Politics: 1946–1958* (University: University of Alabama Press, 1985), 173–76; Carl Grafton and Anne Permaloff, *Big Mules and Branchheads: James E. Folsom and Political Power in Alabama* (Athens: University of Georgia Press, 1985), 173–76.

8. Grafton, "James E. Folsom and Civil Liberties in Alabama," 12–14; Mac-Donald Gallion interview, Montgomery, 19 September 1986; *Birmingham News*, 4 August 1954; *Gadsden Times*, 4, 5 August 1954; *Alabama Magazine*, 21 May 1954.

9. *Montgomery Advertiser*, 2, 3, 4 June 1954; Strickland and Wortsman, *Phenix City*, 152–59.

10. *Alabama Magazine*, 21 May 1954; John Patterson interview, 29 December 1984; Albert L. Patterson, WBRC-Radio, Birmingham, May 1954 tape recording; Charles Meriwether interview, Birmingham, 13 December 1984; *Dothan Eagle*, 2 June 1954.

11. *Montgomery Advertiser*, 5 June 1954.

12. John Patterson interview, 29 December 1984 (quotation); John Benefield to C. O. Revel, Columbia, South Carolina, 1 January 1957; J. Noel Baker to John Patterson, Montgomery, 24 January 1957.

13. *Birmingham News*, 20 June 1954; Albert Patterson Files, John Patterson Papers; *Gadsden Times*, 19 June 1954; Strickland and Wortsman, *Phenix City*, 142, 156, 159–61 (quotation); Frank B. Embry to Ray Acton, Pell City, Ala., 7 May 1981.

14. Sandra Baxley Taylor, *Faulkner: Jimmy, That Is*, (Huntsville, Ala.: Strode, 1984), 1051–107; Sims, "The Little Man's Big Friend," 313; Hilda Coulter interview, Phenix City, 8 December 1985; Mae Patterson McKathan interview, 20 December 1984, Montgomery (quotation).

15. Strickland and Wortsman, *Phenix City*, 161–62; *Birmingham News*, 19, 30 June 1954; Quinnie Kelley interview,1959.

16. Quinnie Kelley interview, 1959.

Chapter 6

1. John Patterson interviews, Goldville, 18 December 1985, 23 March 1986. See also Robert Clem, *John Patterson: In the Wake of the Assassins*, Waterfront Pictures, 2007. In this ninety-minute documentary film, Clem looks at the Phenix City tragedy and John Patterson's career.

2. Charles M. Meriwether interview, Birmingham, 13 December 1984.

3. *Dothan Eagle*, 25 June 1954; *Huntsville Times*, 25 June 1954; John Patterson interview, 23 March 1986.

4. *Sunday (Columbus, Ga.) Ledger-Inquirer*, 20 June 1954; *Atlanta Constitution*, 22 June 1954; *Birmingham News*, 20 June 1954; *Dothan Eagle*, 25 June 1954.

5. Ray Jenkins interview, Baltimore, Md., 11 November 1985.

6. *Columbus (Ga.) Ledger*, 24, 27, 29 June 1954; *Atlanta Constitution*, 23 June 1954; *Gadsden Times*, 23 June 1954.

7. John Patterson interview, 23 March 1986; *Atlanta Constitution,* 23 June 1954; *Birmingham News,* 23, 24, 27 June 1954; "I'll Get the Gangs That Killed My Father!" *Saturday Evening Post,* 27 November 1954.

8. *Columbus (Ga.) Ledger,* 24, 25 June 1954; Strickland and Wortsman, *Phenix City,* 14–15; Joe Robertson interview, Montgomery, 18 December 1984.

9. "Memorandum Report," Oscar F. Coley to L. B. Sullivan, Director of Department of Public Safety, 21 July 1954; *Columbus (Ga.) Ledger,* 15 July 1954; Ray Acton interview, Montgomery, 27 December 1985; state investigator's personal report (Joe Smelley's briefcase is in the possession of John Patterson); *Birmingham News,* 4 August 1954.

10. *Columbus (Ga.) Ledger,* 30 June, 8 July 1984; Emmett Perry, "The Story behind Phenix City: The Struggle for Law in a Modern Sodom," *American Bar Association Journal* 142 (1956): 1178–179; Strickland and Wortsman, *Phenix City,* 114–17; *Birmingham News,* 10 July 1954 (quotation).

11. Ray Jenkins to Harold Martin, Montgomery, 1 December 1974; M. Lamar Murphy interview, Phenix City, 12 August 1985; *Columbus (Ga.) Ledger,* 3 December 1954.

12. Strickland and Wortsman, *Phenix City,* 238–42 (quotation); *Columbus (Ga.) Ledger,* 30 June 1954; *Birmingham News,* 21 June 1954.

13. *Columbus (Ga.) Inquirer,* 14 July, 1 August 1954; the Jefferson County Democratic Party resolution is in the Albert Patterson File, John Patterson Papers; Lamar Murphy interview, 23 February 1986.

14. Ray Acton interview, 27 December 1985.

15. *Gadsden Times,* 27, 28 June 1954; "I'll Get the Gangs That Killed My Father!" *Saturday Evening Post,* 27 November 1954; John Patterson interview, 23 March 1986; Charles M. Meriwether interview, Birmingham, 13 December 1984; "Proceedings of Meeting of State Democratic Executive Committee of Alabama," Birmingham, The Redmont Hotel, Emerald Room, Saturday, 26 June 1954, in Albert L. Patterson Files, John Patterson Papers.

16. *Birmingham News,* 3 July 1954; *Sunday (Columbus, Ga.) Ledger-Inquirer,* 18 June 1954; John Patterson interview, 23 March 1986; Claude Prier interview, Dothan, 17 August 1991.

17. Paul Jackson Miller Jr. interview, Phenix City, 15 May 1986; *Dothan Eagle,* 17 July 1954; John M. Patterson Papers, Alabama Department of Archives and History, Montgomery.

18. *Gadsden Times,* 2 November 1954; *Birmingham News,* 29 September 1954; *Columbus (Ga.) Ledger,* 9 December 1954 (quotation); interviews with John Patterson, 23 March 1986, and Claude Prier, 17 August 1991.

Chapter 7

1. *Birmingham News,* 16, 17, 18 January 1955; *Birmingham World,* 4 January 1955 (quotation).

2. Interviews with John Patterson, Goldville, 12 June 1986, and Mary Joe Patterson, Montgomery, 9 January 1986.

3. Interviews with MacDonald Gallion, Montgomery, 29 June 1986, and John Patterson, 12 June 1986.

4. *Albert Fuller vs. State of Alabama*, Supreme Court of Alabama, Sixth Division, vols. 1–4, Alabama Department of Archives and History, Montgomery.

5. *Columbus (Ga.) Ledger*, 12 March 1955; *Gadsden Times*, 9, 10, 11 March 1955.

6. *Columbus (Ga.) Ledger*, 13, 18–22, 25–27, 29–30 April, 1–4 May 1955; *Albert Fuller vs. State of Alabama*.

7. M. Lamar Murphy interview, Phenix City, 12 August 1985; *Montgomery Advertiser*, 11, 12 October 1955; *Birmingham News*, 5 May 1955; *New York Times*, 18 June 1974; *Birmingham Post-Herald*, 11 October 1955 (Garrett quotation). Arch Ferrell died of a heart attack in Phenix City, August 1993.

8. *Birmingham News*, 19 June 1955; publicity materials for the motion picture *Phenix City: Then and Now*, Allied Artists, 1955; interviews with Ray Jenkins, Baltimore, Md., 11 November 1985, Charles Meriwether, Birmingham, 13 December 1984, and Hilda Coulter, Phenix City, 12 August 1985.

9. Hugh Sparrow and W. W. Ward, "The Man Who Inherited Dynamite," *Front Page Detective*, August 1957, 56–66; interviews with Charles Meriwether, Birmingham, 25 July 1986, and Ray Jenkins, 11 November 1985.

10. *Gadsden Times*, 23 November 1955; John Patterson interview, Goldville, 29 December 1985.

11. *Sylacauga Avondale Sun*, 14 November 1955; *Gadsden Times*, 23 November 1955; *Centreville Press*, 29 September 1955; *Decatur Daily*, 2, 14 October 1955; *Saint Clair (Ala.) News-Aegis*, 27 October 1955.

Chapter 8

1. John Patterson interview, Goldville, 8 June 1986 (first quotation); *Columbus (Ga.) Ledger*, 19 September 1955 (second quotation).

2. Clarence Cason, *90° in the Shade* (Chapel Hill: University of North Carolina Press, 1935), 16–19; Hillel Black, *Buy Now, Pay Later* (New York: William Morrow, 1961), 154–55; *Birmingham News*, 6 September 1957.

3. Interviews with Goodloe Rutland, Birmingham, 17 August 1986, and Douglas Arant, Birmingham, 17 August 1986; Black, *Buy Now, Pay Later*, 156.

4. Interviews with John Patterson, 8 June 1986 and Noel Baker, Opelika, 18 September 1986; *Birmingham News*, 24 October 2006; *Montgomery Advertiser*, 24 September 1955.

5. *Alabama Lawyer* 24, no. 4 (October 1963); John Patterson interview, 8 June 1986; *Alabama Lawyer* 41, no. 1 (January 1980).

6. *C. J. Larson/Tide Finance Company vs. State of Alabama*, Supreme Court of Alabama (97 Southern Reporter 2nd series), 26 July 1957.

7. Black, *Buy Now, Pay Later*, 157–58.

8. *Birmingham News*, 16 May 1957; Black, *Buy Now, Pay Later*, 157–59.

9. *State of Alabama vs. I. S. Odell*, 7 October 1957; *State of Alabama vs. C. H. Bright*, 11 December 1957; *State of Alabama vs. Mutual Finance and Thrift*, 7 December 1957; *State of Alabama vs. GAC Finance Corporation*, 7 December 1957, Circuit Court records, Calhoun County Courthouse. *Personal Finance Law Quarterly Report* 13, no. 4 (Fall 1959): 120–22; *Anniston Star*, 9–11 December 1957, 9 April 1958 (quotation 9 December); *Birmingham Post-Herald*, 6 April, 19 September, 5 December 1958.

10. *Anniston Star*, 12 December 1957; *Personal Finance Law Quarterly Report* 13, no. 4 (Fall 1959): 123; *Sylacauga News*, 3 November 1955 (quotation).

Chapter 9

1. *Montgomery Advertiser*, 4 November 1955; Charles M. Meriwether interview, Birmingham, 13 December 1984.

2. Sims, *The Little Man's Big Friend*, 189–95 (quotation); interviews with Ernest Stone, Jacksonville, Ala., 24 September 1986, and John Patterson, Goldville, 27 September 1986; Grafton and Permaloff, *Big Mules and Branchheads*, 202–4.

3. Barnard, *Dixiecrats and Democrats*; Bob Ingram, *That's The Way I Saw It*, (Montgomery: B and C Press, 1986), 48–49.

4. *Montgomery Advertiser*, 19, 26 September 1956, 4 January 1957; interviews with John Patterson, Goldville, 27 September 1986, and Joe Robertson, Montgomery, 18 December 1984.

5. *Glencoe Paving Company, Inc. vs. John Graves, State Comptroller*; Supreme Court records, 20 February 1957; Sims, *The Little Man's Big Friend*, 198–99; Grafton and Permaloff, *Big Mules and Branchheads*, 213.

6. John Patterson interview, Goldville, 8 June 1986; *Montgomery Advertiser*, 4 January 1957.

7. *Birmingham Post-Herald*, 10 December 1958 (quotation); John Patterson interview, 8 June 1986.

8. *Peggy Finch vs. State of Alabama*, Supreme Court of Alabama, 1 December 1960; *Tri-State Corporation vs. State of Alabama*, Supreme Court of Alabama, 3 December 1964; *Birmingham Post-Herald*, 10 December 1958; *State of Alabama vs. Claude D. Kelley*, Supreme Court of Alabama, 25 January 1963; John Patterson interview, 8 June 1986.

9. *Tri-State Corporation vs. State of Alabama*, Supreme Court of Alabama, 30 March 1961; John Patterson interview, 8 June 1986; *South Magazine*, 20 October 1958; Sims, *The Little Man's Big Friend*, 199.

10. *Birmingham News*, 7, 16 September 1956, 5 October 1956; *Montgomery Advertiser*, 6 September 1956.

11. *Dallas (Tex.) Times Herald*, 20 January 1957; *Columbus (Ga.) Ledger*, 6, 7 January 1956; *Selma Times-Journal*, 9 September 1956.

Chapter 10

1. James T. Harris, "Alabama's Reaction to the Brown Decision, 1954–1956: A Case Study in Early Massive Resistance" (PhD diss., Middle Tennessee State University, 1978), 12; Virginia Van der Veer Hamilton, "The Albatross of Race," *Alabama Law Review* 36 (Spring 1985): 856; Thomas J. Gilliam, "The Second Folsom Administration: The Destruction of Alabama Liberalism: 1954–1958" (PhD diss., Auburn University, 1975), 99–100; Numan V. Bartley, *The Rise of Massive Resistance: Race and Politics in the South during the 1950s* (Baton Rouge: Louisiana State University Press, 1969), 77; John Patterson interview, Goldville, 27 November 1986.

2. Grafton and Permaloff, *Big Mules and Branchheads,* 165, 186.

3. J. Mills Thornton III, "Challenge and Response of the Montgomery Bus Boycott of 1955–1956," *Alabama Review* 33 (July 1980): 199–200; Martin Luther King Jr., *Stride toward Freedom: The Montgomery Story* (New York: Harper and Row, 1958), 110–11; E. D. Nixon interview, Montgomery, 22 December 1986; Richard Blake Dent, "The Man behind the Movement," *American History Illustrated* (December 1985): 4–6; Bartley, *The Rise of Massive Resistance* 177; Freeman W. Pollard, *E. D. Nixon: The Life of a Resourceful Activist* (Montgomery: Junebug Books, 2003), 68–84; *The Papers of Martin Luther King, Jr.* (Berkeley: University of California Press, 1997), 429; Fred Gray, *Bus Ride to Justice* (Montgomery, Ala.: New South, 2002), 28–29.

4. John Patterson interview, 27 November 1986; *Alabama Journal,* 28 March 1956.

5. Thornton, "Challenge and Response," 213–14; King, *Stride toward Freedom,* 160.

6. Harris, "Alabama's Reaction," 250; John Patterson interview, 27 November 1986.

7. Gilbert Isofsky, *The Burden of Race* (New York: Harper and Row, 1967), 498; Gilliam, "Second Folsom Administration," 273–75, 308 (quotation); *Time,* 12 March 1956, 97; John Patterson interview, 27 March 1986; E. Culpepper Clark, *The Schoolhouse Door: Segregation's Last Stand at the University of Alabama* (New York: Oxford University Press, 1993), 151–63; Sims, *The Little Man's Big Friend,* 181–82.

8. Harris, "Alabama's Reaction," 60, 181, 185, 218; Sims, *The Little Man's Big Friend,* 176–77, 186; Gilliam, "Second Folsom Administration," 101.

9. John Patterson interview, 27 March 1986; Gilliam, "Second Folsom Administration," 422; *Montgomery Advertiser,* 10 February 1956.

Chapter 11

1. John Patterson interview, Goldville, 27 March 1987; *Virginia vs. NAACP,* United States Supreme Court, 8 June 1959; "Virginia Legislative Investigation," *Race*

Relations Law Reporter (29 September 1956): 1020; Diane McWhorter, *Carry Me Home: Birmingham, Alabama: The Climactic Battle of the Civil Rights Revolution* (New York: Simon and Schuster, 2001), 107–8; Frye Gaillard, *Cradle of Freedom: Alabama and the Movement that Changed America* (Tuscaloosa: University of Alabama Press, 2004), 52.

2. *Birmingham News,* 29 March, 1 June 1956 (quotation); *Anniston Star,* 1 June 1956; *Montgomery Journal,* 1 June 1956; John Patterson interviews, 27 March, 8 June 1986; J. Mills Thornton III, *Dividing Lines: Municipal Politics and the Struggle for Civil Rights in Montgomery, Birmingham, and Selma* (Tuscaloosa: University of Alabama Press, 2002), 89–91.

3. Gordon C. Rodgers interview, Anniston, Ala., 27 July 1986; *Birmingham World,* 30 June 1956; John Patterson interview, 8 June 1986; *Birmingham News,* 27 June 1956; *NAACP vs. Alabama,* United States Reports, vol. 377, October term 1963 (Washington, D.C.: U.S. Government Printing Office, 1964), 288–310; William D. Workman Jr., *The Case for the South* (New York: Devin-Adair, 1960), 193, 203; Gilliam, " Second Folsom Administration," 426–34; *King Papers,* 3:47.

4. *Talladega Daily Home,* 3 June 1956; John Patterson interview, 27 March 1986; *Mobile Press,* 2, 3 June 1986; Reed Sarratt, *The Ordeal of Desegregation: The First Decade* (New York: Harper and Row, 1966), 182; J. Harvie Wilkinson III, *From Brown to Bakke: The Supreme Court and School Integration, 1954–1978* (New York: Oxford University Press, 1979), 79; Howard I. Kalodner and James J. Fishman, eds., *Limits of Justice: The Court's Role in School Desegregation* (Cambridge, Mass.: Ballinger, 1978), 599; Gilliam, "Second Folsom Administration," 433; Gaillard, *Cradle of Freedom,* 56; Bernard Taper, *Gomillion Versus Lightfoot: The Right to Vote in Apartheid Alabama* (Tuscaloosa: University of Alabama Press, 2003), 17, 20–21.

5. Robert J. Norrell, *Reaping the Whirlwind* (New York: Alfred A. Knopf, 1985), 90–91; Gray, *Bus Ride to Justice,* 4–5 (Gray quotation); *Birmingham Post-Herald,* 31 July 1957; *Talladega Daily Home,* 26 July 1957; *Montgomery Advertiser,* 26 July 1957; John Patterson interview, 8 June 1986.

6. John Patterson interview, 8 June 1986; Norrell, *Reaping the Whirlwind,* 97–99, 101; *Montgomery Advertiser,* 27 July 1957 (quotation); Gray, *Bus Ride to Justice* 114–24.

7. Norrell, *Reaping the Whirlwind,* 111; Thomas R. Brooks, *Walls Come Tumbling Down: A History of the Civil Rights Movement, 1940–1970* (Englewood Cliffs, N.J.: Prentice-Hall, 1974), 134–37; *Statutory History of the United States: Civil Rights* (New York: Chelsea House, 1970), 840–998; Gilliam, "Second Folsom Administration," 549; *Birmingham News,* 1 February 1957, 21 March 1956 (first quotation).

8. *Birmingham News,* 4 February 1957.

9. *Birmingham News,* 6, 8 February 1957; *Washington Evening Star,* 8 February 1957.

10. Interviews with John Patterson, Goldville, 8 March 1986, Charles M. Meriwether, Birmingham, 10 January 1987.

Chapter 12

1. Gilliam, "Second Folsom Administration," 581; William D. Barnard interview, Birmingham, 2 May 1987.

2. Taylor, *Faulkner*, 114; Marshall Frady, *Wallace* (New York: World, 1968), 106–7 (quotation).

3. Frady, *Wallace*, 108–9.

4. Taylor, *Faulkner*, 111, 107 (quotation); George C. Hawkins interview, Gadsden, Ala., 24 April 1987.

5. Frady, *Wallace*, 81; George C. Wallace, *Stand Up for America* (Garden City, N.Y.: Doubleday, 1976), 62–63; Wayne Greenhaw, *Watch Out for George Wallace* (Englewood Cliffs, N.J.: Prentice-Hall, 1976), 116–17; Sandra Baxley Taylor, *Me 'n' George* (Mobile: Greenberry, 1988), 15.

6. John Patterson interview, Goldville, 27 March 1987; *Montgomery Advertiser*, 5 June 1954; Grover C. Hall Jr. to Mrs. Albert F. Fuller, Montgomery, 19 July 1955; Avon Fuller to Grover Hall, Phenix City, June 1955; Avon Fuller to Grover Hall, Phenix City, 14 January 1956. These letters were discovered by Ray Jenkins when he became editor of the *Advertiser* following Grover Hall's tenure; Jenkins gave copies of the letters to Patterson.

7. John Patterson news release, Montgomery, 28 January 1958; interviews with Charles M. Meriwether, Birmingham, 24 May 1987, and John Patterson, Goldville, 1 March, 20 May 1987; *Birmingham Post-Herald*, 4, 6 February 1958; *South Magazine*, 10 February 1958; *Birmingham News*, 3, 7 February 1958.

8. Interviews with John Patterson, 20 May 1987, and Charles Meriwether, 24 May 1987; James Sheppard Taylor, "An Analysis of the Effect of John Malcolm Patterson's Campaign Speaking in the 1958 Alabama Democratic Primary" (PhD diss., Florida State University, 1968), 28–29.

9. Interviews with Maurice Patterson, Birmingham, 11 March 1987, Charles Meriwether, 26 February, 24 May 1987, Ralph Harden, Tuscaloosa, 9 May 1987, and Irby Keener, Centre, Ala., 6 August 1985.

10. *Montgomery Advertiser*, 11 February 1987; James W. Franklin interview, Montgomery, 27 May 1987 (Franklin was a member of the "Sunny Valley Boys" band).

11. Taylor, "An Analysis of the Effect of John Malcolm Patterson's Campaign Speaking," 77–79; *Messages and Addresses of John Patterson* (Montgomery: State of Alabama, 1963), 167–68 (Patterson had his speeches as attorney general and governor assembled by Harry Cook, then printed and bound by the state); *Montgomery Advertiser*, 20 April 1958.

12. Joe Robertson interview, Montgomery, 22 December 1986; *Birmingham Post-Herald*, 20 February 1958; John Patterson interview, Goldville, 30 May 1987.

13. John Patterson televised speech, May 1958, in the possession of Tommy Giles, Montgomery; *Gadsden Times*, 6 April 1958.

14. *South Magazine*, 21 October 1957; Maurice Patterson interview, 11 March 1987.

15. *Life*, 5 May 1958, 53–62.

16. Shorty Price, *Alabama Politics: Tell It like It Is* (New York: Vantage, 1973), 61; Bernie Reese interview, Enterprise, Ala., 4 May 1987; *Montgomery Advertiser*, 11 April 1958.

17. John Patterson interview, 30 May 1987.

18. *Montgomery Advertiser*, 5 April 1958; A. W. Todd interview, Russellville, Ala., 4 May 1987; *Birmingham Post Herald*, 7 April 1958; John Patterson interview, 30 May 1987.

19. Interviews with John Patterson, Montgomery, 9 January 1987, and Charles Meriwether, Birmingham, 6 June 1987.

20. *Greene County Democrat*, 10 April 1958; John Patterson interview, Montgomery, 9 January 1987, and Charles Meriwether interview, 6 June 1987; *Centreville Press*, 10 April 1958; *Birmingham Post-Herald*, 10 April, 1, 3 May 1958; *Dothan Eagle*, 29 April 1958.

21. Interviews with Robert E. Blackwelder, Piedmont, Ala., 14 February 1987 and George Hawkins, 24 April 1987.

22. *Montgomery Advertiser*, 7 May 1958; *Gadsden Times*, 13 May 1958; *Birmingham News*, 7 May 1957; John Patterson interview, Montgomery, 9 January 1987.

Chapter 13

1. John Patterson interview, Goldville, 20 June 1987; *Montgomery Advertiser*, 7 May 1958; *Birmingham News*, 7 May 1958.

2. Interviews with John Patterson, 20 June 1987, and Charles Meriwether, Birmingham, 21 June 1987.

3. Charles Meriwether interview, 21 June 1987.

4. *Gadsden Times*, 7 May 1958; Gilliam, "Second Folsom Administration," 581–83.

5. *Montgomery Advertiser*, 10 May 1958; Gilliam, "Second Folsom Administration," 583 (quotation).

6. John Patterson interview, 20 June 1987.

7. *Gadsden Times*, 20 May 1958; "Patterson for Governor," *South Newsreel*, produced by Roy Marcato, directed by Jim Atkins. Copies of the Patterson film are in the possession of Patterson's photographer Tommy Giles, Montgomery; John Patterson interview, 20 June 1987.

8. *Montgomery Advertiser*, 12, 28 May 1958; John Patterson interview, 20 June 1987.

9. *Montgomery Advertiser*, 15 May 1958; *Birmingham News*, 16 May 1958; *Anniston Star*, 16 May 1958; *Huntsville Times*, 16 May 1958; *Mobile Register*, 16 May 1958; Gilliam, "Second Folsom Administration," 581; Bob Ingram interview, Montgomery, 16 July 1987.

10. *Montgomery Advertiser*, 16, 17 May 1958; *Birmingham News*, 16, 17 May 1958; Greenhaw, *Watch Out for George Wallace*, 114–15.

11. Interviews with Robert M. Shelton, Northport, Ala., 9 May 1987, John Patterson, 20 June 1987, and Charles Meriwether, 21 June 1987; *Birmingham News*, 16 May 1958.

12. Interviews with Robert Shelton, 9 May 1987, and Ralph Harden, Tuscaloosa, 9 May 1987.

13. *Montgomery Advertiser*, 16, 17 May 1958; *Birmingham News*, 16 May 1958, *Birmingham Post-Herald*, 22 May 1958.

14. *Montgomery Advertiser*, 27 May 1958; Charles Meriwether interview, 21 June 1987.

15. *Montgomery Advertiser*, 23, 29 May 1958.

16. *Montgomery Advertiser*, 29 May, 2 June 1958; *Gadsden Times*, 25 May 1958; *South Magazine*, 18 May 1958.

17. *Birmingham Post-Herald*, 8 May, 4, 6 June 1958; Alabama Department of Archives and History, *Alabama Official and Statistical Register, 1959* (Alexander City, Ala.: Outlook Publishing, 1959).

18. *Columbus (Ga.) Ledger*, 8 June 1958; *Birmingham News*, 4 June 1958.

19. Gilliam, "Second Folsom Administration," 586; *Montgomery Advertiser*, 1 June 1958.

20. Frady, *Wallace*, 127.

Chapter 14

1. *Birmingham News*, 29 December 1958; *Gadsden Times*, 29 December 1958; John Patterson interview, Goldville, 29 December 1958.

2. Interviews with John Patterson, Goldville, 11 July 1987, and Charles Meriwether, Birmingham, 21 June 1987; *Birmingham News*, 7 December 1958.

3. *Montgomery Advertiser*, 4 June 1958.

4. John Patterson interview, 11 July 1987; *Birmingham News*, 16 November 1958.

5. Interviews with Charles Meriwether, 21 July 1987, John Patterson, 11 July 1987, Maurice Patterson, Birmingham, 11 March 1987, and Mabel Amos, Montgomery, 22 July 1987.

6. John Patterson interview, 11 July 1987; *Birmingham Post-Herald*, 11, 20, 21, 23 November, 2, 4 December 1958; *Gadsden Times*, 12 December 1958.

7. *Birmingham Post-Herald*, 23 November 1958; *Birmingham News*, 9 November 1958; John Patterson interview, 11 July 1987.

8. John Patterson interview, 11 July 1987; Grafton and Permaloff, *Big Mules and Branchheads*, 165–66, 185, 187; interviews with Vaughn Hill Robison, Montgomery, 30 July 1987, John Casey, Heflin, Ala., 29 July 1987, and McDowell Lee, Montgomery, 29 July 1987.

9. *Alabama Official and Statistical Register: 1959*, 620; Grafton and Permaloff, *Big Mules and Branchheads* 187; *Birmingham News*, 9 December 1958.

10. *Birmingham News*, 6 August, 16 November 1958; *Birmingham Post-Herald*, 4 August 1958.

11. *Birmingham News*, 17 January 1958; John Patterson interview, 11 July 1987.

12. John Patterson interview, 11 July 1987; *Montgomery Advertiser*, 20, 21 January 1959; *Birmingham News*, 20, 21 January 1959; *South Magazine*, 12 January 1959; *Messages and Addresses of John Patterson*, 3–10.

13. *Birmingham Post-Herald*, 20 January 1959; John Patterson interview, 11 July 1987.

Chapter 15

1. John Patterson interview, Goldville, 3 August 1987; John Patterson press releases (courtesy of Harry Cook, Washington, D.C.); *Messages and Addresses of John Patterson*, 11–16; Sam Engelhardt interview, Montgomery, 11 August 1987; *Gadsden Times*, 4 February 1959.

2. John Patterson interview, Montgomery, 11 August 1987; *Birmingham News*, 3 May 1959; *Gadsden Times*, 3 May 1959; *Messages and Addresses of John Patterson*, 20.

3. *Tuscaloosa News*, 27 August 1961; Harry Haden interview, Huntsville, 21 August 1985; *Montgomery Advertiser*, 27 August 1961; *Birmingham News*, 11 August 1961; *Birmingham Post-Herald*, 21 July 1961.

4. Patterson press release, 15 April 1959; *Alabama Journal*, 31 December 1959; *Birmingham News*, 23 August 1959.

5. *Messages and Addresses of John Patterson*, 38–39; *Montgomery Advertiser*, 24 June 1959; John Patterson interview, 11 August 1987; University of Alabama Center for Business and Research, *Economic Abstract of Alabama, 1975*, 53–54; *Alabama School Journal*, September 1959, 8–11.

6. *Messages and Addresses of John Patterson*, 44–45; *Birmingham News*, 3, 4 May 1959; *Gadsden Times*, 5, 6, 7 May 1959.

7. *Alabama Laws*, Legislature of Alabama, Act No. 99, 295; Act No. 110, 336; Act No. 118, 363; Act No. 126, 369; interviews with John Patterson, 11 August 1987 (quotation) and Joe Robertson, Montgomery, 22 December 1986; *Birmingham Post-Herald*, 1 September 1959.

8. Patterson press release, 22 June 1959; *Montgomery Advertiser*, 11 July 1959; *Anniston Star*, 12 July 1959; John Patterson interview, Goldville, 22 August 1987.

9. Joe Robertson interview, Montgomery, 18 December 1984; Patterson press release, 6 September 1959.

10. Interviews with Ralph Mead, Centre, Ala., 28 August 1987, and Joe Robertson, 18 December 1984; *Birmingham News*, 5 September 1959.

11. *Journal of the House of Representatives*, regular session, 1959, 803–36; William H. Sadler Jr. "Alabama Adopts Small Loan Act," *Personal Finance Law Quarterly Report* 14, no. 1 (Winter 1959): 4–39; *Journal of the Senate of the State of Alabama*, regular session, 1959, 1067, 1121–42, 1149–58, 1193, 1175, 1591, 1597; *Gadsden Times*, 18–19, 24 September, 3–6 November 1959; *Birmingham News*, 11 September, 6 November 1959; *Credit Union Bridge*, August 1959, 10–13; Black, *Buy Now, Pay Later*, 157–59.

12. *Montgomery Advertiser*, 7 November 1959; *Anniston Star*, 7 November 1959; Patterson press release, 12 November 1959.

13. *Alabama Journal*, 31 December 1959; *Opelika Daily News*, 30 December 1959; *Decatur Daily*, 31 December 1959; *Tuscaloosa News*, 31 December 1959; *Leeds News*, 6 August 1959; *Birmingham News*, 23 August 1959; John M. Collier, *Earl McGowin of Alabama: A Portrait* (New Orleans: Faust Publishing, 1986), 59–61.

14. Interviews with Joe Robertson, 18 December 1984, John Patterson, 11 August 1987, Ralph Mead, 24 August 1987, Gordon Wooddy, Piedmont, Ala., 9 February 1987, and Mabel Amos, Montgomery, 22 July 1987.

15. *Birmingham News*, 18, 22 March 1957, 15 June 1959. Robert Kennedy claimed to have introduced Patterson to his brother John, which Patterson disputes. Patterson said he met John Kennedy and was later introduced to Robert. Kennedy's speech in Patterson Papers, Alabama Department of Archives and History; Robert Kennedy, *Robert Kennedy: In His Own Words* (New York: Bantam, 1988), 90.

16. *Montgomery Advertiser*, 14 June 1959; Joe Robertson interview, 11 August 1987; Stephan Lesher, *George Wallace: American Populist* (New York: Addison-Wesley, 1994), 114–15; *Birmingham Post-Herald*, 15, 17–18 June 1959.

17. Interviews with John Patterson, Goldville, 22 August 1987, Charles Meriwether, Birmingham, 4 December 1984, and Joe Robertson, Montgomery, 18 December 1984.

18. Ralph Smith interview, Guntersville, 28 November 1984; Theodore C. Sorensen to author, New York City, 12 March 1985.

19. Interviews with Charles Meriwether, Birmingham, 4 December 1984, and Ralph Smith, Guntersville, Ala., 28 November 1984; *Birmingham Post-Herald*, 17 June 1959.

20. *Birmingham News*, 17, 21 June 1959; *Montgomery Advertiser*, 18 June 1959; Charles Meriwether interview, 18 June 1959.

21. *Birmingham Post-Herald*, 18 June 1959; *Birmingham News*, 3 July 1959.

22. *Methodist Christian Advocate*, 21 June 1959; *Birmingham News*, 24, 28 June 1959.

23. *Birmingham News*, 10 August 1959; *Montgomery Advertiser*, 10 August 1959.

Chapter 16

1. John Patterson press releases, 5–7, 13, 27 April 1960; *Anniston Star*, 14–15 April 1960; *Birmingham Post-Herald*, 20 January 1960.

2. Alvin Prestwood interview, Montgomery, 11 August 1987.

3. "Alabama Business," Bureau of Business Research, University of Alabama, 15 February 1960; *Birmingham News*, 8, 10 April 1960.

4. Levi Watkins, *Fighting Hard: The Alabama State Experience* (Detroit: Harlo Press, 1987), 28–37; *Montgomery Advertiser*, 2–4 March, 8, 9, 12, 15–17, 19–20, 27–28, 31 April, 1 June 1960; John Patterson press release, 4 February 1960.

5. John Patterson interview, Goldville, 20 September 1987; Watkins, *Fighting Hard*, 33; *King Papers*, 3:25–26; Thornton, *Dividing Lines*, 113–17.

6. John Patterson interview, 20 September 1987; Watkins, *Fighting Hard*, 35, 36, 39, 43; "Minutes of the State Board of Education," Montgomery, Alabama, 20 July 1960; John Patterson press release, 5 May 1960; *Montgomery Advertiser*, 3–7 May 1960.

7. *Birmingham News*, 6, 8 April 1960; Arthur M. Schlesinger Jr., *Robert Kennedy and His Times* (Boston: Houghton Mifflin, 1978), 207–10; Gray, *Bus Ride to Justice*, 150–59; Interviews with John Patterson, 20 September 1987, and Charles Meriwether, Birmingham, 27 October 1987; McWhorter, *Carry Me Home*, 150–51.

8. *Gadsden Times*, 8 April 1960; interviews with John Patterson, 20 September 1987, Charles Meriwether, 27 October 1987, and Sam Engelhardt, Montgomery, 28 October 1987; "Alabama Election Statistics; Democratic Primary Election, 1960," 637.

9. Herbert S. Parmet, *Jack: The Struggles of John F. Kennedy* (New York: Dial Press, 1980), 409; Sam Engelhardt interview, 28 September 1987; Ralph G. Martin, *A Hero for Our Times* (New York: Fawcett Crest, 1983), 102; Victor Lasky, *J.F.K.: The Man and the Myth* (New York: Macmillan, 1963), 253–54, 256.

10. Kenneth P. O'Donnell and David Powers, *Johnny, We Hardly Knew Ye* (Boston: Little, Brown, 1970), 180–81; Theodore C. Sorensen, *Kennedy* (New York: Harper and Row, 1965), 158; John Patterson interview, 20 September 1987.

11. Peter Wyden, *Bay of Pigs: The Untold Story* (New York: Simon and Schuster, 1979), 59–64; David Wise and Thomas B. Ross, *The Invisible Government* (New York: Random House, 1964), 338–47; Sorensen, *Kennedy*, 294–309; John Patterson interview, Goldville, 4 October 1987.

12. Joe Shannon interview, Birmingham, 2 October 1987. Alabama Air National Guard pilots Thomas Willard Ray, Leo Francis Baker, Riley W. Shamburger Jr., and Wade Carroll Gray were killed 19 April 1961, flying combat missions at the Bay of Pigs, Cuba. *Birmingham News*, 13 April 1986; Haynes Johnson, *The Bay of Pigs* (New York: W. W. Norton, 1964), 47–64; John Patterson interview, 4 October 1987.

13. John Patterson press release, 5–7, 13, 27 April 1960; Joe Shannon interview, 2 October 1987.

14. John Patterson interview, 4 October 1987; Wise and Ross, *Invisible Government*, 74–90.

15. Interviews with Tina Patterson, Goldville, 2 October 1987, Joe Robertson, Montgomery, 18 December 1984, Mary Joe Patterson, Montgomery, 9 December 1985, and Mabel Amos, Montgomery, 22 July 1987.

Chapter 17

1. Interviews with John Patterson, Montgomery, 3 November 1987, Mary Joe Patterson, Montgomery, 9 January 1985, Charles Meriwether, Birmingham, 13 December 1984.

2. John Patterson interview, Goldville, 22 August 1987; Harry N. Cook interview and memorandum to author, 16 November 2005.

3. *Montgomery Advertiser*, 10 March 1961; *Huntsville Times*, 1 February 1961; *Mobile Register*, 6 March 1961.

4. Charles Meriwether interview, 13 December 1984; *Montgomery Advertiser*, 10 March 1961; *Huntsville Times*, 3, 5 March 1961.

5. *Mobile Register*, 8 March 1961; *Birmingham News*, 8, 9 March 1961; Charles Meriwether interview, Birmingham, 4 December 1984.

6. Charles Meriwether interview, Birmingham, 13 December 1984.

7. *Huntsville Times*, 9, 10 January 1961; *Birmingham News*, 11, 12 January 1961.

8. John Patterson interview, Goldville, 8 November 1987; Sarratt, *The Ordeal of Desegregation*, 189.

9. Interviews with Henry L. Andrews, Tuscaloosa, 2 February 1987, and Charles D. McGlamery, Birmingham, 2 February 1987.

10. John Patterson interview, 8 November 1987; Wesley Critz George, *The Biology of the Race Problem*, prepared by commission of the governor of Alabama, 1962; Ralph Smith interview, Guntersville, 10 November 1987; *Birmingham Post-Herald*, 25 October 1956; Ray Jenkins interview, Baltimore, 11 November 1985.

11. *Messages and Addresses of John Patterson*, 46–77; *Huntsville Times*, 3, 4, 5 May 1961.

12. John Patterson interview, 8 November 1987; *Birmingham News*, 11 May 1961.

13. William H. Stewart Jr., "Reapportionment with Census Districts: The Alabama Case," *Alabama Law Review* 24 (Fall 1974): 693–713; "Message of Governor John Patterson to Joint Session of the Alabama Legislature at Special Session, June 12, 1962," Alabama Supreme Court Library; *Sims vs. Frank*, 208F Supp. 431 (M.D. 1962).

14. *Birmingham News*; 3, 5, 7 May 1961; *Official Statistical Register: Second Primary*, 2 June 1964, 544; *Huntsville Times*, 11 May 1961; Albert Rains interview, Gadsden, 16 November 1987; *Montgomery Advertiser*, 14 June 1964; *Messages and Addresses of John Patterson*, 52–54.

15. Thornton, *Dividing Lines*; "A Conversation in Alabama," *New Yorker*, 16 July 1961; Juan Williams, *Eyes on the Prize: American Civil Rights Years, 1954–1965* (New York: Viking Press, 1987), 148; Clark, *The Schoolhouse Door*, 151.

16. Floyd Mann interview, Montgomery, 17 November 1987; Harris Wofford, *Of Kennedys and Kings: Making Sense of the Sixties* (New York: Farrar Strauss Giroux, 1980), 153; John Patterson interview, 3 November 1987; Peter Collier and David Harowitz, *The Kennedys: An American Drama* (New York: Summit Books, 1984), 274.

17. Williams, *Eyes on the Prize*, 148; Floyd Mann interview, 17 November 1987; *Anniston Star*, 15, 16 May 1961; Charles Lam Markmann and Mark Sherwin, *John F. Kennedy: A Sense of Purpose* (New York: St. Martin's, 1961), 330; *Birmingham News*, 15, 16 May 1961.

18. John Seigenthaler oral history, John F. Kennedy Library, Boston; Alan F. Westin and Barry Mahoney, *The Trial of Martin Luther King* (New York: Thomas Y. Crowell, 1974), 39–40; *Birmingham News*, 15–16 May 1961.

19. Articles by Howell Raines in *New York Times*, 17–18 February 1980; Robert Shelton interview, Northport, 14 December 1987; deposition of Gary Thomas Rowe Jr., 17 October 1975, in "Senate Select Committee to Study Governmental Operations with Respect to Intelligence Activities."

20. Interviews with John Patterson, 8 November 1987, and Floyd Mann, 17 November 1987.

21. Reg Gadney, *Kennedy* (New York: Holt, Rinehart and Winston, 1983), 110–11; Arthur M. Schlesinger Jr., *A Thousand Days* (Boston: Houghton Mifflin, 1965), 936; Wofford, *Of Kennedys and Kings*, 152–54; interviews with Floyd Mann, 17 November 1987, and John Patterson, 8 November 1987.

22. John Patterson interview, 8 November 1987; *Montgomery Advertiser*, 17 May 1961; Thornton, *Dividing Lines*, 121–22.

23. Floyd Mann interview, 17 November 1987; Wofford, *Of Kennedys and Kings*, 153; John Seigenthaler oral history, 312–22; interviews with John Patterson, 8 November 1987, Charles Meriwether, Birmingham, 4 December 1987, and Ralph Smith, Guntersville, 4 December 1987; Gaillard, *Cradle of Freedom*, 80–81, 96–109.

24. John Patterson interview, 8 November 1987; John Seigenthaler oral history, 325–26; interviews with Charles Meriwether, 4 December 1987, and Floyd Mann, 17 November 1987; Westin and Mahoney, *Trial of Martin Luther King*, 40–41; *Montgomery Advertiser*, 20–21 May 1961.

25. Williams, *Eyes on the Prize*, 155–56 (quotation); Stephen B. Oates, *Let the Trumpet Sound: The Life of Martin Luther King* (New York: Harper and Row, 1982), 174–75; Diane McWhorter, *A Dream of Freedom: The Civil Rights Movement from 1954 to 1968* (New York: Scholastic, 2004), 61–65; John Patterson interview, 8 November 1987; Fred Powledge, *We Shall Overcome: Heroes of the Civil Rights Movement* (New York: Scribner, 1993), 43–45; *Montgomery Advertiser*, 22 May 1961; Burke Marshall, oral history, John F. Kennedy Library, 28–29; *Time*, 2 June 1961; Tommy Giles interview, Wetumpka, Ala., 5 February 2006.

26. John Patterson interview, 8 November 1987; Harvard Sitkoff, *The Struggle for Black Equality, 1954–1980* (New York: Hill and Wang, 1981), 106–12; Carl Brauer, *John F. Kennedy and the Second Reconstruction* (New York: Columbia University Press, 1977), 100; *Montgomery Advertiser*, 21–22 May 1961; *Messages and Addresses of John Patterson*, 287–302 (the complete transcript of the meeting is included); Thornton, *Dividing Lines*, 122–23.

27. Williams, *Eyes on the Prize*, 158; Theodore C. Sorensen to author, New York City, 27 February 1985; Arthur M. Schlesinger Jr. to author, New York City, 12 March 1985; Harry Cook interview, Washington, D.C., 12 November 1985; Dan T. Carter, *The Politics of Rage: George Wallace, the Origins of the New Conservatism, and the Transformation of American Politics* (New York: Simon & Schuster, 1995), 229–30.

28. John Patterson oral history, John F. Kennedy Library, 37; Burke Marshall, *Federalism and Civil Rights* (New York: Columbia University Press, 1964).

29. Brauer, *John F. Kennedy and the Second Reconstruction*, 103; Schlesinger, *Robert Kennedy*, 296; *Birmingham News*, 21 May 1961; *Montgomery Advertiser*, 21 May 1961.

30. *Messages and Addresses of John Patterson*, 21 May 1961; *Birmingham News*, 19–22 September 1961; John Patterson interview, 8 November 1987.

Chapter 18

1. John Patterson press release, 17 January 1962; John Patterson interview, Montgomery, 3 November 1987.

2. "Alabama Business," Bureau of Business Research, University of Alabama, 15 February 1963; "Message by Governor John Patterson to the State Legislature," 8 January 1963.

3. John Patterson interview, 3 November 1987; *Anniston Star*, 18–19 January 1962; *Montgomery Advertiser*, 16 May 1957 (Folsom's speech at Governor's Day, University of Alabama).

4. *Birmingham News*, 5 April 1962; *Montgomery Advertiser*, 2 April 1962; John Patterson press releases, 30 March, 4 April 1962.

5. *Montgomery Advertiser*, 21 May 1962; *Gadsden Times*, 2, 3 May 1962.

6. Stewart, "Reapportionment with Census Districts," 693–99; *Birmingham News*, 11 July 1962; *Messages and Addresses of John Patterson*, 86–94.

7. John Patterson interview, 3 November 1987; *Montgomery Advertiser*, 6–11 July 1962.

8. *Anniston Star*, 16 July 1962; *Montgomery Advertiser*, 15, 16, 21, 22 July 1962; John Patterson interview, 3 November 1987; *Sims vs. Frink*, Alabama Records, Alabama Supreme Court Library, 431–51.

9. *Montgomery Advertiser*, 12 July 1962; Ray Jenkins interview, Baltimore, 30 December 1987.

10. John Patterson interview, 3 November 1987; John Patterson press release, 12 July 1962; *Montgomery Advertiser*, 13 July 1962.

11. Interviews with Ray Jenkins, 30 December 1987, and MacDonald Gallion, Montgomery, 29 December 1987. John Patterson's personal files reveal correspondence to all parties concerned with the contract, but no replies explaining the problem were found.

12. Maurice Patterson interview, Birmingham, 27 December 1987; *Montgomery Advertiser*, 12, 13 June 1962.

13. MacDonald Gallion interview, 29 December 1987; *Montgomery Advertiser*, 20, 21 December 1962; Maurice Patterson interview, 27 December 1987; *Newsweek*, 27 August 1962.

14. *Montgomery Advertiser*, 9–10 August, 19–22 November 1962; John Patterson interview, 3 November 1987; *Alabama Journal*, 20–21 November 1962; *Birmingham Post-Herald*, 27 February 1963.

15. Interviews with John Patterson, 3 November 1987, Maurice Patterson, 27 De-

cember 1987, and Randolf Lurie, Montgomery, 18 January 1988; *Newsweek*, 27 August 1962.

16. *Birmingham News*, 1, 6, 7 October 1962; *Birmingham Post-Herald*, 23 December 1985; interviews with John Patterson, 3 November 1987, Charles R. Lowman, Andalusia, 8 February 1988, and John Hill, Andalusia, 9 February 1988.

17. *Birmingham News*, 13 January 1963; *Alabama Journal*, 28 July 1961; John Patterson interview, 3 November 1987.

18. McDowell Lee interview, Montgomery, 29 June 1987; *Birmingham News*, 13 January 1963.

19. John Patterson interview, 3 November 1987.

Chapter 19

1. Interviews with Charles Meriwether, Birmingham, 1 March 1988, and John Patterson, Goldville, 12 February 1988.

2. Interviews with Charles Meriwether, 1 March 1988, and John Patterson, Goldville, 10 March 1988.

3. *Journal of the House of Representatives of the State of Alabama: Third Extraordinary Session of 1965*, 4–51.

4. Interviews with George Hawkins, Gadsden, 1 March 1988; Kenneth Hammond, Valley Head, Ala., 6 March 1988; and John Patterson, Goldville, 12 February 1988.

5. *Journal of the Senate of the State of Alabama: Third Extraordinary Session of 1965*, 4–108; Tom Shelton interview, Jacksonville, Ala., 16 September 2006; *Montgomery Advertiser*, 2, 5–9 October 1965; *Gadsden Times*, 14, 15 October 1965; *Birmingham News*, 23 October 1965; McDowell Lee and H. E. Sterkx, *George Corley Wallace: A Legislative Legacy, 1946–1986* (Troy, Ala.: Troy State University Press, 1986), 20–21.

6. Kenneth Hammond interview, 6 March 1988; Frady, *Wallace*, 203–5.

7. Charles Meriwether interview, 1 March 1988.

8. Interviews with John Patterson, Goldville, 12 February 1988, and Joe Robertson, Montgomery, 2 March 1988.

9. *U.S. News and World Report*, 16 May 1966; *Newsweek*, 16 May 1966; Jack House, *Lady of Courage* (Montgomery: League Press, 1969), 46; Phillip Crass, *The Wallace Factor* (New York: Mason/Charter, 1975), 88–89; Greenhaw, *Watch Out for George Wallace*, 200–201.

10. *Birmingham News*, 4 May, 9 November 1965; *Anniston Star*, 4 May 1965; John Patterson interview, Goldville, 12 February 1988.

11. Interviews with John Patterson, Goldville, 12 February 1988, and Ted Rinehart, Montgomery, 11 April 1988.

12. *Birmingham News*, 22 April 1970; Neal R. Pierce, *The Deep South States in America* (New York: W. W. Norton, 1974), 109; John Patterson interview, Goldville, 12 February 1988.

13. John Patterson interview, Goldville, 12 February 1988; *Birmingham Post-Herald*, 30 March 1970; *Montgomery Advertiser*, 20 February 1970.

14. John Patterson interview, Goldville, 12 February 1988; *Huntsville Times*, 9 April 1970; *Centreville Press*, 16 April 1970.

15. *Birmingham News*, 6 May 1970; John Patterson interview, Goldville, 12 February 1988.

16. Interviews with Charles Meriwether, 1 March 1988; John Patterson, Goldville, 12 February 1988; Ted Rinehart, 11 April 1988; Joe Robertson, Montgomery, 2 March 1988 and 18 June 2006; and Mary Joe Patterson, Montgomery, 9 January 1985. Mary Joe Patterson died of heart congestion 12 June 1985, in Montgomery.

17. John Patterson interviews, Goldville, 12 February 1988, 21 September 2006; Ralph W. Adams to author, Troy, Alabama, 25 April 1988; *Birmingham News*, 17 December, 2003, 27 January 2004.

18. *United States vs. Roy S. Moore*, 18 November 2002; United States Court of Appeals, *Eleventh Circuit vs. Roy S. Moore*, 1 July 2003.

19. *Roy S. Moore vs. Judicial Inquiry Commission*, 30 April 2004. John Patterson interviews, Goldville, 12 February 1988, 18 December 2004, 12 August 2005.

Index

Page numbers in italics refer to photographs